Second Edition

Business and Professional Communication

Second Edition

Business and Professional Communication

A Practical Guide to Workplace Effectiveness

Kathryn Sue Young

Professor, Department of Communication and Theatre, Mansfield University

Howard Paul Travis

Emeritus, Mansfield University

Long Grove, Illinois

For information about this book, contact:
Waveland Press, Inc.
4180 IL Route 83, Suite 101
Long Grove, IL 60047-9580
(847) 634-0081
info@waveland.com
www.waveland.com

10-digit ISBN 1-4786-3977-6
13-digit ISBN 978-1-4786-3977-0

Printed in the United States of America

7 6 5 4 3 2 1

About the Authors

Kathryn Sue Young has taught at the college level for over 30 years at The Pennsylvania State University, Clarion University, University of Central Arkansas, and is currently a full professor and chair of the Department of Communication at Mansfield University. She has published *Group Discussion: A Practical Guide to Participation and Leadership*, 4th edition, with Wood, Phillips, and Pedersen, which is also available in Korean. She has also published numerous articles, including an article in a joint American-Russian publication, and has presented numerous papers at national conferences.

Howard Travis taught at the university level for 39 years. His former students work nationally and globally in media as on-air talent, writers, producers, directors, technicians, sales executives, lawyers, public relations/promotion practitioners, media managers, and media CEOs. He retired early from his teaching career in 2002. Mansfield University of Pennsylvania awarded him professor emeritus status, and he holds the rank of Honorary Professor of Communication, Volgograd State University, Volgograd, Russia.

Together they have published four editions of *Oral Communication: Skills, Choices, and Consequences*, as well as *Communicating Nonverbally: A Practical Guide to Presenting Yourself More Effectively*. Currently they are writing a book on the practical principles of persuasion.

Contents

Preface

Did you ever purchase a puzzle to work on for relaxation and entertainment? If so, you understand that it takes time to put it together. The puzzle you select normally catches your eye due to the image presented on the box cover. As you open the box and dump its contents on a flat surface, you begin to notice the size and shapes of its pieces as well as the total number of pieces to assemble for completion of the image. Then you begin the process of turning each piece over to examine where it might fit in the total design, arranging pieces by color so they relate to specific areas within the picture. You quickly realize that putting the entire image together is going to take more time than you originally planned. Some puzzles are quite complex and take days or weeks to complete. Puzzles are a problem-solving exercise.

Solving a puzzle is a great metaphor for the time and effort you need to spend on yourself preparing for a career in business and other professions. Just as you choose a puzzle based on the image on the box cover, you need to create a personal image (brand) that employers recognize as a good fit for their company. Image is rooted in appearance, specific skills, and abilities. The skills that attract the attention of employers initially are your academic credentials, employment record, physical appearance, sense of movement and physical style, and extemporaneous use of language in a variety of settings. These "pieces" of your personal brand help strangers remember your name and give them a sense of what you will be like as a colleague. These skills assist you in getting a job, but other skills will allow you to succeed.

Skills that cement your brand in the minds of colleagues include: excellent writing, consistent use of language (verbal and written), problem-solving abilities, solid use of technology and social media, enthusiasm for work and people, a moral and ethical foundation, the ability to adapt quickly to new ideas, and being a role model for others. Mastery of these skills and abilities can propel you toward a position as a manager and leader within an organization. These skills are part of your brand, but because they take time to reveal themselves, others do not "see" your true image until they work with you over a period of time.

The skills of every working person need constant monitoring, adjustment, and improvement. A career spans decades. Therefore, your skill set will be constantly challenged by new technology, a changing corporate culture, and a diverse workforce. This book will encourage change by helping you recognize and strengthen the communication skills necessary throughout your career.

Acknowledgments

This book was a joyful writing experience. Its many concepts became a mirror in which my entire career reflected back to me. Perhaps the best reflection of all was one of a business door opening wide, thus allowing me to join the ranks of the employed. My working life began with a generous person giving me the chance to prove myself. As I walked through my professional open door, I met Howard Scammon. Mr. Scammon, Chairman of Theatre and Speech at The College of William and Mary, was a true Southern gentleman whose constant smile, gracious use of language, welcoming personality, and insightful mentoring made me see the possibilities of life as a teacher. His constant encouragement and words of wisdom made my time in Williamsburg truly memorable. I trust my academic career reinforced his faith in me because I am not sure what I would have done with my life had it not been for the door he opened. Thank you, Mr. Scammon.

—HPT

I echo Howard's comments. Three of my professors—Arlie Parks, Dennis Gouran, and Gerald M. Phillips—opened doors for me. Dr. Parks showed me the road to graduate school when I was an undergraduate student. I would never have made it there without her guidance. When I was a young, inexperienced graduate student close to PhD completion, Dr. Gouran told me I would present a paper at the National Communication Association convention. I had never flown or done anything of that magnitude, and I was terrified, but he pushed me forward. Dr. Phillips handed me my first job interview in a department where he knew someone. That piece of networking along with the skill and knowledge that I had developed under his mentorship resulted in my first university position. After that I was ready to fly on my own. I will always treasure their willingness to believe in me.

—KSY

Connections in the business world are invaluable as well as essential. Through a connection we met our publishers, Carol and Neil Rowe at Waveland Press, Inc. Carol and Neil are the most remarkably warm people you could possibly meet. Their constant encouragement throughout the writing process can never be repaid. If we could pick a couple to live next door to us, we would pick them. Our conversations simply flow, and the laughter is not to be believed. What a team! Thanks to them for all they do to make writing such a pleasure. And, many thanks for hiring such a talented staff at Waveland Press, Inc.

Specifically, we need to thank Carol for making the process of bringing this edition to life an absolutely wonderful experience. The second edition is enriched by her meticulous editing talents. She is delightful to work with in sharing ideas and finding professional solutions to communicate ideas. Carol possesses warm interpersonal skills as well as surgeon-like language skills. Working with a great editor like Carol made this edition an absolutely remarkable experience.

In addition, we must thank several enthusiastic students who assisted us with the second edition of this textbook. We were grateful to add information contributed by Chelsea Thomas, Christie Buyer, Breanna Murphy, Dean Marker, Emily Schamel, and Erica Frank. Sharing research, editing decisions, and creative ideas with students made this text a collaborative effort. Each one of us grew personally through our honest discussions regarding how to make content effective for today's students.

We hope the material in this text encourages you to craft a career marked by the acquisition of valuable skills, active listening, energy, and professionalism.

CHAPTER
ONE

Communicating for Career Success

Goals

- Explain the importance of communication.
- Describe the components of communication.
- Analyze problems and propose correctives to communication situations.
- Select the appropriate channel for your communication.
- Explain how noise influences communication.
- Explain and practice the four communication situations.
- Analyze the four principles of communication.

Welcome to the world of business and professional communication. Preparation for the professional world is not difficult if you are willing to acquire the communication skills necessary for success. We hope this book will serve as a guide for the entire process of analyzing yourself to determine what type of employment to seek, steps to secure a position, and how to succeed in your chosen profession.

Most people reading this book are about to embark on a job search. The search process is much more than just applying for jobs. It begins with in-depth strategic planning prior to applying for an initial job interview. It is important to analyze yourself and your career goals as you decide where to apply for that first job. Obtaining an interview is only the first hurdle to clear in a competitive marketplace, and securing an interview by no means indicates you will be selected for the job.

Presenting yourself through a résumé and cover letter, digital portfolio, or an online application creates a number of challenges. Your writing must be impeccable, and your personality should be evident. Capturing the interest of the hiring manager is a must if you want to move forward through the interview process.

A job interview is one of the most important persuasive speeches you'll ever give because it attempts to convince others of your value as an employee. You'll make your employment journey easier when you recognize the value of communication skills, which include perceived warmth, comprehensive verbal ability, appropriate appearance, expansive writing skills, cooperative interpersonal qualities, and technical abilities (transmitting your ideas through electronic message sharing). Potential employers notice these communication skills immediately. Having excellent interpersonal skills and being able to give memorable answers to questions (both verbal and written) during an interview places you ahead of other job applicants.

Technology is changing the interview process for most available positions. Rather than face-to-face or phone interviews with an employer, you may receive an email invitation to an on-demand (one-way) video interview. You choose when to arrange to record your answers to prescripted questions using your computer's webcam. Employers later review the recorded videos, sometimes prescreened by artificial intelligence software to select the most likely candidates. Some employers continue to use resumés, which can also be prescreened by software to select the applicants for in-person interviews.

Once you receive and accept a job offer, there are a multitude of unknowns that will flash through your mind as you approach your new office space for the first day: Will you enjoy the job? Will you be prepared for the work that is handed to you? Will you be able to personalize your work space? How will you get along with your colleagues? How will your use of time affect your success? Will your attire be appropriate, and what does it communicate to others? Will you make a good first impression? Good communication skills provide a solid foundation for positive answers to these questions.

Whether you are seeking a job or have been in a position for a while, future advancement in an organization is critical for sustaining a productive, professional career. A typical career is approximately forty years in length. It is important to establish a strong foundation for your career and to build success with solid annual achievements. Strong communication skills will be your most valuable personal tool in life. Whether you are leading a team project, sending a mass email or report to clients, or participating in a virtual meeting, every piece of communication will help demonstrate that you are a professional communicator and valuable colleague. Remember, promotions and/or careers have been derailed by sloppy, impulsive, inappropriate, or unprofessional communication whether in person or on a digital platform. The material in the following chapters will help you avoid such pitfalls.

This book blends the theories of intrapersonal communication, interpersonal communication, nonverbal communication, gender communication, public speaking, group communication, organizational communication, and intercultural communication to focus on the essential skills for communicating appropriately in today's business setting. Let's begin with a basic review of the communication process to establish the foundation for professional business communication.

Communication Essentials

Communication is an interactive process between individuals where they share meaning verbally and/or nonverbally. The definition of communication is quite simple, but its execution is rather complicated since participants vary in culture, language usage, career background, and ability to use technology. You are familiar with verbal messages and their intended meaning, but nonverbal messages—every gesture you make, the clothes you wear, or even just the way you walk around the office—also communicate information to colleagues observing and evaluating you. Personal observation is an ongoing process, and the judgments made about you are cumulative and rarely forgotten.

We categorize communication as **intentional** or **unintentional**. For example, can you remember making a remark you never intended for someone else to hear—but they did? While unplanned communication may or may not have had long-lasting consequences in a junior high school setting, the consequences of unintentional communication in a business setting can be devastating. Everyone who hears a word or phrase of unintentional or thoughtless communication remembers it. Your verbal carelessness could haunt you in the future.

ETHICAL ENCOUNTER

You are in the restroom and overhear unflattering information about something your boss did. You treat this as fact and pass it on to another colleague. Later you find out you misheard the information. How do you fix this situation? What should you do differently?

It is important to understand that your goal in communicating is to share meaning effectively. Communication occurs whether others interpret it correctly or incorrectly. When someone interprets the meaning of language incorrectly, we call it miscommunication, but it remains communication nevertheless. If you become known as someone who can't exchange ideas clearly in a professional setting, you are establishing a pattern of unprofessional behavior that may lead to eventual career failure.

To communicate effectively in business, you must first understand:

- the importance of appropriate communication;
- the communication components;
- communication situations; and
- communication realities.

THE IMPORTANCE OF APPROPRIATE COMMUNICATION

Good communication skills help individuals feel comfortable and confident in their ability to exchange ideas in a timely, concise manner. Word selection when making a business presentation can tip the balance between a positive or negative reaction toward a presenter and the presentation itself.

REALITY ☑

It is important to develop career speech that eliminates local dialects and grammar that occasionally prevent careers from maturing because an employee's language usage doesn't meet the demands of the employer's national/global, diverse clientele.

It is not enough to be educated and to know your academic area well; you must be able to present your thoughts professionally in spontaneous situations. Communication training assists career-seeking individuals with strategies to help them better present their ideas—and themselves. Business recruiters look for individuals with the communication skills to step into a position immediately as well as fit into the corporate environment with other employees.

On a personal level, we communicate in business to accomplish tasks, get things we want, negotiate a raise, conduct business conversations, meet people, function in teams, learn new concepts, and prove our value to an organization. A key strategy to being successful—and earning a satisfactory income—is to practice communication skills that assure others of your professionalism and your value to the company. The more effective you are in using language and professional behavior, the better the potential career outcome.

Business reports consistently list communication as one of the ten essential skills an employee should possess—typically one of the first three skills listed. The inclusion of communication skills is no accident when you consider the daily contact you have with colleagues: interpersonally, nonverbally, technically, socially, and in formal presentations. Professionalism involves improving your speaking style, behavior, written ability, time management, and technical proficiency so business colleagues see you as someone who adds value to the company. Solid communication skills allow you to maneuver in the business world with self-confidence and a feeling of personal accomplishment.

Communication Components

Communication is an ongoing, cumulative process. For this reason, you need to polish every aspect of your communication style prior to entering the business community. To be successful at communication, coworkers must effectively share meaning with one another. Sharing meaning involves one person comprehending the intended meaning of another person's language and nonverbal behavior. However, comprehension is challenging when you consider that verbal style often evolves from individual family backgrounds, education, culture, and ethnicity. Technology makes it possible to work globally. Therefore, you must adapt to colleagues whose use of English is slightly different than your own because this is their second or third language.

Nonverbal communication can be misinterpreted easily as well. Before you can fully understand communication complexities, you need to consider the elements that make up an ordinary interpersonal interaction. Every interaction consists of the following **communication components**: communicators, messages, a channel, circumstances, feedback, and, in some instances, noise. A good communicator analyzes each of these components prior to making the best possible language choices for each business interaction.

Communicators

Communicators are the people involved in a verbal/nonverbal/written exchange. Each individual simultaneously sends and receives messages. For example, a coworker who briefly stops by your office transmits both nonverbal (smiles, hand gestures, eye contact) and verbal messages (the task material they talk about). In addition, you send messages to your coworker by maintaining eye contact, writing notes, or perhaps yawning during conversation. Everyone communicates something when they are in an environment with other people, whether or not they are aware of it. Effective communicators recognize that they intentionally and/or unintentionally send and receive messages; they constantly monitor and reflect on their verbal and nonverbal behavior as well as on the behavior of those around them while fine-tuning their skills. You can't control the communication style of another person, but you certainly can control and improve your own style so that you are perceived as a responsible, professional person.

For example, Laura notices that Rowan is distracted when she walks into the office. He is missing his usual quick smile and lively "good morning!" He is staring at the wall and belatedly utters a faint greeting after Laura reaches her desk. She perceives the difference in his usual nonverbal/verbal communication and proceeds based on that recognition. Laura sits at her desk and politely asks Rowan if anything is wrong. His verbal and nonverbal responses to her question will dictate where their conversation goes next.

Messages

Messages can be either verbal or nonverbal. **Verbal messages** include all spoken language; **nonverbal messages** are utterances and actions without words plus physical attributes. Nonverbal messages include our gestures, the way we use our voice (loud, soft, high or low pitch), the way we move, the clothes we wear, and the car we drive. When we enter an office, our clothes, gestures, haircut, and personal possessions send nonverbal messages to colleagues. But remember, nonverbal messages have the potential to be decoded incorrectly by others. A handshake when meeting someone may be a polite gesture to you, but someone in a position of greater authority may see your action as inappropriate. Some individuals of higher status prefer to extend their hand first to initiate physical contact.

Verbal and nonverbal communication require the continuous encoding and decoding of messages. This process begins with a thought a person wishes to communicate. The person encodes the thought into words and/or physical actions. **Encoding** means a communicator reviews all of the available symbols (words) and/or actions that could best represent her thought and selects the most effective method of expression. Then, the person selects a channel to send those words or actions to other communicators. The other communicators receive the words or actions and decode the message prior to responding. **Decoding** means analyzing and reacting to received symbols or actions, applying meaning to them, and consolidating them into a usable thought for an appropriate timely response.

The more effective we are at encoding our thoughts, the more likely other communicators are able to decode the meaning of our messages properly. You will have a better chance for shared meaning and understanding in interpersonal and group situations when you employ good encoding and decoding skills. It is important for communicators to be aware that anyone can decode a meaning that wasn't intentional. For instance, someone might decode another's pause before speaking as, "the following statement is not true." However, communicators may pause simply because they are trying to find the best word choice to start the next phrase or sentence. We should constantly be aware that some of the meanings we decode could be inaccurate; thus we need to analyze messages thoroughly before responding.

In the business world, you may enhance language encoding by using professional jargon. **Jargon** is specialized language used to communicate within a specific discipline or corporation. For instance, camera operators call the horizontal movement of a camera lens a "pan," while to a performer a pan is a bad review; for a chef, a pan is something entirely different. Every profession uses its own jargon, and you must shift your use of jargon to accommodate understanding during professional communication. Using incorrect jargon signals a lack of experience working in a specific profession.

REALITY ☑

We have an alum who went to work at a global corporation. She reported needing to carry a small notebook during the first week to record all of the jargon and acronyms used at the company. Quizzing herself at night allowed her to get up to speed quickly, to interact meaningfully with her coworkers, and to make a good impression in her first few days at work.

On the other hand, you must remember to eliminate technical jargon when you are talking to someone outside of your field of expertise. Your ability to flow in and out of jargon serves you well as long as you evaluate your intended audience. In other words, you can't use professional jargon when speaking to a community volunteer organization unrelated to your professional career. Language needs to match the background of an audience for them to clearly understand your message.

Delivery (how you say something) can enhance or hinder the effective decoding of a verbal message. The vocal characteristics we use in delivery include tone, pitch, rate, and variations in projection. All of these vocal characteristics color our words and phrases to emphasize or de-emphasize key thoughts in a presentation. If we don't deliver messages appropriately, our meaning may be distorted and decoded incorrectly by audience members.

Channels

Messages must travel through a specific medium—a **channel**—to get from one communicator to another. Each channel targets a different sensory receptor, so you must select the appropriate channel to accomplish your intended goal. The many channels include phones, handheld devices, computers, websites, newspapers, radio, television, books, notes, blogs, social networking sites and apps, sound systems, and face-to-face interaction.

When you choose a channel for various communication events, think about the purpose of the communication and the consequences of the message you send to make sure you have made the best decision. The choice of channel impacts how an audience receives a message. Some situations warrant direct involvement with the intended receiver of your message even though a technical channel might be more convenient and more comfortable.

For example, your department manager wants to fire your office mate, Anthony. She logs onto her computer and types, "The department is restructuring, and your position is terminated. Please clean out your desk by noon." She hits "send," then summons security to escort Anthony out of the building at noon. Is using email an appropriate channel in this situation? What will Anthony think of her action?

Familiarity with navigating technical channels like websites, blogs, social media, apps, and texting prepare you for the contemporary workforce. Each technical channel uses specific jargon for communication. Companies use each of these channels to reach internal and external receivers. You need to move quickly from one channel to the next while maintaining the appropriate language required for each channel. Although the business world still uses traditional channels like letters and presentations, the increasing reliance on **technical convergence** (developing messages for multiple platforms) requires greater analysis and response speed for targeting language to specific receivers.

Many companies also monitor your public and social behavior to protect their image in the community. For example, if you are talking to a community group, you will be seen as a representative of the company. So make sure that when you are communicating via public channels, you always act in the best interest of the company. If you engage in any negative chatter about the company, make ***sure*** the channel is private. Negative comments made in a bar/restaurant or on social media become public information. Privacy is evaporating quickly in the digital age. Be careful.

Circumstances

Circumstances refer to the context of a communication situation and to the fundamental nature of the communicators, which includes a communicator's background, attitudes, beliefs, and values. All of these elements influence verbal and nonverbal message choices and reactions to messages when decoded. A heated discussion in a business meeting may be threatening to some colleagues and yet invigorating to others. The fundamental nature of each participant determines his or her personal reaction to a heated discussion.

Attitudes, beliefs, and values all influence how we communicate to others. Think of the divided political world in which we live. Chances are that you work with people who do not have the same attitudes or beliefs as you. Highly-charged topics are best kept out of the workplace. Even an innocuous joke about taking home a workplace pen can upset someone who values honesty and believes this to be stealing. Be aware that everyone decodes your communication differently.

Context also contributes to the meaning of a message. What you say in one situation to a particular group of colleagues may not be appropriate with different colleagues. Every circumstance and its participants are unique and call for targeted messages and responses. For example, you and your colleagues feel comfortable using jokes and calling each other names. In the context of your office environment, you are all satisfied with this banter. However, you may feel uncomfortable or be offended if someone from outside your group makes the same comments to you. Analyzing your circumstances, including your own fundamental nature and the context of a situation, allows you make appropriate choices before uttering a verbal response or reacting to a particular comment. Think carefully about whether previous communication choices apply to your current situation and respond accordingly.

Feedback

Feedback is the response one communicator gives to another. It can be verbal, nonverbal, or a combination of the two. Feedback is essential during the communication process; it acknowledges the presence of the other person, lets the communicator know you received the message, and demonstrates that the communication is valued. The lack of feedback is one negative aspect of on-demand video interviews. Applicants frequently have no idea whether their responses were effective; there is no interviewer providing verbal and/or nonverbal feedback.

Feedback is not limited to face-to-face interactions. For example, a simple gesture like leaving a colleague's favorite cup of coffee on his or her desk as you return from a personal break provides feedback; it signals that you appreciate sharing the workload. Your colleague may never return the favor, but you have communicated a team-oriented approach.

Random acts of kindness in the workplace can go a long way to improve morale and good will.

You can improve your feedback by remembering to be timely. Responding to someone as soon as possible regarding a message so that they don't have to track you down helps to improve your business credibility. There are times when the sender can perceive any delay by the receiver as an inability to answer a question or as an avoidance tactic.

Immediacy behaviors are another key component to being perceived as a friendly employee. People who smile and look attentive, have positive body posture, and lean toward the other person when someone is talking are perceived to be giving positive feedback that keeps the conversation going. Obviously, sometimes you don't want to give that impression, but being open and friendly in your nonverbal feedback in general will help you to appear engaged and as if you are listening and interested.

Noise/Distractions

Noise consists of any distractions that interrupt communicators from encoding, sending, receiving, and/or decoding a message properly. There are three types of noise you need to consider as you communicate: physical, personal, and semantic.

PHYSICAL NOISE

Any external, distracting sound present during communication—from a humming light fixture to a bug flying around your desk while you are editing a document—constitutes physical noise. Physical noise distracts us and competes with our thought processes. As a communicator, you must concentrate harder on your remarks to avoid the external distraction whether you are speaking or writing. This is one reason why we turn down the car radio while trying to locate a client's office for the first time. It's easier to concentrate on your driving and spot a location when physical noise is minimized.

PERSONAL NOISE

Personal noise refers to ongoing thoughts or concerns in our minds. There are three types of personal noise that can distract our attention while focusing on a task.

- Prejudice.
- Closed-mindedness.
- Self-centeredness.

Prejudice occurs when we have a preconceived, often negative, view of someone or something. If, for example, you have biases against public school education, you may have a negative impression regarding the intellectual ability of anyone trained in a public environment. If you learn a colleague is from a public university, you may underestimate his or her ability. Conversely, if you are prejudiced toward private education, you could overestimate the ability of a colleague trained in a private environment. You should always be aware of personal prejudices and choose to eliminate them as you evaluate messages, people, and situations. Failure to do so could result in costly mistakes for your career.

Closed-mindedness occurs when we refuse to listen to another person's point of view. Think about your position on a topic like the virtual office: employees working from their home. Chances are you feel very strongly about the topic. Could you learn something by hearing information from the opposing side? Of course you can. However, many people who believe they are right refuse to listen to any information that conflicts with their own beliefs. This rigidity harms the communication process. In business, you could easily get into a heated discussion about such a topic. If you are arguing closed-mindedly, you could destroy another person's confidence in your ability to be reasonable and fair.

Self-centeredness occurs when we focus more on ourselves than on the other person during communication. How often do you zone out in meetings thinking about your own schedule, a meeting you have in two hours, your weekend activities, a fight with your significant other, or even what you will have for dinner? You may have learned the art of smiling, nodding and/or looking attentive during a presentation even though you are not paying the least bit of attention to the message. This personal distraction can easily lead to making a serious mistake at work (for example, failing to use a new technical protocol discussed at the department meeting). This attention failure can cost you your position. While you may have been able to zone out in college lectures and get by, you'll need to change this behavior to succeed in business.

You can practice tuning out personal noise by taking notes in class. This activity will help you pay attention, retain important information, and build good habits for the workplace.

SEMANTIC NOISE

The third type of noise is semantic noise. Semantic noise occurs when the person you are communicating with speaks a different language, uses technical jargon, and/or resorts to emotionally charged words. As the corporate sector expands globally, the potential for problems caused by different languages increases. Some of your colleagues may not use English as effectively as you do, just as you may not use their language as effectively as they do. Adding technical jargon to your communication increases the confusion. If one communicator knows the terminology and the other does not, sharing meaning is difficult if not impossible.

Emotionally charged words also block the communication process. The listener may fixate on a word rather than paying attention to the complete message. For example, in some regions of the United States, the terms "Ma'am" and "Sir" refer to people who are in positions of authority, even if they are only 30 years old. However, in other areas of the United States, those terms conjure up images of senior citizens. The term "Ma'am" might offend a 30-year-old woman in northern California—just as a 30-year-old woman in Arkansas could be offended if a younger person didn't use "Ma'am" while addressing her. Business language should always be respectful; effective business language involves knowing the customs of a particular locale and adapting to its style.

Every step of the communication process is important in establishing your credibility with others. Select your message and channel carefully. As a communicator, you must be aware of the entire chain of events your words or actions initiate; accept responsibility for the choices you make throughout a conversation. Always consider the circumstances of the people around you as you evaluate a message and select the appropriate channel for its delivery. You should be aware of noise in every interaction and work to eliminate it whenever possible. And you should do your best to provide proper feedback to the requests of colleagues. These personal communication choices make professional interactions as smooth and effective as possible. To be an effective communicator, you should strive to make wiser verbal and nonverbal choices as you become more aware of how interactive the process truly is.

Post-analysis of every interaction can help you evaluate a poor communication experience. Ask yourself: "Was it me?" "Was it the other person?" "Was it the channel?" "Was my message worded incorrectly?" "Was there noise?" You can improve future interactions by examining personal word/behavioral choices that work or don't work.

Communication Situations

There are four basic communication situations.

- Intrapersonal communication is communicating within yourself.
- Interpersonal communication is communicating with another person.
- Small group communication is communicating with 3–20 people (with 5–8 as the ideal size) who have a common goal.
- Public communication is communicating with a large audience.

When we mentally review, rehearse, or analyze conversations or experiences internally, we are engaging in **intrapersonal commu-**

nication. Think how often you do a mental review of content or organizational structure prior to an important meeting or presentation. Before you meet with a manager, do you think about what you are going to say in the time given to you? When your alarm goes off in the morning, do you think, "If I hit the snooze button, I can give up the shower and sleep for another 18 minutes"? We use intrapersonal communication constantly as we meditate, reflect, and strategize. Intrapersonal communication helps us to know ourselves, to practice important communication scenarios, to analyze everything around us (including our own actions), and to think critically of past and future events.

In contrast to the internal dialogue of intrapersonal communication, **interpersonal communication** takes place whenever two people speak or see one another in addition to a written exchange of ideas, no matter how brief the exchange. Examples include: the discussion you had with a coworker about office expenses; the complaints you shared with someone about an office colleague; the person you acknowledged in the cafeteria; a boss you spoke to regarding a raise. You should be able to list at least 20 exchanges you had with others in the last 24 hours. We use interpersonal communication constantly to help create and maintain our relationships, both personal and public.

Interpersonal communication becomes **small group communication** when the number of people increases; groups ideally have five to seven members but can sometimes be constructed with three to twenty. Group members generally have a sense of belonging and usually share common beliefs, goals, or reasons for getting together. Group members work together to accomplish task, organizational, and/or relationship goals.

Groups with task goals meet to solve a problem or complete an assignment. You can find this type of group in the workplace or in volunteer organizations. Task groups normally consist of five to seven people. When your company asks five of you to develop a marketing plan for the distribution a new product, you are a part of a task group. Another function of groups is the relationship goal, which fulfills the personal needs of conversation and belonging. These groups may consist of close friends who eat dinner together occasionally or colleagues who go to a movie at the end of the week simply to unwind. Sometimes groups have both task and relationship goals. These blended groups could include a social group, book club, and/or a religious gathering. In addition to relationship functions, these groups also perform tasks such as fundraisers, social service projects, reading assignments, and so forth.

Teams are a specific type of small group. Teams work on tasks designed to accomplish a specific goal. Members of teams employ a standard procedure to accomplish their goal. Teams are prevalent in numerous workplace environments. In this text, we focus exclusively on communication within teams rather than on the broader concept of small group communication. Solid teamwork results in job satisfaction, overall productivity, personal fulfillment, and professional advancement.

Public communication occurs when a communicator informs, persuades, and/or entertains a large group of people. Speakers have an organized message to deliver, an official audience, and they prepare for an event. Typically, public communication comes in the form of training seminars, oral presentations, a keynote address at a conference, and corporate announcements via in-house media, as well as messages delivered through digital media. You may think you will never have to give a speech after graduating from college; however, public communication is definitely in your future. You should learn the skills for effective public speaking so that you are better prepared when opportunities arise in both your professional and personal life. Once you have employment, your public performance reflects on your employer. You should always deliver the presentations you make with superior performance standards. Professional success is more probable when you function at your best consistently.

> With the prevalence of social media, you will need to think carefully about the kinds of posts you make and how they might jeopardize your position at your company.

Communication Principles

Improving your communication skills takes time, practice, and dedication. It involves thinking before acting, research, making the best verbal and nonverbal choices for public behavior, and dealing responsibly with the consequences of those choices. Below are four principles to keep in mind when thinking about communication.

- We cannot not communicate.
- Communication is irreversible.
- Communication is an ongoing, cumulative process.
- Communication involves ethical considerations.

WE CANNOT NOT COMMUNICATE

Someone, somewhere, receives and interprets everything we do. Even if we isolate ourselves, thinking we won't have to communicate, the very act of not interacting with people you've known for a long time communicates a specific message to them. We communicate with family members, friends, coworkers, peers, professors, salespersons, significant others, and many more. We constantly put our communication skills to the test every minute of every day.

COMMUNICATION IS IRREVERSIBLE

If you say something or do something that upsets another person, whether it is intentional or unintentional, you can't change it. Once the words are out of your mouth or you complete an inappropriate action, the damage is done. You can apologize and hope to lessen the impact of your words or behaviors, but you can't change the initial impression you made. When you choose certain words or act a certain way, there are consequences—some positive and some negative. Effective communicators understand this principle and, therefore, think carefully before they speak or act. They monitor and reflect on all of their communication.

COMMUNICATION IS AN ONGOING, CUMULATIVE PROCESS

The bits of information we collect internally become part of our fundamental nature and affect our future communication. By being more aware of why we say the things we do, we can improve our professional speech style and learn numerous new diverse perspectives. We each experience the world a little differently, so in addition to understanding and improving our own style, we need to remember that other people have their own unique styles as well. No one is a perfect communicator; instead, we have varying degrees of success in different situations. Effective communicators are flexible because they adapt their messages to the circumstances they encounter. Improving your communication skills is a lifelong commitment to building an excellent professional image. You already possess basic communication skills; by increasing your performance repertoire (verbal, nonverbal, written, and use of technical channels), you will be able to handle the numerous diverse situations you encounter daily. You don't need to imitate others or to compromise your values and ethical standards to be successful. However, polishing language skills (verbal and written) allows you to communicate effectively and to adjust to unexpected circumstances.

COMMUNICATION INVOLVES ETHICAL CONSIDERATIONS AS WELL

As you think about the fact that communication is an ongoing process and that it is irreversible, you want to think about its ethical considerations. "Ethical issues may arise in human behavior whenever that behavior could have significant impact on other persons, when the behavior involves conscious choice of means and ends, and when the behavior can be judged by standards of right and wrong" (Johannesen, Valde, and Whedbee, 2008, p. 1). You will find ethical questions to consider/analyze throughout this book. These ethical issues provide opportunities for reflection and for discussion with your classmates.

Many communication situations we face on a daily basis in business include ethical choices. For example, do we pass along a piece of gossip we hear about a peer? Or do we take the time to investigate the comment prior to making a decision regarding its truthfulness and passing it along? Or do we refrain from sharing the information altogether? On another day, do we refrain from communicating that we disagree with a policy decision? Or do we hide our feelings by remaining silent? Each of these choices has considerable ethical consequences related to credibility and professional judgment.

We can also use communication to uphold personal ethics and moral standards in everyday life. We do so, for instance, in a grocery store when we inform the clerk that the register undercharged us, or when we tell a server that the dessert we ordered is missing from the bill. Our conduct projects our personal ethical standards to those around us in these daily situations.

The better you know yourself through intrapersonal examination, and the more you practice communicating interpersonally, the better equipped you will be to handle challenging business situations.

REALITY ☑

Which of the four communication realities have you seen in action in the workplace?

Final Thoughts

Someone is always observing your behavior, listening to your communication style, and analyzing your abilities. Any home with electronic monitoring, TVs or artificial intelligence devices (ie. Alexa, Google, etc.) is being monitored by complete strangers. Every movement or sound in these homes is being heard/recorded somewhere. Judgments of others are cumulative and, in numerous professional situations, never revealed to you. Professional advancement is rooted in judgments that others make about you and your abilities on a daily basis. Therefore, you should do your best to be consistent with your language and behavior at all times. The knowledge you gain from this book will help you to review and to improve your current skills so that you become a more successful communicator in a variety of situations. Every new situation is as simple and as complicated as walking into your office space on the first day of a new job while being evaluated by colleagues. Chapter 2 will help you analyze your communication and behavior so that you will be more aware of your fundamental nature as you continue your journey toward becoming a business professional.

Key Terms

Channel
Circumstances
Closed-mindedness
Communication components
Communicators
Decoding
Encoding
Feedback
Interpersonal communication
Intrapersonal communication
Jargon
Messages (verbal/nonverbal)
Noise
Personal noise
Physical noise
Prejudice

Public communication
Self-centeredness
Semantic noise
Small group communication
Teams
Technical convergence

Exercises

1. Divide the class into small groups. Each group will build and maintain a weekly blog discussing and updating the material in the book as it's covered.
2. Research a current business publication online to find a Top 10 list of the skills professionals feel are necessary to obtain a job. How many of the skills listed are communication skills? Why are these skills important to a corporation?
3. What are your strongest and weakest communication skills? How can you improve your weakest skill?
4. What channel do you prefer for most communication? Why? What channel do you like least? Why?
5. What communication challenges are present when addressing someone twenty or more years older? Discuss the differences in addressing a parent versus an employer the same age as the parent.
6. Wear professional attire to class for a week. Does your attire change the way you feel?

CHAPTER
TWO

Intrapersonal Examination

Goals

- Describe the three steps of the perceptual process.
- Analyze the differences in people's varying perceptions.
- Practice the perception checking skill.
- Explain how perception relates to self-concept and self-esteem.
- Choose and rank values that are important to you.
- Assess your strengths and weaknesses.
- Assess your intrapersonal qualities.
- Appraise your communication skills, predict your success, and plan for improvements.

When we think of going out into the work world, we often focus on what interactions we may encounter with others. We often neglect our intrapersonal communication in that thought process. Whereas **interpersonal communication** is communication between two or more people, **intrapersonal communication** is the dialogue and thought process that goes on internally. We are acting as our own receiver during intrapersonal communication.

As you begin to think about a career, it is important to have a thorough understanding of yourself through extensive intrapersonal communication and self-assessment. You need to be able to assess your job skills, communication skills, personal values, qualities, and goals. What kind of person are you? Does your perception of who you are match the perception strangers have when they meet you? What career do you want to pursue? Do your answers to these basic questions about yourself match the qualifications for the career you wish to pursue?

The world of technology has everyone exchanging messages, befriending total strangers, tweeting and blogging, but few individuals are really looking at or analyzing the motivation behind their message exchanges. Effective communicators allow verbal and nonverbal messages to be a true reflection of who they are and what they think; it is essential to know who you really are. On a personal level, are you energetic, lazy, enthusiastic, boring, innovative, or dull? Are you a needy person or independent? Do you take charge of a situation or drag your feet in making decisions? The answers to all of these questions are extremely important to consider as you prepare for your working career. Professional people must project a credible image by consistently matching verbal and nonverbal messages with what they know to be true about themselves. Audiences are more at ease when speakers are perceived as authentic—confident about who they are, genuine, trustworthy, and sincere.

Personal perception is the foundation of self-esteem and self-concept. Analyzing your nonverbal and verbal skills allows you to create a credible persona for professional growth and advancement. Other people decide if you are worth knowing or employing. Therefore, it is worth your time to comprehend perception as it applies to communication and your potential for success.

Imagine attending a business/social meeting in which you and your colleagues are locked in a heated, hour-long discussion with your boss. The discussion is frank, and voices are raised. As you return to your desk after the meeting, one colleague comments about enjoying the invigorating discussion. Another colleague, however, is visibly shaken, feeling targeted by the yelling. How can two colleagues react so differently to the same meeting? Although both participated actively in the discussion, they did not perceive the session's significance in the same way. It is useful to remember that personal perception is more than its dictionary definition (awareness of the elements of the environment through physical sensation). **Perception** is the act of sorting through external stimuli and assigning meaning to them. Chapter 1 discussed the term "fundamental nature." It is an important term to keep in the back of your mind during all of your communication with others. Because people have different life experiences as well as expectations, they perceive events and personal behaviors differently. Competent communicators assess potential communication difficulties that result from perceptual differences. Perception affects how individuals encode and decode messages, and savvy communicators are aware of these differences.

THE PERCEPTUAL PROCESS

You are asked to attend a meeting to discuss financial restraint. Departmental expenses are too high and need to be lowered for the next two fiscal quarters. Employees must find a way to slash the current operating budget by 20%, or management will eliminate a position. Everyone attending the meeting is apprehensive about how to manage current departmental responsibilities and duties with such a significant financial decrease while trying to save everyone's job. Tom suggests that the department limit photocopying; Kay immediately opposes the idea. She is uneasy with his suggestion because photocopying is an extremely important part of her business routine. If she can't have unlimited photocopying, she will not be able to meet her clients' needs. Kay is quite assertive and not afraid to voice her opinion loudly. Shareese, a quiet young woman, perceives Kay's boisterous communication style as "attitude" and feels that Kay is yelling at group members even though Kay thinks she is simply defending her position. The varying reactions of employees reveal the perceptual differences based on individual fundamental natures. Differing perceptions of how a verbal discussion should be conducted makes professional communication challenging.

Another colleague, Rick, considers what he can do to lower costs but doesn't share his ideas. He isn't really paying attention to the comments of Tom, Kay, or Shareese. He is mentally focused on what he can do to help. A little later, however, Kay makes a snide remark to Tom regarding Rick's unwillingness to enter the discussion. Her zinger is somewhat funny but also hurtful. Na'eem overhears the remark and smiles; Shareese is totally unaware of the exchange. Rick has a negative personal reaction to Kay's remark because it reminds him of how his wife snipes at him at home. The tone of the discussion begins to shift as Rick allows his negative reaction to her remark to color his professional judgment and subsequent communication with his colleagues. The personal perceptions of each individual in this scenario influence and affect the behavior of everyone else. This makes it difficult to remain focused on the topic itself.

There are three steps in the **perceptual process**:

- selection,
- organization, and
- interpretation.

In the first step of the perceptual process—**selection**—your mind decides which of the numerous stimuli during communication to recognize. Rick hears Kay's snide remark, while Shareese does not. Shareese notices Kay's tone of voice, which Tom doesn't consider threatening in any way. Tom notices that Shareese is withdrawing nonverbally, shrinking physically by slouching in the chair and crossing her arms. No one else pays attention to her nonverbal behavioral shift.

Meanwhile, there are other distractions (physical noise) in the room that no one notices: the coffee maker is dripping, the fluorescent light is humming, and street noise is swirling in through an open window. If we acknowledged all of the sensory stimuli around us, we'd be overwhelmed and have trouble concentrating on the tasks in front of us. Perception helps us sort through external stimuli for relevance as we focus on the immediate task(s). The process of focusing on specific stimuli (language, behavior, sound, color, temperature, etc.) and ignoring everything else is called **selective attention**. While numerous other stimuli are present in every environment, we normally focus on the primary tasks before us (although personal reactions may color our perceptions) while eliminating secondary distractions.

In the second step of the perceptual process—**organization**—your brain takes the stimuli you receive and organizes them by mentally grouping them together in meaningful, organized ways. You may have seen the example that follows:

> aoccdrnig to a rscheeahcr at an Elingsh uinervtisy, it deosn't mttaer in waht oredr the ltteers in a wrod are, the olny iprmoetnt tihng is that frist and lsat ltteers be at the rghit pclae. The rset can be a toatl mses and you can sitll raed it wouthit porbelm. Tihs is bcuseae we do not raed ervey lteter by itslef but the wrod as a wlohe.

This example demonstrates how quickly our minds analyze and reorganize information. Almost everyone can read the paragraph above with little or no trouble. If you receive a partial message, you fill in the holes in written language automatically. This is an amazing ability of the brain, but you should be very careful in professional communication to make sure your written material is accurate. Even though someone may not notice a mistake because they "fill in" your error perceptually, you can't count on that. People who do see the error may ignore the content of your message because they assess you as less capable.

While you are in college, get into the habit of reading your material out loud. It is easy to miss errors when proofreading because your mind corrects mistakes or omissions. It's easier to locate errors spoken aloud. This may save you from embarrassment in the work world.

Accurate spelling and grammar send clear signals to others about your competence and credibility in communication. Written errors are a sign of incompetence in the professional world.

REALITY ☑

Sometimes multiple people can proofread something and still miss an error. We recently saw an invitation that read:

> Happy Holidays
> CEO John Smith & and Jane Doe
>
> Cordially invite you and your guest to
> a Holiday Open House

You should be able to identify two errors in that extremely short message.

We organize the relevance of messages by comparing them to information we retain from previous experiences. Thinking about similar situations, incidences, or behaviors allows us to use them to categorize new information prior to assigning meaning. It's frequently assumed that future events in our lives possess similarities to previous experiences. The past is the foundation of selective attention that helps us select and organize stimuli for a response, but it can also limit our ability to perceive new information properly. When we fail to view new perceptual input with an open mind, it is difficult to be an effective, nonjudgmental communicator. We may recognize only similarities rather than noticing subtle nuances of difference in the input. Previous judgments can be a guide to selecting good language/behavior responses, but they can also easily cloud our willingness to remain open to analyzing new information properly when we feel pressured to make a hasty decision.

Once you organize stimuli by grouping it into categories and comparing it to your previous experiences, you move into the third step of the perceptual process—**interpretation and response**. You interpret all stimuli you receive and assign meaning to it. This third step is where you reflect your fundamental nature. Influences from your family, community, religion, learning experiences, and relationships affect how you interpret a specific perceptual event and respond to it verbally and nonverbally.

Let's return to the business meeting example. Rick's cell phone rings, and he decides to answer it. You pay attention to the call for a moment and then become annoyed because you perceive that Rick thinks the financial discussion is less important than his incoming call. That is the meaning you assign to Rick's nonverbal communication. Your attention shifts away from him once again after a brief period and returns to the financial conversation, but you remain very annoyed with Rick based on your perceptual interpretation of his lack of cell phone etiquette. However, others don't interpret Rick's act in the same way.

Varying Perceptions

People's perceptions of the same sensory input are not identical to yours for a variety of reasons. The cell phone incident is one example of the complexity of perception. You perceive Rick's actions as offensive, while Tom is busy eavesdropping. He perceives the call as a welcome distraction from the heated, cost-cutting discussion.

Shareese is glad to have something else to focus on other than Kay's shrill comments. Na'eem is the youngest colleague in the room, and he grew up using a cell phone and new media. He perceives the phone interruption as necessary. He is comfortable answering a cell phone no matter when it rings because he thinks he can handle multiple conversations and respond appropriately to each of them.

So why do perceptions vary? How can two individuals assign meaning differently when they experience the same stimuli? Think back to the communication process and our discussion of circumstances. We talked about the fact that all participants in the communication possess different backgrounds and experiences. As you add that personal component to the perceptual process, you can begin to appreciate the complexities of communication. In the organizing step, we are comparing sensory stimuli to our past experiences. When colleagues have different experiences, it is reasonable to deduce that they can have different interpretations for stimuli while engaged in interpersonal communication. Therefore, it is important to make sure that others clearly understand your communication style.

REALITY ☑

The concept of perception applies not only to individuals but also to departments within companies as well as businesses. Professionals can brand a specific department in their own organization as ineffective: troublesome personalities, don't meet deadlines, don't keep promises, do shoddy work, etc. If you wind up working in such a department, your corporate colleagues may automatically consider you to have poor skills because you are part of the "bad" department. Perception can override reality.

Perception Checking

Because the interpretation phase of communication leaves us vulnerable to misunderstanding, perception checking is a skill you can use to double-check your comprehension of what is going on with another person. **Perception checking** consists of three parts.

- First, you give an objective description of what you sensed.
- Second, you give an interpretation of what the situation meant to you.
- Finally, you ask a question to clarify for accurate meaning.

In the previous example, you could say to Rick, "I noticed you answered your cell phone during the meeting. I felt your conversation to be disruptive and showed that you were not interested in the department's future. Is this the case?" This is a theoretical example of perception checking; no one really speaks this way. How could you rephrase those thoughts in a way that sounds more natural but still incorporates the three steps? The goal of perception checking is clarity. You could try, "Hey Rick, I see you kept getting calls during the meeting. Do you have an important deal that you need to finalize?"

It is useful to remember that you should only use perception checking if there is a chance your attribution of meaning is incorrect. In the following example, it would be inappropriate to use perception checking.

> *Shareese:* Na'eem, would you please close the door so we can avoid distractions?
>
> *Na'eem:* I'm getting the sense you would like to have the door closed. Would you?

Overusing perception checking is inappropriate. Think of how annoying it would be to have someone constantly checking to see if you are mad at them. Sometimes people use perception checking inappropriately as a communication tool for conversational clarity when they really need to stop and spend some time analyzing the communication. In our initial example of the communication differences between Kay and Shareese, if Kay is speaking in an excited or intense voice, why is Shareese's first perception that Kay is yelling (angry)? Why wouldn't Shareese assume Kay feels strongly about the topic? Some people tend to think that everything is their fault when in reality they need to think of other possible reasons that might trigger the behavior and discover the reasons for their perception of the behavior.

You should use perception checking when you truly want to understand what is going on with another person. If a colleague is in a bad mood and you work closely with her, you can choose to ignore her language or behavior and stay out of her way until her mood improves. But if a situation continues to bother you, then you need to clarify whether you are the cause of her foul mood before simply assuming you are. Perception checking is a tool of resolution in this situation.

REALITY ☑

Lots of things bother people. A poignant journal entry from a former student talked about the fact that her father had died when she was in middle school. It was sad and hurtful to hear other people talk about their fathers. However, she knew that it wasn't right for her to tell everyone to stop. Instead it was she who needed to find a way to cope.

In the business world, however, you can't always figure out the dynamics of every interaction. Sometimes people say hurtful things, and you simply need to move on. What if you perception check with someone, and he says that he had no hurtful intentions. He was resolving another situation in his mind and didn't think before saying something to you. However, you still feel hurt. There is no easy way to resolve this. Some people want everyone to know when they are hurt or offended by words or actions. This response is not perception checking, because it does not ask for communication clarity. The response is an emotional reaction asking for an apology, not clarity.

> We don't need to voice every injustice. Sometimes people just say things that are hurtful and sometimes you need to let it go. Your (possibly inappropriate) response could create conflict. Move on.

The fact is, some businesspeople care if they've hurt your feelings, and others simply don't care at all. You need to know your emotional self well before you ask for clarity from others. You may be perceived as emotionally weak if you are constantly offended by colleagues. This perception could prevent promotion within an organization as well as lead to your termination.

REALITY ☑

Some people are emotionally fragile and feel hurt by everything. Is this you? As part of an intrapersonal assessment, you need to ask yourself how often you feel hurt by another person's remarks or actions. Can you take constructive criticism and fix the problem, or do you perceive any criticism to be malicious or hurtful (they don't like me)? Why?

Finally, there are many people who feel awkward using the perception-checking skill. It does take some practice if you haven't used it a great deal. Some people are reluctant to use perception checking because it is easier to assume what another person means than to ask for clarity. You may think you will appear to be weak if you ask for clarity. Although asking someone to explain his or her behavior may be initially awkward, the value of accuracy in communication—personal and professional—is immeasurable.

Ethical Encounter

There are moments in a professional career when you can use perception checking to reveal personal beliefs and/or principles. You must determine within yourself if a personal principle is worth revealing as you ask someone for clarity. In other words, what are the consequences for your future? For example, it is definitely worth asking, "I'm not sure what you mean by that?" if someone makes a racist, sexist, or homophobic remark. If they respond with an "Awww come on, I was just joking around!" you may need to reply with a request, "Ok, please don't talk that way around me." This response clearly lets the other person know how you wish to be treated. But if the remark is a small, inconsequential one about a situation at work or the disorder on your desk, it may be best to ignore the remark and move on. If you call attention to the remark, you will enhance its significance for yourself and the other person will remember you for speaking up. Each of you alters your perception of the other based on the remark, and an offhand interaction will influence all future communication with each other. What principles do you hold that are worth perception checking?

Perception Related to Self-Concept

Another way perception relates to each of us is through its connection to self-concept. **Self-concept** refers to what we know about ourselves (positive and negative), including our physical attributes (short or tall, big or small), our aptitudes (good managerial skills, getting along with others), our physical coordination (good athlete, proficient at yoga), our skills (creativity, analytical reasoning, writing), and our knowledge of a specialty area (computer programming, graphic design). We assess our self-concept in three ways.

- Facts that we observe about ourselves.
- Feedback that we get from others.
- Comparison of ourselves to others.

When we examine our performance, we are assessing facts about ourselves. We recognize whether we are tall or short, effective in interpersonal relationships, type 100 wpm, speak well, write well, and so forth. These conclusions are the result of intrapersonal assessment and evaluation. Some people, however, cannot accurately assess themselves. They think they are talented at things when they are actually deficient, or they are hypercritical of themselves even when they are good at what they do. While being confident and/or humble are both terrific qualities, accurate **self-assessment** allows you to interact with others without being annoying. No one wants to listen to or be around a braggart or a whiner.

We also assess ourselves through the feedback we get from others, both verbally and nonverbally. Personal evaluations made by teachers, family members, significant others, friends, siblings, other relatives, coaches, and religious leaders impact our sense of self, and they need to be analyzed for accuracy in order to improve on weaknesses we perceive as valid. If, as a child, you hear someone say that you are "pretty" or "smart" or "stupid" or "lazy," these verbal labels shape your perception of yourself. Nicknames such as "chubby," "slim," "bubba," or "princess" also affect self-concept. If we see ourselves through the labels given to us by others, we may develop a self-concept based on illusion rather than reality. These labels can influence the way you present yourself to business colleagues as an adult. Do you see yourself as a "Bubba" on the way to a job interview? Do you see yourself as a "princess?" If so, how will the human resources director evaluate your behaviors as you act out these perceptions? It is better to see yourself as professionally qualified rather than as a Bubba or princess to market yourself appropriately.

REALITY ☑

Placing too much value on labels from others can be problematic. If you were unlucky enough to have verbally abusive parents who constantly told you that you were incapable of doing anything right, you need to make sure that you don't live up to the negative label they placed on you. People, even parents, can be mean and wrong. Someone else's opinion is simply that . . . an opinion—it is not a fact. Emotional stability is based on fact and what you can actually do.

Lastly, we assess through comparison with others. Have you ever found yourself with a very low grade, but you felt much better after learning that everyone else received a similar grade? That is comparison. We can improve ourselves if we realize that we are not up to par with our colleagues in a certain skill. We can practice, take an outside course, or get experience elsewhere. Try not to pay attention to comparisons that don't matter.

REALITY ☑

During the intrapersonal evaluation process, write a description of yourself centering on the various aspects of self-concept. What are your strengths and weaknesses? Once you examine your self-concept truthfully, you can begin to strengthen each skill you possess and to correct perceived weaknesses.

Naturally, self-concept influences your communication skills with the external world. Presentational style, use of nonverbal communication, ability to interact on an interpersonal level, or the ability to function in a team environment evolves from self-concept. If our self-concept is one of shyness, we are likely to have non-animated nonverbals, a quiet disposition, a subdued presentational style, and we may be reluctant to participate in teams. On the other hand, if our self-concept is one of confidence, we stand tall, speak effectively (grammar and tone), and willingly participate in teams.

Before you venture into the business world, it is important to have a realistic grasp of your self-concept to avoid placing yourself in professional situations you are not prepared to handle.

Share your assessment with a trusted friend to check for accuracy.

Perception Related to Self-Esteem

Self-esteem refers to the value we place on our self-concept while observing and interacting with the environment around us. For example, Rachel is 5′1″ tall; part of her self-concept is that she's quite short. Her self-esteem related to this concept depends on the value she places on height. In U.S. culture, research shows that tall people have an advantage over competitors in interviews, presidential elections, and promotions (Andersen, 2008, pp. 320–321). If Rachel thinks only tall people are attractive and competent, her self-esteem will probably be low because there is nothing she can do to change her height. However, if she believes competency does not depend on height, then being 5′1″ tall will not affect her self-esteem as she interacts with other people.

It is easy to be your own worst enemy. However, you can choose to be either extremely critical or extremely supportive of yourself. How you communicate intrapersonally affects your self-esteem. What do you say to yourself when you miss a project deadline? Do you say, "I can't believe how stupid I am! I can never do anything right." This negative internal communication can damage your self-esteem and affect future behavior. Or, do you say something positive to yourself, "Wow. I can't believe I didn't make that deadline. I need to figure out what to do differently so I can improve my performance and keep this job." Your intrapersonal communication can harm or improve self-esteem. It is important to remain positive in self-criticism so you can solve your problem(s) and improve performance.

Be positive and gentle with yourself. Unless, of course, you need a kick in the pants for motivation. Be adaptable enough to know the difference.

Self-esteem and self-concept influence our willingness and ability to communicate effectively. If you feel good about yourself, you are more likely to meet new people, to assert your ideas in a team situation, to stand confidently before an audience as you speak, and to experiment with new communication strategies. If you don't trust yourself to discover new inner abilities and instead rely only on past skills that make you feel comfortable, you constrict personal growth and hinder potential marketability. If you feel you need to strengthen your self-concept or self-esteem, there are numerous books and articles outlining ways to improve. Seeking professional assistance is another option. Thorough awareness of both concepts (self-concept and self-esteem) is extremely useful before venturing into the workplace.

Values, Personal Qualities (Skills), and Communication Assessments

In addition to understanding the concept of perception and how it relates to your self-concept and self-esteem, you should also do some work assessing your values, personal qualities (skills), and communication skills.

Values

The first thing to do in this assessment of self is to take a serious look at the things you value. Matching your **values** to a potential job will help you make better employment decisions. A career is challenging enough; working in an environment that doesn't match your personal values will increase stress. There are a number of different values and numerous lists to research for assistance. The following list offers a good start in assessing your personal values (Roberts, n.d.). Underline the words that are important to you; review the values you underlined and circle the five that are the most important to you. Discuss your choices with classmates and look for similarities and differences when comparing the results.

Achievement	Financial gain	Physical challenge
Advancement and promotion	Freedom	Pleasure
Adventure	Friendships	Power and authority
Affection (love and caring)	Growth	Privacy
Arts	Having a family	Public service
Being around people who are open and honest	Helping other people	Purity
Challenging problems	Helping society	Quality of what I take part in
Change and variety	Honesty	Quality relationships
Close relationships	Independence	Recognition (respect from others, status)
Community	Influencing others	Religion
Competence	Inner harmony	Reputation
Competition	Integrity	Responsibility and accountability
Cooperation	Intellectual status	Security
Country	Involvement	Self-respect
Creativity	Job tranquility	Serenity
Decisiveness	Knowledge	Sophistication
Democracy	Leadership	Stability
Ecological awareness	Location	Status
Economic security	Loyalty	Supervising others
Effectiveness	Market position	Time freedom
Efficiency	Meaningful work	Truth
Ethical practice	Merit	Wealth
Excellence	Money	Wisdom
Excitement	Nature	Work under pressure
Fame	Order (tranquility, stability, conformity)	Work with others
Fast living	Personal development	Working alone

What is the most important value you possess according to the list you just created? Does the business you are interested in match your personal values? For instance, if money is your number one value, then you may be willing to work under pressure, supervise others, and place your family second to the job. On the other hand, if family is the most important thing to you, you may need to realize that you can't have a fast-paced, travel-filled, high-pressure job that keeps you at the office at all hours or on-call 24-7.

REALITY ☑

How will the values you selected affect your ideal job choice? Be specific.

If you accept a job at a company with values significantly different from your own, you may regret the decision eventually. For example, we knew someone who went to work at a huge corporation. It seemed like a dream job with a clothing allowance, a high salary, and lots of prestige. However, our friend soon realized that the company expected him to be available for any and all events. There were mandatory happy hours, mandatory golf weekends, etc. He soon found that his time was not his own (not to mention that he hated golf). The company paid time-and-a-half for these events but the money did not compensate for the dissatisfaction. Our friend valued his independence and alone time. He discovered he had to leave the company after only 9 months. Most importantly, he discovered that his initial assessment of money as his most important value was inaccurate. He found that he valued independence and free time more than the money he was making. He approached his next employment possibility armed with a much more informed assessment of his values.

Personal values can shift with time and experience. This is not a frustrating concept or an example of personal failure. It simply indicates personal and professional adjustment as you gain experience and more self-awareness. Periodic self-examination highlights possible changes and corresponding shifts in emphasis.

Ethical Encounter

What happens when you encounter others in the workplace whose values differ from your own? How will you handle the communication?

Personal Qualities (Skills)

Before you go looking for a new job, it is important to figure out how good you are at what you want to do. If you've been actively preparing for your career, you've done an internship in your area of interest as a student, part-time work that supports your career choice, or volunteer work to gain experience working with others. The following questions may help pinpoint your **personal qualities/ skills** and the type of employment for which you are best suited. Are you comfortable in diverse situations? Do you have experience in virtual meetings? Can you plan large social events? Do you consistently send thank you notes to people who make a difference in your daily routine?

Julie Jansen (2016), a career and executive coach, identifies 11 keys to success that any individual can develop. These are all qualities that help us to be successful people.

1. **Confidence:** belief in oneself based on a realistic understanding of one's capabilities and circumstances.
2. **Curiosity:** an eagerness to know and learn; exhibiting constant interest; paying special attention to the less obvious.
3. **Decisiveness:** making a choice and taking action.
4. **Empathy:** seeking to understand someone else's feelings and situation; demonstrating caring.
5. **Flexibility:** responding positively to change; being adaptable and able to deal with ambiguity.
6. **Humor:** not taking yourself too seriously; being amusing and amused; viewing the world with enjoyment.
7. **Intelligence:** thinking and planning before acting; working efficiently. (Jansen stresses that this skill differs from one's IQ.)

8. **Optimism:** focusing on the positive aspects of a situation; expecting good outcomes.
9. **Perseverance:** persistence and hard work with passion, energy, and focus to achieve results.
10. **Respect:** treating others considerately and courteously; protecting the self-esteem of others.
11. **Self-awareness:** monitoring and observing yourself; consciously changing your thought processes and behaviors.

How many of the 11 qualities do you possess? What steps could you take to improve some of the qualities you consider weak? Awareness of each quality can assist you in strengthening your ability to project these skills to others—but remember that you want people to perceive the attributes as genuine. Coaches/mentors can help individuals develop the desirable qualities, which is why people often use the terms "qualities" and "skills" interchangeably.

REALITY ☑

Identify two of the personal qualities on the list that you exhibit enthusiastically and one that needs improvement. How would you do that?

Communication Skills

The final assessment you should do concerns your verbal and nonverbal **communication skills**. Communication skills are often hard to assess yourself, so be sure to ask others around you about specific concerns. There are many self-assessment instruments on the internet that you can use as a checklist. We have included a brief assessment instrument below to help you start thinking about the communication skills you currently possess.

Ethical Encounter

How ethical is it to say that you have good communication skills (oral, written, or technical) when, in fact, you do not?

Communication Skills Self-Assessment Exercise

Answering questions about your communication skills is somewhat difficult since personal perception can differ from reality. To best analyze yourself, answer the questions; then, ask a trusted friend and/or colleague if they think that your answers are accurate. Remember that you can work to change any area of communication weakness if you choose to do so.

1. Is your nonverbal communication appropriate for business and appealing to others? Think specifically about your handshake, eye contact, and your facial expression.

   My nonverbal communication is:

Excellent **Sufficient** **Needs Work** **Embarrassing**

[When someone meets you, they will immediately notice a firm and confident handshake, direct and appropriate (not creepy) eye contact, and a pleasant and approachable facial expression. If you do these things well, you increase your chances of a good first impression.]

2. Do you have the confidence and initiative to introduce yourself to people in the office if your boss does not do so?

   My communication initiative to make a solid first impression is:

Excellent **Sufficient** **Needs Work** **Embarrassing**

[In many companies, someone will take you around and introduce you to colleagues, but in other companies you are left to your own devices to make introductions. Having the initiative to introduce yourself to others can make you appear confident and approachable—two positives for a good first impression.]

3. Do you possess good listening skills? Think specifically about: whether you can listen to directions once and be able to follow them precisely;, whether you "zone out" when someone is talking to you; and whether you can be sympathetic to what is being said when that is appropriate. In addition, factor in whether you listen critically (analyzing what you hear) or if you just believe everything you hear.

   My listening skills are:

Excellent **Sufficient** **Need Work** **Embarrassing**

[If you have to ask for clarifications numerous times because you weren't listening effectively, your perceived competence as a professional person suffers. Also, not believing everything you hear can be a good quality, as long as you have sufficient background to ask reasonable questions for clarification. Listen carefully and critically; ask questions when comments don't make sense.]

4. Do you have the skill to receive criticism gracefully and the strength to issue a critique when the job calls for it? Can you avoid making excuses or getting defensive?

   My communication skills for issuing and receiving criticism are:

Excellent **Sufficient** **Need Work** **Embarrassing**

[Many people get defensive when someone critiques or criticizes their ideas or skills. If you can issue a "Thanks, I'll take that under consideration" and seriously do so, you'll be far better off than people who give a million excuses for why they do what they do. Analyzing critiques or criticism thoroughly allows you to improve quickly and remain a valued colleague. The flip side of receiving a critique is giving feedback to someone else. If that thought makes you somewhat uneasy, you want to remind yourself that the workplace only gets better when people actively evaluate what is going on and perform tasks competently.]

5. Do you have strong conversational skills? Think about whether you monopolize verbal time, have balanced conversations, or don't talk at all. Do you keep conversation topics pleasant, or are you always complaining? Do you ask other people about themselves to show interest and to keep the conversation flowing?

   My conversational skills are:

Excellent **Sufficient** **Need Work** **Embarrassing**

[Being a good conversationalist often makes the workplace more pleasant. Being upbeat, positive, asking questions that show you want to get to know another person while keeping conversations balanced are ways to accomplish this verbal task. People who are always complaining or exuding negative energy are very difficult to work with.]

6. Do you think carefully about your own communication and the communication around you? Think specifically about whether you monitor (thinking about what you are saying before you say it and reviewing what you said after you say it) or whether you jump to conclusions without gathering factual information.

My communication analysis skills are:

Excellent **Sufficient** **Need Work** **Embarrassing**

[People who monitor their communication figure out what is working, what didn't work, what should be said, and what shouldn't be said. Don't be the person who says the first thought that pops into your mind. Also, get the facts. If you hear a piece of gossip, gather factual information. You can get into a lot of trouble in the workplace by jumping to conclusions and acting on rumors.]

How do your skills measure up? You can analyze your intrapersonal skills long before you enter the workplace. Conversations and careers are stronger when you approach language as a positive force for personal growth and change. Each of us feels we are good at analyzing the communication issues (verbal/nonverbal) of others, but how often do we think about why we react to others the way we do? You can't always count on another person to communicate effectively, but you can choose to communicate appropriately yourself. We hope the course you are taking will help you to do further analysis of your communication style. This textbook also provides more discussion of some of these skills in upcoming chapters.

Final Thoughts

Understanding the perceptual process and related perception concepts is critical to becoming an effective communicator. You must understand why you assign meaning the way you do to words, actions, situations, and people, so you can improve your communication style and avoid miscommunication. Once you understand your own perceptions and how the perceptual process works, you'll be better able to analyze why other communicators perceive phenomena and assign meaning the way they do.

There are fascinating challenges waiting for you as you acclimate to business situations—perhaps new regions of the country or another culture. As you work through the perceptual process of organizing and assigning meaning to unfamiliar behaviors and events, you must always be aware of the potential for saying or doing the wrong thing. As you gain a more acute awareness of yourself and your ability to communicate effectively with other people, don't jump to conclusions regarding the verbal and nonverbal behavior of others especially when English is a secondary language. A simple question can assist you in understanding; seeking clarity through perception checking will help you become a more effective communicator and colleague.

Do your best to manage your own perceptual process so others consistently see you as a solid, credible communicator and someone they would like to get to know better. Your credibility is anchored by a thorough understanding of who you are, your values, and your ethical decision-making skills applied in a consistent, fair manner. This is why a thorough intrapersonal examination of who you really are is vital to successful communication. Take nothing for granted. Be constantly aware of your own skills and qualities as well as those of everyone around you.

Key Terms

Communication skills
Interpretation and response
Interpersonal communication
Organization
Perception checking
Perceptual process
Personal qualities (skills)
Selection
Selective attention
Self-assessment
Self-concept
Self-esteem
Values

Exercises

1. How do other people perceive your strengths and weaknesses? Ask the opinion of at least five people.
2. What skills do you feel you possess that match an employer's needs? Do these skills target your career area?
3. What computer and electronic communication skills can you offer an employer?
4. Discuss how your two best personal qualities fit with your career interest.
5. What do you value most in life?
6. Analyze your perceptions of a classmate. What past experiences assisted you in making these judgments? Which perceptions might be inaccurate?

CHAPTER
THREE

Job Searches, Résumés, and Cover Letters

Goals

- Identify all relevant information and experiences for a résumé.
- List the sections of a résumé.
- Understand the ethics of misrepresenting yourself.
- Select unique language to enhance the résumé.
- Create and design an effective résumé format.
- Identify what information must go in your cover letter.
- Gather appropriate examples and develop job focus for a cover letter.
- Create and design an appropriate cover letter.
- Identify the parts of a LinkedIn profile.
- Create and design an appropriate LinkedIn profile.
- Analyze your social networking information and make changes where necessary prior to your employment search.

Your self-assessment (chapter 2) covered your interests, self-esteem, values, personal qualities, and communication skills. Analyze your assessment carefully as you begin to think about an initial employment position and the various companies who have employment possibilities for your skills and interests. You should also consider the areas of the country where you would enjoy living—warm/cold; east/west/north/south; urban/rural, etc. Knowing where you want to live and the kind of people you want as neighbors and colleagues can assist you in making better decisions about the companies to pursue during a job search. Do not send résumés to potential employers if you have no interest in working for them or living in the region in which they are located. While it is fine to apply to something you think you might like given what you find out during an interview, if you know that you could never live in a cold climate, don't apply there. You do not want employers to feel they have wasted their time and money pursuing you just to have you reject them at the last minute. The corporate world is interconnected, and word gets around. On the other hand, if you are interested but realize after an interview that the job isn't what the company advertised or you don't like the people or environment, there is no obligation to accept.

REALITY ☑

What concerns you about securing your first career job?

A thorough analysis of job titles and employee responsibilities within a company is also necessary when matching your skills to advertised positions. Companies often use the same titles to describe a position, but the personal skill base required can be completely different. Without researching a company, you may find yourself applying for a position that sounds promising in an ad, but the facts suggest you do not possess the necessary skills. You can avoid embarrassment during an interview by a website search and/or an informative phone interview with someone in human resources or another individual within the company. The goal of the preliminary job investigation is to appear as professional as possible. This research takes initiative on your part, but it can also pay off as you apply for a position that suits your abilities rather than one that is totally wrong for your skills, values, and personality.

Once you have identified where you want to live and the responsibilities you'd like to assume—and you've researched the ad and the company—your next task in a career search is preparing a résumé. As you think about what to include on a résumé, it is useful to ask family members, friends, and former employers to tell you what they think are your greatest assets. Listen carefully to the information people share without reacting to any of their views or suggestions. This is not a time to argue or get defensive—it is a time to gather information. Once you talk to other people about your strongest assets and values, you can analyze their statements and compare this list of perceptions to your self-assessment. Every point of comparison that matches your assessment gives you a better idea of a "selling point" to mention in your résumé.

Wendy Enelow and Louise Kursmark (2010) offer some suggestions when deciding what to include in your résumé or cover letter.

- If you are graduating from college and do not have much work experience, highlight professional skills you developed while working on team projects at school.
- Look at your academic experiences for leadership skills, which are important in a work environment and illustrate your potential.
- Highlight academic achievements, which indicate both your intelligence and competitiveness.
- Most importantly, be sure to connect your skills, experience, and interests to what the employer needs. Communicate that you understand business priorities and are ready to contribute to the success of the company.

With this employment research and skills research behind you, you can now begin writing your résumé.

Résumés

A **résumé** is a document that reflects your skills, knowledge, and work history. You send it to potential employers, and they determine, based on how you present yourself on this single sheet of paper or digital version, whether they are interested in contacting you for an interview. You should choose descriptive words carefully and include information that makes the reader want to meet you. Since the résumé leads to an interview and employment, it is extremely important to present yourself effectively, accurately, and persuasively.

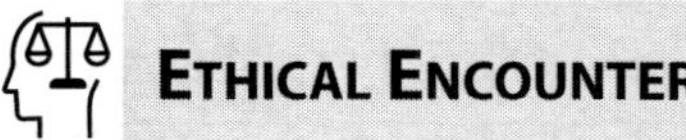

You decide to list an academic discipline as a minor area of study even though you did not take all of the required courses to qualify for an official minor designation on your transcript. Is this decision a good one?

Most employers only spend about 10 seconds glancing at your résumé. Imagine trying to read 60, 150, or over 1,000 résumés to fill one opening in a company. The task is daunting. In order to whittle a pile of applicants down to a manageable size, employers look through the stack of résumés very quickly to see if they can initially eliminate any candidates who do not fit the posted job requirements. A résumé immediately goes into the discard pile if it is not visually attractive, easy to read, free from typos, or relevant for the position.

Résumé Sections

So where do you start? The first thing to do is to gather all of the information about your school, work, and volunteer experience as well as any special skills you have or projects you completed. There are a variety of sections you might include on your résumé.

- Objective OR summary of skills/qualifications
- Employment history
- Work-related experience
- Specific skills you have that are unique (i.e., proficiency in a specific software application, but do not list general knowledge of commonly used software)
- Fluency in languages
- Community service
- Honors and awards

- Organizational memberships
- Leadership opportunities
- Social media handles, LinkedIn address
- Certifications
- References (if you choose to include them)

As you develop these sections, you should not include high school awards. Most employers are only interested in what you have done in college, work, or life.

OBJECTIVE OR QUALIFICATIONS?

So what information should be at the top of a résumé? Remember, the material you select will be the first impression you make on potential employers, so it needs to be good. In making a decision about whether to use an objective or qualifications/skills summary, you should consult with professionals in your field. An **objective** is what you hope to achieve. It is one sentence—not a paragraph. If you do decide an objective is important, you must write a brilliant one that resonates with potential employers. Human resource personnel know your objective is to get a job. Don't state the obvious. You must highlight your abilities with solid writing in the objective.

Targeted objectives generally use a format that highlights the applicant's strongest skills.

> *Objective:* An xxx position in an organization where yyy and zzz would be needed.

Xxx is the name of the position you seek. Yyy and zzz are the most compelling personal qualities, abilities, or achievements that will make you stand out from competing applicants. The research you have previously done to find out what is most important to the employer will guide your choices when deciding yyy and zzz. For example:

> *Objective:* A software sales position in an organization where a consistent record of generating new accounts, exceeding sales targets, and enthusiastic customer relations is needed.

The objective is an attention-getting device; it immediately showcases your best skills. When written well, the objective invites further exploration of the résumé. Consider the difference between the two objectives below.

Ineffective: To get a video-editing position.

Effective: To obtain a video-editing position in a company where enthusiasm, technical skill, and self-motivation are desired.

The effective objective would be a persuasive statement at the top of the résumé because it sells your qualities of enthusiasm and self-motivation and alludes to the fact that you have technical skill.

More common today is a **skills or qualifications summary**. The format is typically a bulleted list at the top of your résumé that highlights what you bring to the table. Make sure that you use the right header. We have seen people who choose "skills summary" and then list an item that is not a skill. A skills summary works for some career areas, while a qualifications summary is better for others.

Note the difference.

A **skills** summary is a list of particular abilities, such as "excellent written and oral communication skills" or "fluent in Spanish."

A **qualifications** summary is a list of what you've done, such as "wrote 14 PSAs and 22 press releases" or "published three articles in Spanish."

Which do you find to be more persuasive?

EMPLOYMENT HISTORY

Your employment history typically includes salaried work. If you have had jobs that don't relate to your degree, you may include them farther down on your résumé to show that you have work experience, but without explanation.

Example:

- Sales Clerk *Dollar Store* 9/19–present
- Ride Operator *Hershey Park* 5/19–8/18 (seasonal)
- Cashier *McDonald's* 9/17–4/19

You don't have to break down a position where duties would be common knowledge. For example, there is no need to list cashier duties.

- Handled cash
- Counted drawer at end of night

The employer knows these responsibilities.

If your paid experience is related to your professional area, then it might be placed higher on your résumé and include specific duties.

Assistant manager *Urban Outfitters* 1/19–present

- Developed employee schedules
- Trained new hires
- Assessed performance; conducted in-person reviews

WORK-RELATED EXPERIENCE

Work-related experience typically includes the acquisition of knowledge and skills related to your field for which you weren't paid. A communication major might spend a semester acting as the General Manager of the campus radio station. It isn't a paid job, but it is definitely work-related experience. Unpaid internships would go in this section as well.

LANGUAGE FLUENCY

If you still have time left in your college career to incorporate study of another language, do so immediately. If you can't fit it into your class schedule, work with language apps or CD programs to learn what you can. Many programs are free; you can learn some conversations basics by spending as little as 10 minutes a day on a language app. In today's global environment, knowing another language (or two or three) will give you a distinct advantage in terms of being hired.

COMMUNITY SERVICE

This category can set you apart from other qualified applicants. For example, one applicant might work full time, go to school full time and have a 4.0. That is great—it shows tremendous work ethic.

But an applicant who works part time, goes to school full time and has a 3.5 grade point average plus volunteers at the local animal shelter the first Friday of every month for two hours might be viewed more favorably. Showing that you are civic minded (having an interest in your community rather than just in yourself) can make an eye-catching difference that gets you an interview.

HONORS AND AWARDS

Seek to attain as many honors and awards as possible while you are in college. Honors might include the Dean's list by earning a qualified GPA. If you secure honors or awards, keep a list so that you do not omit an achievement or forget the specifics. For instance, listing "Award for outgoing and dedicated first year student" is not as impressive as including the full citation: "Arylene M. Garrity award for an outgoing and dedicated first year student." Be aware of opportunities and apply. Awards may remain unclaimed at some universities because no students submit an application.

ORGANIZATIONAL MEMBERSHIPS

Do your best to join at least one organization while at college. If you can handle more, do so. A journalism major should be a member of the campus newspaper. A business major should be a member of the business organizations and clubs. There is typically an HR club for human resource majors. If you belong to nothing, that says something about your passion or lack thereof for a career. Seriously assess your time. If you are scrolling cute cat videos on social media, then you have time to be a member of a club.

> One caveat here. You will want to assess whether to add organizations that reveal social or religious affiliations. Sometimes this gives an employer information that they may use to discriminate against you.

LEADERSHIP EXPERIENCE

Leadership opportunities are another way to make yourself stand out. If you can be the president of something, do it. You can gain a lot of useful experience by running a club or organization. If you are shy, tired, overcommitted, etc., a leadership role that doesn't put you in the spotlight can be a great alternative. You might apply for a treasurer or secretary position, which are both valuable roles but don't take as much time, energy, and skill as a presidential position.

SOCIAL MEDIA HANDLES

If the type of job you are applying for requires a knowledge of social media, then include this as a section. Some job advertisements will say that social media experience is desirable. If so, they mean targeted social media, not personal accounts. Let's say you ran Twitter for your campus bookstore. Include the handle, how long you were in charge, the increase in followers that happened while you were there and other relevant facts. If you simply use Instagram to post full-body selfies of your flat stomach, then don't include the information. Use common sense and clean up your social media accounts. Potential employers may scan those accounts. Having a locked or private account can also raise a red flag, since the assumption might be that you are trying to hide something.

CERTIFICATIONS

There may be certifications that are valuable for your major. For example, safety science majors need a number of certifications to enhance their chances for a job. A CPR certification might be valuable for a number of majors. If you have certifications, by all means list them. It shows that you have made an extra effort beyond normal academic activity.

RELATED COURSEWORK

Sometimes (particularly if you are having a hard time getting to a full-page résumé you might want to include a list of courses that exceed usual expectations for a major. For example, an accounting major would not list "Accounting I and Accounting II." That's obvious. But if you took a gender course or a business communication course that could help you to perform well in the workplace, that might be a selling point for an accountant. Your choices should be specific to the job for which you are applying.

REFERENCES

Some professions will accept the line "References Available Upon Request." Others expect you to list references (name, title, relationship, company, contact information). You need to let every reference and/or employer listed on your résumé know that you mentioned them. Never list someone as a reference without gaining permission to do so. This professional courtesy guarantees that they can talk intelligently about you with human resources personnel when a prospective employer contacts them to discuss your abilities.

Always ask permission to use someone as a reference and then let them know an employer might be calling. We have been surprised many times by someone calling for a reference for a student who had a mediocre record or for someone who graduated years earlier whom we vaguely remembered. The hesitation on our end as we struggled to figure out what to say because we had been caught off guard was detrimental to the chances of that person being hired.

Misrepresentation on a Résumé

Once you have gathered the information, you write each of the sections for the résumé. The most important advice is to be clear, accurate and truthful. There is never a good reason to be dishonest (Doyle, 2018). All of your résumé's information can be checked by human resources personnel or an interviewer prior to contacting you and/or after they have spoken to you.

For example, various organizations require a community service component of all employees. It may be tempting to list your community service activity on your résumé without mentioning that it was mandatory, but this is not a wise decision. If an interviewer checks with people at the volunteer organization to find out what you actually did and they can't remember your name, the interviewer knows you have exaggerated this work claim and may assume other material on your résumé is exaggerated also. This fact usually eliminates you from job consideration. The volunteer project might look better on the résumé by describing the skills acquired during the work effort rather than simply mentioning the name of the organization. It is important to find unique words to describe yourself—but not at the expense of truthfulness.

REALITY ☑

How should you list a service project?

Five hours of Adopt-A-Highway service (October 15, 2020) as part of the Phi Sigma Pi Honor Fraternity

Or

Developed leadership skills during a group project (October 15, 2020) to clean the highway near the university campus.

Exaggerating your accomplishments to get the reader's attention is not only unethical but it also can cost you your credibility and your position should you be hired. Employers may review your résumé even after you have been working at a company when they consider you for advancement. A misstatement on your résumé that wasn't questioned during initial employment can catch up with you at this phase of your career. Termination often follows—even if you've had good performance.

Language on a Résumé

Today's employment marketplace is fluid and volatile. Industries sometimes turn to technology for additional profit with fewer employees. They want employees who can make money for the company. Look at yourself and your skills in a professional way as you select the appropriate words to express actual accomplishments on paper. The language you use needs to be concise, descriptive and exciting.

Be concise. Once you have a rough draft of your résumé, look for words to eliminate. Is anything repetitive? Are you rambling? Written materials can usually be edited for conciseness.

REALITY ☑

Imagine a potential employer reading the following statement:

"Spent long hours working in the back room of McDonald's counting every box, bag, and supply and putting that information on a spreadsheet."

How would you revise? (Hint: Inventory is the simplest, most recognizable term to describe the activities.)

Be descriptive. What are you really good at doing? Does your work and volunteer history demonstrate this passion and talent? Words need to reflect your unique qualities to enable someone who reads your résumé to see immediately what you are capable of doing. In addition, a reader should have an idea of what to expect when you walk into their office for an interview.

REALITY ☑

Being descriptive will make you more persuasive. Both of the following statements represent the same activity completed by senior Public Relations majors in their capstone course.

Applicant A: Created, developed, and led a campaign for a local, nonprofit organization. This campaign included social media use, contacting local media, and holding a community event.

Applicant B: Developed a public relations campaign to increase awareness in the local community about Wellsboro Montessori Children's Center. Surveyed 95 people in the community to determine the focus of the campaign and an appropriate special event. Created promotional materials—two PSAs, a logo, a poster, a newspaper ad, a press release, rack cards, a fact sheet, and a promotional video. Recruited eight sponsors for the campaign and received $300 in donations. Hosted a special event, which attracted 200 community members.

Which applicant seems like the better choice?

Used with permission of Amanda Tanner and Keri Edsall.

In examining the example above, you may find the Applicant B comment to violate the rule of being concise. Be concise in your words, but if you have specific examples, numbers, or other descriptive terms that help a potential employer to see what you did, then by all means include details.

Be exciting. Examine the sections of your résumé for exciting language. Look for ways to make your résumé stand out. Begin phrases with strong, action verbs (Doyle, 2019d). "Designed and created flyers" is more active and exciting than "I made flyers."

Never use the word "I" in the résumé. "I have experience with" becomes "Experience with . . ." Edit out pronouns and articles.

There are a number of action verbs to make your résumé stand out (Indeed, 2017). Avoid passive verbs and jargon; use a variety of action verbs.

Verbs for accomplishments	Verbs for duties, activities, and responsibilities	Verbs for creative positions	Verbs for sales positions	Verbs for management positions	Verbs for financial positions	Verbs for technical positions
Achieved	Accelerated	Authored	Captured	Advised	Audited	Advanced
Capitalized	Accomplished	Brainstormed	Conserved	Arranged	Classified	Architected
Deciphered	Analyzed	Briefed	Converted	Augmented	Collected	Automated
Discerned	Assembled	Communicated	Earned	Centralized	Equalized	Coded
Drove	Founded	Conceptualized	Generated	Championed	Dispensed	Deployed
Enacted	Created	Curated	Maximized	Differentiated	Halted	Detected
Endeavored	Constructed	Derived	Negotiated	Directed	Investigated	Devised
Established	Delivered	Designed	Won	Empowered	Lowered	Diagnosed
Exceeded	Developed	Diagramed		Endorsed	Maintained	Discovered
Sharpened	Executed	Drafted		Ensured	Minimized	Formulated
Shattered	Expanded	Edited		Forecasted	Recognized	Installed
Sparked	Finalized	Illustrated		Fostered	Secured	Launched
Spearheaded	Forged	Imagined		Identified		Networked
Steered	Guided	Influenced		Integrated		Planned
Stimulated	Handled	Intensified		Leveraged		Programmed
Supervised	Headed	Modeled		Reconciled		Rewrote
Surpassed	Improved	Proofread		Reduced		Refined
	Increased	Published		Replaced		Tested
	Initiated	Researched		Resolved		Troubleshoot
	Implemented	Strategized		Orchestrated		Upgraded
	Instituted	Storyboarded		Optimized		
	Produced	Translated		Predicted		
	Simplified	Visualized		Renovated		

There are a number of articles on "overused verbs" on the internet. Take a moment to check those articles and remove those verbs from your résumé. Also, remember to choose a variety of action verbs; repeating even powerful words detracts from the reading experience. Take time to evaluate each word. Making active and exciting verbal adjustments can boost your résumé's appeal and set you apart from other candidates seeking the same job.

Formatting and Layout

Once you have gathered information and written each of the sections, you need to figure out the format you want to use. There are multiple templates available. However, because many people use them, you may look like everyone else applying for the job. A unique, personalized format can set you apart.

Listed below are essentials to remember when constructing your résumé.

- Make the page visually attractive.
- Proofread carefully to eliminate all typos and errors.
- Showcase your qualities, strengths, and experience.
- List specific instances where you accomplished what you say you can do.
- Follow the format required by your professional area.

Résumé requirements vary from person to person and/or from profession to profession. You will need to make the following decisions.

- What to include in the header.
- Whether to limit the résumé to one page.
- Whether to use white paper, off-white, or another color.
- Whether to use multiple fonts.
- Whether to use graphics.
- Whether to include a personal picture (typically only for actors and models).

INITIAL DECISIONS

Headers typically include at least your name and contact information (usually a cell phone number and an email address). Most companies won't be sending you mail at this stage in the application process, so including your address is optional. If appropriate, you might include the url to your LinkedIn profile and social media handles.

HEADER EXAMPLES

Kathryn Sue Young

kyoung@gmail.com ◆ 570.123.4567 ◆ www.linkedin.com/in/kathrynsueyoung

Sydney L. Hartman

Email: hartl04@mansfield.edu Phone: 570-555-1212
LinkedIn: linkedin.com/in/sydhart

Jenna Buhite

1166 Mockingbird Lane, Stepway, Pennsylvania 15853
jbuhite@gmail.com | 814-123-9876

Page limitations are another area where you need to check résumé standards in your field. At one time, résumés were only one page in length; that is still true in many fields. One of our former students wanted to work on Capitol Hill. She sent out 100 copies of a two-page résumé. She was bewildered when she did not get a single inquiry. After doing more research she found that the norm on Capitol Hill (in her field at that time) was a one-page résumé. Apparently, anything over one page went into the trash immediately. She retooled her résumé to one page and received a number of interviews. A two-page or longer résumé may be perfectly acceptable in certain fields. In these professions, you would not want to limit yourself to only one page if you had enough relevant information to include—but be certain that everything you list is, in fact, relevant to the position for which you want an interview.

Also make sure that you aren't using two pages with tons of white space. Sometimes a résumé needs to be graphically redesigned to make it fit on one page. Conversely, if a one-page résumé looks too crowded, it is time to streamline by cutting some material. Never go to a second page unless you have at least a full 1/3 of the page to fill.

Once you have determined what you want to say, think about how to present it—that is, how to format your résumé. Potential candidates for positions have about 10 seconds to capture the attention of reviewers. Presentation is important; the résumé should be concise yet compelling.

PRESENTATION

There are as many résumé styles as there are personalities and specific jobs. Blueskyresumes.com is one place to consult for ideas. Your résumé should look professional, which does not necessarily mean fancy fonts, graphics, or a lot of bells and whistles. If you are sending a résumé via email or replying via a website, the original formatting may be lost. If you have the option of attaching the document, send it as a pdf file, which will retain the formatting. A pdf file isn't easily altered, which makes it a wise choice. The list that follows provides guidelines.

- Use standard margins.
- Single space between items, and double space between sections.
- Highlight items using **boldface** or *italics* rather than changing fonts. Bold the items that you want to stand out, such as your name, employer's name, the name of the institution, or the position you held.
- Use bullets to highlight accomplishments. Bullets make a résumé look clean, clear, and crisp.
- Use indentations for emphasis. Résumés that are all flush left don't lead your eye anywhere.
- Make sure items line up vertically. If dates are on the right, make sure they are in a straight line.
- List items in reverse chronological order.

PROFESSIONAL EXPERIENCE

Member Service Representative Corning, NY
Corning Community YMCA September 2018–present

- Assisted senior director by proofreading YMCA newsletters, brochures, and additional communication materials as well as screening calls and recording and delivering messages for staff directors
- Communicated YMCA policies and services to members, responded to member questions and concerns, promoted membership and program sales to visitors, and conducted facility tours
- Responsible for membership and program registrations, daily accounting, maintaining accuracy of electronic database, determining scholarship membership eligibility, and opening/closing facility

Additional Résumé Strategies

Even if your word choice and layout are intriguing, you can sabotage that positive impression immediately if there are typos in your résumé. Spell-check can catch some spelling and grammatical errors, but it will not tell you if you have used the wrong word (Indeed, 2017). Proofread very carefully—word by word. Ask someone else to proofread your résumé; another person may see things that you missed. You and a friend could take turns reading the résumé aloud to identify errors.

As you craft your résumé, it is helpful to cross-reference its claims with the information you've created on social networking sites. The social perceptions you share on the web need to match the perceptions you create with your résumé. A potential employer may check your site (see discussion in a following section).

Bring extra copies of your résumé to the interview. You look extremely competent if the interviewer cannot find your résumé, and you are immediately able to hand them a copy. Many companies are shifting to online applications (see discussion below); however, there is often a place to attach a formatted résumé.

Placing yourself on the job market is an excellent time to review the professional nature of the email address on your résumé as well as the message on your voice mail. These two items can make a good impression on a stranger when they see/hear them while considering you for a position with their company. You should clearly shape your email address to reveal that you are prepared for a career (not hotvanillachick@hotmail or gasgiant@gmail). Your voice mail message should be polished and articulate, with no background distractions like funky music or silly sayings. We recommend that you update both of these items for professionalism prior to sending out the first résumé. In addition, you should also reexamine your social media sites as if you were a professional trying to evaluate you for career potential.

You also want to think about ways to make your résumé look unique and stand out, but without compromising professional quality. For example, we had a student who tried to make her résumé look unique by incorporating heart-shaped bullets. While we admired her creativity, it was too "cutesy" for corporate America.

For generations, capturing the attention of hiring managers was critical; businesses were constructed around helping applicants create résumés that would signal an applicant was right for the job. Today, the average corporate opening attracts 250 applicants; only about half of whom have the necessary qualifications (Hatfield, 2017). Many large companies scan printed résumés and store the files on a computer. These files and online applications can be scanned by software—applicant tracking systems (ATS)—to analyze and classify résumés. This means no human being looks at your résumé initially. About 95% of Fortune 500 companies use ATS, which is increasingly being used by smaller businesses. About 40% of employers use ATS, which filters out 75% of applicants (Bell, 2018).

If using ATS software, recruiters or hiring managers choose keywords and rank their importance. The software then searches a résumé for the key words to match the skills, experience, and education of applicants with the position. Therefore, it is important to use the key words of job advertisements when describing your work history.

REALITY ☑

What key words would you want to incorporate for the job advertisement placed by Winding River Productions (which appeared on Indeed, 2019)?

Production Animator

Winding River Productions

Are you looking to grow your career in a fun, fast-paced environment and work with a great, supportive team? Do the latest advances in the field of medicine fascinate you? Then look no further than Winding River Production (a subsidiary of US HealthConnect)!

We are currently seeking a qualified candidate to fill our full-time Production Animator position in our Fort Washington office. Our ideal applicant will have 3 to 5 years' experience in editing, animation, and graphic design, as well as possess excellent problem-solving skills.

About the Position

- Must work on location at our Fort Washington, PA office
- Full-time, salaried position
- Specific responsibilities include (but are not limited to):
  - Managing projects from pre- to postproduction
  - Offering creative consultation with internal and external clients
  - Providing audio and video editing, graphic design and animation services
  - Delivering projects on time and within budget
  - Addressing edits in a timely fashion
  - Setting up and operating equipment in the recording studio
  - Working collaboratively with various departments involved in the preplanning and completion of each project
  - Creating and monitoring project schedules to ensure timely delivery
  - Working to improve planning processes and looking for solutions to improve efficiencies, where needed
  - Traveling (domestically and internationally) to execute projects onsite and/or to participate in client meetings, when necessary

Skills and Experience Required

Qualified candidates must:

- Have 3–5 years' experience in audio and video editing, graphic design, and animation
- Have a bachelor's degree (B.S.) or equivalent
- Have experience in graphic/animation design (Motion Graphics – 2D Animation – 3D Animation)

(continued)

- Have linear editing experience in Adobe Premiere (video editing)
- Have advanced experience in Adobe After Effects (animation and motion graphics)
- Possess recording studio experience and expert knowledge of videography
- Lighting (live, hard set, and green screen)
- Camera operation
- Knowledge of DSLR
- Have corporate design sensibilities (Photoshop and Illustrator)
- Experience creating vector assets in Illustrator
- Keep up to date on current design trends
- Put a premium on customer service
- Be a strategic thinker
- Be flexible and independent while working in a fast-paced environment
- Have excellent attention to detail as well as verbal and written communication skills
- Possess strong organizational skills with the ability to prioritize and manage multiple projects at once
- Be able to work extended hours as needed

What Qualified Candidates Can Expect from Us

- A modern working environment with a culture that supports work/life balance
- A competitive salary and benefits package
- Onsite gym at no cost to employees

Interested? Please submit your résumé and salary requirements. **Submissions without salary requirements will not be considered. No phone calls please.**

Job Type: Fulltime

Experience:

- Adobe Illustrator: 2 years (Required)
- 3D Animation (Cinema 4D and 3DS Max or Maya): 2 years (Required)
- 2D Animation: 2 years (Required)
- 3D Modeling, Texturing, Lighting: 1 year (Preferred)
- Adobe After Effects: 2 years (Required)
- Video Editing: 2 years (Required)

Some people place a list of keywords at the bottom of their résumés, but once a human being looks at the résumé and notices the trick, they may have an unfavorable reaction and discard the résumé. In addition, fancy formatting and marbled papers do not scan well. Those choices would put you immediately into the discard pile. If the company requires electronic submission, you may need to submit your résumé in a sans serif font without any formatting (such as bold or italics), no bullets, and left justified. Most company websites explain their review process and formatting requirements for résumé submissions.

Be sure to read all the requirements in a job ad. One student applied for a DJ position; in the application instructions, it said to put the following statement at the bottom of the résumé: "I am a professional DJ." That may seem like a small item, but omitting it shows that you did not read the instructions and do what was asked. Can you determine what must be included when responding to the Winding River ad?

Remember our advice about bringing extra copies of your résumé to an interview? The advice applies even if you submitted your résumé online. You could create two versions of your résumé—one to meet the constraints of online submission and the ATS process and the other formatted as described above to appeal to human reviewers. Bringing printed copies to the interview allows you to distribute them to the various individuals you meet on-site. Some of these people have not seen your résumé in advance, and a paper copy gives them a chance to scan the material as they converse with you. In addition, they can scan your résumé in detail after you leave if you've made a strong impression on them interpersonally.

Cover Letters

Now that you've written your résumé, you need to write an appealing cover letter to accompany it. Whereas the résumé is a list of experiences, skills, and qualifications, a **cover letter** is a description of you and your qualifications in narrative form that allows you to convince an employer that you possess the experience and skills to fill a specific advertised position. Every job description lists the necessary requirements for the advertised position. The résumé lists your best skills and experiences; the cover letter gives you the opportunity to present why you are an excellent candidate. Therefore, you write a new cover letter to describe your match for the requirements of each specific job for which you apply—making sure the cover letter addresses the specifics of posted necessities for the position.

Typically the cover letter highlights the portions of your résumé that reinforce the various skills an employer is looking for. Some employers read cover letters first, and if they are impressed by what they read, they'll consult your résumé for more information. As described above, other employers use computers to scan your résumé. If you possess the basic qualifications for the position, the employer then reads your cover letter. Make sure to use well-worded phrases and descriptive sentences to showcase the specific skills/experiences on your résumé that match the advertisement. Your cover letter should be concise, creative, and direct.

Cover letter writing is a complex process. You need to analyze the company and to address all of the specifics in the job advertisement (or at least as many as you can). Simply listing your strengths is not enough. You can't simply state, for example: I am an organized, creative, self-motivated, and enthusiastic professional with exceptional verbal and written communication abilities as well as excellent multitasking, time-management, and web-design skills. Your claims are meaningless without illustrating them through examples, stories, and explanations.

Preparing for Writing a Cover Letter

The first thing you need to do is gather the information you want to include in your cover letter. Find out more about the company where you are applying by looking at its website, the Twitter feeds of its executives, and profiles of its employees on LinkedIn (Gallo, 2014). This information can reveal the culture of the organization and help you decide on the tone for your cover letter. If your tone matches the culture of the organization, you improve your chances of gaining an interview.

Understanding why the company is hiring helps you write a compelling cover letter that addresses the company's specific needs (Slack, 2019). Your research may point to trends in the industry or challenges faced by companies in that industry. People who can help solve problems are attractive hires. If something in your experience would apply to the challenges faced by the company, mention that briefly in your cover letter. In short, the more you know about the company, the better you can describe why you would be a good hire.

Now gather the personal information that best fits the position. Analyze what the ad asks for and then determine which of your experiences best demonstrate each requirement. Listed below is a sample advertisement, followed by a worksheet.

Media Relations/Public Relations Professional

- **About the Job**

This position is responsible for leading our local/regional media relations and public relations efforts to increase public and brand awareness.

Media Relations: Primary duties include writing press releases, pitching to media, managing press coverage/clips, implementing PR campaigns, and serving as liaison with managers, administrators, reporters and other external parties. Position also researches and writes releases, fact sheets, news pitches, bylined articles, position papers, op-eds, press kits, background information, talking points, and other press materials. Other duties include increasing press activity—including proactive media outreach and pitches, identifying and preparing spokespersons for interviews, and maintaining company newsroom page.

Public Relations: Supports company PR activities and events. This position will cultivate relationships internally and externally, including local media.

Social Media: Leverages social networks to communicate messages and build relationships with internal and external parties—including the media. Contributes parallel media/social media content/posts for publication.

- **Position Requirements**

Background: Seeking seasoned professional with 1–3 years related experience in media relations and public relations within a fast-paced business environment, with the ability to multitask. Must be media savvy, connected to current industry news events, and a self-starter. Creative mind with a track record of generating and implementing new ideas and story angles. Excellent media, PR, writing, proofreading, editing, and pitching skills required. Must be proficient in MS Office products with a high level of proficiency in MS Word.

Education: Minimum 4-year degree in Mass Communications, Marketing or related field.

Other Skills: Public relations and Web/new media experience preferred. Ability to research, read, comprehend, and write complex communications. Ability to present information effectively in large and small group environments. Must have excellent communication and interpersonal skills. Analytical skills, Excel and Power Point proficiency a plus. Must have demonstrated multitasking skills and be able to work both independently and with a group.

WORKSHEET FOR THE LETTER OF APPLICATION/COVER LETTER

What responsibilities or qualifications does the ad require?	What experience do I have to demonstrate this?
1-3 years related experience in media relations and public relations within a fast-paced business environment	Worked in the media relations office of my university designing PR materials and monitoring social media
Must be media savvy, connected to current industry news events	Familiar with all social media platforms. Specialize in Twitter for the university. Read blogs and follow PR influencers
A self-starter	Started a summer lawn care service building to 45 clients in two years
Creative mind with a track record of generating and implementing new ideas and story angles	Suggested a new way to approach campus recruiting
Excellent media, PR, writing, proofreading, editing, and pitching skills required	Earned high marks in every writing and speaking course. Proofed papers as a side business in college
Must be proficient in MS Office products with a high level of proficiency in MS Word	Skilled in Word, PowerPoint, Excel. Understand headers, styles, graphics, charts, images, and commands
Four-year degree in Mass Communications, Marketing or related field	Graduating in May with a degree in Mass Communication with an emphasis in public relations
Public relations and Web/new media experience preferred	Created four videos designed for distribution on FB to help connect alums to the university
Ability to research, read, comprehend, and write complex communications	Experience with lengthy research papers and journal article research. Completed a 25-page final project for capstone
Ability to present information effectively in large and small group environments	Gave informative and persuasive presentations in every communication class. Kept groups updated on research info
Must have excellent communication and interpersonal skills	Earned high marks on every communication assignment
Analytical skills, Excel and Power Point proficiency a plus	(stated above)
Must have demonstrated multitasking skills and be able to work both independently and with a group	Participated in multiple group projects throughout school. Effectively managed full-time college with two part-time jobs. Able to meet all deadlines without fail.

Once you have this information, it is time to figure out how to turn it into narrative prose.

Formatting the Cover Letter

The cover letter should be less than one page in length (Doyle, 2019a). It complements the résumé; don't just repeat your résumé information. The cover letter is a persuasive document to market your credentials and to make an impression that invites an interview. Include specific information about your match for the job requirements.

After the address information (see chapter 6), begin with a greeting such as "Dear Ms. Rice." If the specific name of a human resource contact isn't listed in the advertisement, check the corporate website or social media for a name or call human resources (Doyle, 2019d). If you can't find a name, the final option is to address the letter to the search committee.

The first paragraph should include a strong opening statement that clearly, professionally, and enthusiastically states why you want the job (Gallo, 2014). Indicate where you found the advertisement; companies appreciate learning where their advertising dollars are most effective. The final sentence of this paragraph should be a concise statement about how you are right for the job and what you can offer the company.

The second and subsequent paragraphs should persuasively match your qualifications to the job itself. These are the "key" paragraphs in your letter, since they show an employer that you've actually read the company's ad and have the specific skills required. Be engaging in telling your story and allow a little of your personality to come through as you describe why you are an exact match for the job. Use as much of the information from your worksheet as possible.

Focus your comments on the position advertised as you write the body of your letter. Use specifics in describing your ability to do what the employer needs. Provide tangible examples that illustrate your accomplishments (Doyle, 2019a). Pull in as many items from the company's list as you can without exceeding the one-page limit.

The final paragraph should thank an employer for taking the time to read your application. Some people advise specifying a time when you will follow up, but our feeling is that such a statement could be perceived as presumptuous. A simple "I look forward to hearing from you" should be effective.

Many companies talk about their application and follow-up procedures in the job ad itself or on their corporate website (another reason for you not to risk a negative impression by stating when you will follow up). Web-generated job ads usually tell you that the company received your material. Some companies send postcards when they receive your material, while many do not notify you at all. The company knows you want a job, so don't state the obvious. Make the final paragraph concise and to the point.

Close with "sincerely" or "respectfully" and your typed name four lines later. Don't forget to sign the cover letter above your typed name. Your typed name must match the name printed on your résumé (middle name, middle initial, etc.). A pen with black ink is the best to use when signing your name because people can read it easily if the employer photocopies your cover letter for internal distribution. It doesn't hurt to make sure your black pen works on scrap paper before you begin to sign the cover letter. Going back over the signature a few times doesn't make a professional impression. If your pen fails, you need to print a new copy of the cover letter and sign it to send with the résumé.

> Do not forget to sign your cover letter! An unsigned cover letter is an easy way to be eliminated from job consideration because you lack attention to detail.

We recommend that you use the same graphic header for your cover letter that you design for your résumé. Consistent design and paper texture ties the cover letter and résumé together as a professional package. It is also useful to an employer should your materials become separated.

Don't forget to apply the information about using language from the previous section on writing résumés. Mara Woloshin (2009, p. 7) suggests an editing technique for cover letters that can put you above the rest of the crowd: "When proofreading, modify your modifiers from insecure thinking terms (I feel, I believe, I hope), to active action terms (I am committed, I am confident that)." Your cover letter demonstrates how well you know the company, the position you are applying for, and how you will contribute. It also gives a first impression of your writing and communication skills.

Writing styles vary from one person to another. The true judge of your written style is the person who reads your material, so spend some time proofing your letter to make sure it's the best it can be. A cover letter allows you to demonstrate your written abilities quite clearly to a potential employer. The cover letter and résumé can open the door to a job that interests you. Make sure to apply for multiple jobs. Two or three will not typically yield results. We recommend at least 25. Once the items are sent, you wait for follow-up communication.

LinkedIn

LinkedIn is a popular professional social network. The official LinkedIn site claims they have 500 million+ members. LinkedIn allows you to connect with past and current colleagues, people you would like to get to know professionally, and potential employers. You can read business articles, join business groups, post business topics, and—most importantly—look for jobs. Creating a LinkedIn profile is a requirement for our students, and we have had a number of them contacted by recruiters to apply for jobs.

LinkedIn has an intuitive computer program to work with, so even if you aren't particularly tech savvy, you can create a solid profile in a few hours. Don't race through the process. Your site must resonate with a reader. This is another "first impression" moment for a potential employer, so your attention to detail is extremely important. There are hundreds of articles on the internet about creating a LinkedIn profile. Use them to your advantage. In the meantime, listed below are some recommendations as you start the process.

1. LinkedIn is a mix between a résumé and cover letter. It requires more narrative writing than your résumé but more segmented info about your skills, experience, etc. than your cover letter. It is fine to use "I" here, or you can avoid it as in your résumé. Just be consistent.
2. Change the URL assigned by LinkedIn to your name. Click "view profile"; next click "edit your public profile." This opens a new window, under the section "edit public profile

url" is an icon that looks like a pencil. Click it and type your custom url in the text box. Click "save."

3. Next go into the privacy settings and change them to public. If you don't do this step, professionals considering you for employment cannot see your full profile.
4. Begin with a professional picture. Never cut yourself out of an existing picture where you were with someone else. Wear appropriate business attire for your field. If you are going into a corporate environment, this is probably a business suit. However, we have had sports information majors post a picture in which they were wearing a polo shirt on the field or holding a camera, etc. Your picture should not look like a mug shot. Try to have a little bit of background rather than a white wall. Let your personality come through visually.
5. Next, change the background banner. Since the template banner is the same for everyone, people know immediately that you didn't bother to change it. Make sure to use complementary colors to your profile picture. There are millions of free images on the internet to choose from. Keep it simple but relevant. For example, a computer engineer might choose a banner of mother boards and electronic components. Be appropriately creative.
6. The summary space is your first opportunity to capture the reader's attention. We encourage you to read current internet articles for summaries. There is no right answer here, and it is different for every field. However, if you don't engage the potential employer with the information and writing, they won't examine the rest of your profile. Resist the urge to simply fill this space with cliché terms that don't demonstrate anything.
7. Start filling in all the details about your jobs, experiences, community service, etc. If you finished your résumé, paste it into LinkedIn. One caveat—if you are fluent in another language, make sure you add it, but do not list English if English is your first language. This just looks silly.
8. Add interest groups, but be careful. Schools, business publications (*Inc.* and *Forbes*), and people in your field are all fine. However, be careful of controversial groups or people.

REALITY ☑

Here are some actual student LinkedIn summaries for you to examine and discuss.

- Mass Communication major with a concentration in Public Relations at Mansfield University of PA, graduating in December of 2018—Highly motivated & driven—Willing to serve my community in any way—Basic Spanish skills
- Over 10 years of video production experience beginning in high school. Gained valuable experience working on numerous personal and team projects.

Produced many different types of video content at Mansfield University, including short films, a music video, a public service announcement, and five documentary-style segments for the university's television show *Into the Northern Tier* in addition to editing 11 episodes of the weekly MU60 video blast, hosting 4 episodes on camera, and contributing video footage to many more.

Overall, participated in over 40 video productions that include newscasts, independent films, and various promotional pieces.

[Note the use of numbers in this profile, as recommended in the résumé section.]

- A multi-sport, play-by-play broadcaster and reporter with ESPN Ithaca. Currently the Voice of Big Red Wrestling and host of the Big Red Wrestling Report in cooperation with Cornell University and ESPN Ithaca. Now the lead play-by-play broadcaster for high school sports on ESPN Ithaca.
- Lead play-by-play broadcaster for Cornell Women's Ice Hockey with ESPN+.
- Formerly the voice of Mansfield University Athletics via Mountie All-Access, part of the PSAC Network. Professional play-by-play broadcaster for RLM Sports and WQLV with broadcasting experience in six different sports.
- Worked in collegiate, summer league, and professional baseball as a play-by-play broadcaster, color commentator, and marketing and social media specialist. Interned with the Florida Collegiate Summer League and Tri-City ValleyCats in consecutive summers, allowing for immersion into professional sports business.
- Captured and distributed photos that were used by Minor League Baseball on MLB.com.
- Accredited parliamentarian with the Society for Agricultural Education Parliamentarians.

What words and phrases do you find to be strong or weak?

The reader makes judgments about you based on who/what your interest groups reveal.

9. Make connections. Start with your classmates and professors. Add any former or current employers and colleagues. Keep building this "networking" profile throughout your career.
10. Read and explore what LinkedIn has to offer. When you read something, it will show up so others can see what you've examined. This can be a way to sell yourself. You can even publish articles on LinkedIn. Check off the settings that you are actively job hunting. This allows recruiters to find you.
11. Now proofread. Please do this multiple times and have friends read and proofread as well. Nothing puts off a potential employer like typographical, grammatical, and writing errors.

LinkedIn is an important part of today's professional social media. Make sure you keep examining and tweaking your profile depending on your current situation. You never know when you might be contacted for an interview.

Social Networking, References, and Job Searching

Once you have created an exciting résumé and cover letter, you send it to a potential employer. Be prepared for scrutiny of the material you place on your résumé and cover letter. Seven in ten employers use social networking sites to research job candidates, and more than half have not hired a candidate because of content found on social media (Hayes, 2018). Eve Tahmincioglu (2009), an award-wining labor and career columnist, writes about important considerations when listing references on your résumé.

- Think very carefully about people you are connected with on your social networking sites. More hiring managers use these sites for information about job candidates, so your contacts should be people you trust who will give you a good recommendation. Use the privacy settings if you don't want a potential employer to see your connections.
- Call your references ahead of time and make sure they know what type of job you're applying for. Make sure they are aware

of why you left your last job so their account matches what you have said. Alert your references to be prepared with facts.

- Ask your references not to exaggerate your qualifications; too much overstatement could raise red flags.
- If a hiring manager tells you he is going to contact a former boss or subordinate who does not appear on your reference list and you know that person is likely to give you a bad review, be honest. You might say something like, "I don't mind you calling Mary, but don't be surprised if she doesn't give you a glowing report. We just didn't hit it off." (Resist bad-mouthing anyone.)

Managers may be reluctant to give recommendations because they fear litigation from former employees if the comments are not positive. In turn, many employees omit employers from their résumés if the comments are likely to be negative. Hiring managers are aware of both problems and use social networking sites such as LinkedIn and Facebook to find information. Some firms ask job candidates to sign waivers promising not to sue former employers if the reviews are negative.

Managing the images and information on your social networking sites is not only good personal marketing but it is also essential for your professional credibility. While some human resources departments may not approve of a social media search, many people in a position to hire will look at your online presence. Fifty-eight percent of employers look for information to support a candidate's qualifications for the job; fifty percent look to see if the candidate has a professional online persona, and thirty-four percent want to know what others have posted about the candidate (Driver, 2018). More than forty-four percent of employers have found content on social networking sites that convinced them to hire the candidate (Salm, 2017). Among the primary reasons for hiring were: candidate's background information supported their professional qualifications

---

REALITY ☑

Make sure to Google yourself periodically. One of the applicants for a job at our university had the same name as a notorious criminal. Aware of this information because of an internet search, the candidate briefly addressed the potential problem in the cover letter.

(thirty-eight percent), excellent communication skills (thirty-seven percent), and creativity (thirty-five percent).

But your online presence can backfire as well. We have seen professional accounts of 30-something professionals who post pictures of their bodies, pursed lips (duck lips), etc. A weight loss journey is one thing, but "look at me" pictures show immaturity in the professional world. Above all, don't completely delete yourself from the internet. Fifty-seven percent of employers are less likely to call someone for an interview if the candidate is a ghost online. The bottom line? Think before you post, because there's always someone watching.

Rosemary Haefner (2009), formerly Chief Human Resources Officer at CareerBuilder, suggests that you think of social media as a skill set that needs to be honed for career success (as opposed to posting what you had for lunch or what you looked at while shopping). Haefner recommends the following DOs and DON'Ts to maintain a positive online image.

1. Clean up digital dirt ***before*** you begin your job search. Remove any photos, content, and links that can work against you in an employer's eyes. [Your authors suggest that while you are in college, don't put compromising information on social networking sites.]
2. Consider creating your own professional group on sites like LinkedIn to establish relationships with thought leaders, recruiters, and potential referrals.
3. Keep gripes offline. Keep the content focused on the positive, whether that relates to professional or personal information. Make sure to highlight specific accomplishments inside and outside of work.
4. ***Don't*** forget others can see your friends, so be selective about whom you accept as friends. Monitor comments made by others. Consider using the "block comments" feature or setting your profile to "private" so only designated friends can view it.
5. ***Don't*** mention your job search if you're still employed. [Your authors also recommend not posting that an interview went well.]

Ethical Consideration

Social networking encourages freedom of expression, but when a corporation accesses an individual's personal information to determine if someone is a good fit for the company, when does an employer's quest to determine your worth to the company become a violation of your right to privacy?

Germany was the first country to draft privacy legislation protecting potential employees as well as employees from eavesdropping employers. They considered legislation to make it illegal for companies to check your Facebook and other social networking sites for personal information about you.

It is important to think about your digital footprint throughout your working life.

Adapted from Jolly, 2010.

If your written persuasion effectively entices an employer to contact you, you need to think about one more piece of personal organization prior to a potential phone call—how you answer the phone! Consider keeping a list of the companies you have contacted to remind yourself of the contacts you've initiated. You may think you will remember, but if time elapses and you have applied at a number of companies, the list is an excellent precaution against any memory loss. It will help you project a professional tone with the corporate person trying to reach you.

REALITY ☑

We have often called a potential candidate to invite them for an interview only to hear them say "Who? What job is this?" This is a terrible first impression.

If your contact number is your personal cell phone, you need to be alert and ready to communicate *every* time it rings. You may want to keep your list of applications in an easy-to reach spot on your phone. If you are in a crowded or loud space, figure out whether you can quickly excuse yourself to quieter surroundings or whether you need to let the call go to voice mail. Reply as soon as possible. When you place yourself on the job market, your future is on the line each time the phone rings, and you need to answer it professionally. If your initial written and mental preparation goes well, you will receive an invitation to continue the interview process through a phone or email request to meet you either in person or via video conferencing.

You occasionally may be interviewed for jobs that don't exist. Human resource personnel are always looking for potential employees, and a good interview can place you in a file entitled "future hires." It is also possible to interview for an advertised position already reserved for an internal candidate. The interviewers know the person within the organization, and he/she possesses an obvious advantage for a position over an "outsider." Sometimes, this happens for legal reasons. They know who they want in the job, but they are legally required to interview a certain number of candidates. Your efforts may be in vain. Then again, an interview can mean future employment if you present yourself in an exceptional manner.

Final Thoughts

Creating a compelling résumé can be a daunting task. One suggestion to make the written process easier is to treat the layout of your information as a board game. Type your name, address, jobs, skills, education, and so forth onto a piece of paper and cut the information into separate strips. Then, begin to move them around on a full sheet of paper until you like the arrangement and order of the material. Now, you are ready to format all of your material into an initial document for final review and editing prior to printing. You might eventually move the education category listed at the top of your résumé to the bottom as your work experience eventually replaces the initial importance of a college degree. Similarly, some work experience eventually will disappear from your résumé because an employer will want to see only your most recent employment and skills.

Each cover letter you write will differ from the previous one because you need to target the specific job you are seeking. You should pull various skills and/or responsibilities from your résumé to feature in every cover letter you write. You shape the letter's information to a position's requirements. Although you write the cover letter creatively, the information you feature is always factual and truthful. The format of a cover letter is just like a good public speech: introduction, body (why your experience/skills meet the requirements of the position), and conclusion. A solid cover letter takes practice, but your writing improves each time you apply for an employment opportunity.

A cover letter and résumé are the most important pieces of persuasive writing you do after leaving school. They need to capture the attention and interest of professional people. Once they have resonated with an employer, you are contacted for an in-person, phone, or VoIP interview. At this time, your oral communication skills and interpersonal skills can open the door to a career. The interview demonstrates to the corporation that you fit into its culture and possess the character and skills required.

Key Terms

Cover letter　　Résumé

Exercises

1. Write your résumé. Use the appropriate format and language of your career discipline.
2. Write a cover letter for two job ads. Attach a copy of the ad to each letter for submission.
3. Research the company of your dreams and analyze the skills necessary to work there. This research also applies to graduate school if that is your next step.

CHAPTER
FOUR

Interviewing

Goals

- Understand the preparation that is necessary for virtual and on-site interviews.
- Select artifacts and behaviors to make a great first impression.
- Define behavioral interviewing.
- Prepare and practice behavioral interview answers.
- Prepare to ask effective questions in the interview.
- Identify illegal interview questions.
- Understand the implications of communicating effectively after the interview.

Interviewing is a process where you demonstrate effective communication skills to obtain employment or a promotion. Interviewing involves perhaps the most important persuasive communication in which you will engage after graduation, or if you decide to change jobs, or if your employment is terminated. Without a persuasive résumé and cover letter, you will not obtain an interview opportunity. Many job applicants who appear terrific in their application don't make a solid first impression during the interview (whether in person or through technology). Your verbal, nonverbal, and written skills must complement one another to complete a successful interview process.

There is no single, perfect communication technique that will impress all employers during an interview. Effective résumé writing and interviewing preparation vary from profession to profession. Therefore, along with the general guidelines we provide, we strongly recommend you do a thorough internet search for interviewing tips within your field. Even with countless how-to guides, your success in gaining employment will depend on key components such as your verbal communication, personality, appearance, and work experience. A knowledgeable faculty advisor or professional mentor is a valuable resource when preparing for an interview.

> You must practice interviewing skills. Unless you interview well, it is hard to get a job. Reading how-to guides provides information, but you must practice how you will present that information. Review your nonverbal behaviors; practice effective gestures, pitch, tone, etc. Ask a friend about your verbal skills. Participate in a mock interview to improve verbal and nonverbal skills.

Once your résumé and cover letter attract an employer's attention, an interview opportunity usually follows. You must diligently prepare for the interview. Some individuals think they can simply talk and be themselves. This casual attitude may be your downfall. Employers prefer concise, logical answers to their questions, and most people cannot speak effectively without practice. The more you practice, the better prepared you will be. Practice will boost your confidence and reduce stress about the interview.

This chapter reviews six elements to help you be effective in an interview.

- Prepare for the overall interview experience.
- Prepare for interviews through technology (phone, on-demand voice, video).
- Prepare for on-site interviews.
- Make a great first impression.
- Answer questions effectively.
- Communicate effectively after the interview.

Preparing for the Overall Interview Experience

The first thing you will need to prepare for is how to answer your phone or email to accept the interview and begin the process. When HR or a search committee decides to contact you, these are the usual communication channels. As we mentioned in the last chapter, once you begin to apply for jobs, you must keep a list of what you have applied for so you know how to answer questions when a specific employer contacts you.

REALITY ☑

One of our alums received a call about a job that he applied for the night before. The first thing asked was "What do you know about what we do as a company?" He couldn't remember a thing and said, "I don't recall any particulars about the company." Needless to say, the interview ended there.

Every phone call should be answered professionally with no background noise. If you are at a party or somewhere where you may not be able to hear well, let the message go to voice mail and return it as soon as you can consult your list of job applications and get to a quiet location. If you receive communication via email, make sure to check and double check your reply to make sure there are no errors in your writing. And please, check your email multiple times a day, even if it isn't your preferred channel for communication. Employers usually do not wait very long for your response to a message. It is easy to move on to the next candidate. If you want a job, you must remain vigilant.

REALITY ☑

We've been surprised in the past few years at how many days can go by where we don't get a response from a candidate that we'd like to interview. When they eventually respond, we are already annoyed.

Accept the employer's suggested time for the interview unless you have an unavoidable conflict. You should be the one making alterations in your schedule to meet an interview request. If you are not a morning person and the suggested time is seven in the morning, figure out how to make that work. Numerous individuals today do not like to be inconvenienced, and they make special requests for accommodations. When you do that, you create a negative first impression.

> Check and double check the time zone for the interview. Do not assume they have provided a time for you that is in your time zone. You must remember where companies are located. There is nothing worse than getting a call an hour or two before you expected it or missing calling in because of a time-zone error.

Let's say you have an interview scheduled via technology. It may be a phone interview, computer-generated written interview, or web conferencing. Digital protocols will continue to expand as employers seek better ways to appraise job applicants. There are a variety of preparations you should do before the actual interview time arrives. These preparations allow you to remain calm and well informed throughout your initial communication.

Research the company thoroughly so you know all of its basic information: size of the organization, product(s), scope (local, regional, national, global), number of employees, mission, etc. It is very likely that you will be asked to answer questions regarding information that is readily available on the web. You also need to think of questions you might ask at the end of the interview. Some of the questions you ask an interviewer should evolve from your personal research about the company and what it produces. Your questions reveal your areas of interest, intuition, intellect, and ability to think on your feet—in addition to your sincere interest in the company. Unfortunately, many job applicants don't do extensive corporate research ahead of time. For example, we once had a job applicant who asked how many students were enrolled at our institution. That immediately told us the person had not done any preparation for the interview.

Next, review all of your personal information carefully. Review the cover letter you sent for that position. Think about all of the experiences you have had that make you marketable as an employee. Look at the actual job ad again so you remember clearly what they are looking for in a candidate. Make lists. Jot notes. Do whatever works for you—but have all of this information fresh in your mind. This is your next opportunity to persuade interviewers that you are the right candidate for the job. You cannot do that if you sound generic. Focus your thought process toward this particular job. If you sound unprepared, you have wasted the opportunity. You can't get this moment back again.

You need to check and double check the instructions for the interview. If asked to use Skype, say yes—not "oh could we use X program that I'm more familiar with?" Learn how to use the suggested program as quickly as possible. Be sure to practice with a friend before the interview.

So are you ready? Let's get to the interview.

Preparing for the Virtual Interview

At one time, the only type of initial contact was the face-to-face interview. Today, interviewers screen candidates via phone, one-way on-demand voice or written interviews, or through two-way web conferencing, such as WhatsApp, Zoom, or Skype (among others) before proceeding to an on-site interview. Initial screenings are handled by humans or through AI (artificial intelligence).

Phone Interviews

Phone interviews add an interesting dimension to the interview process. This is a good news/bad news situation. The good news is you don't have to worry about your attire or posture. You can use interview notes with answers to potential questions and lists of skills or qualities that you don't want to forget. The bad news is your vocal technique, vocabulary, and verbal style are all scrutinized. Your paralanguage (the vocal techniques you use to emphasize and give meaning to words) is even more important on the phone. Because the listener has no visual cues, your "ums/uhs," pitch, tone of voice, and rate are the focus of the conversation. Speaking too quickly makes you sound nervous. Too many "ums/uhs" make you sound unsure of yourself. Practice using a conversational style for answering questions before you have a phone interview. Concentrate on your grammar, articulation, and expressing yourself in a concise manner. Stand up while you talk during a phone interview so you have the best breath support for energy and vocal quality. You can tape your notes and résumé on the wall in front of you if necessary. Also remember you will receive no nonverbal feedback in a phone interview. You cannot tell whether the interviewer is smiling, nodding or looking disgusted. Imagine the interviewer with a positive, friendly face to help yourself remain calm and confident.

Many of our students have had success with attaching a large smiley face to the wall to look at as they answer questions. It sounds silly, but it helps establish a good mental outlook.

One-Way On-Demand Vocal and Written Interviews

Technology is progressing rapidly. Job candidates may encounter an on-demand voice or written interview as an initial screening tool to whittle down applicants for actual interviews. With this technology you are interviewing, one-way, with a computer program. For example, you access the program, and a series of questions come up on the screen one at a time. You are required either to speak into your computer mic/phone to answer the question or write your answer into a box that is supplied on your screen. Technology now is sophisticated enough that it can include video, which records the way you look and your nonverbal communication as well.

If you are used to looking at people when you speak, this type of interview can be unnerving. The smiley face on the wall or above your computer might help you here too. Try to stay calm. We heard of one company that makes the interview go dark in the middle of the process, which makes you think you lost the connection. Then it records your reaction. An "OH NO!" is much different from an "OH EXPLETIVE!" so you need to be on your toes during the entire digital experience.

Often the responses are timed. You might be allowed to have one do-over where you can delete your original answer and try again, but rarely do you get unlimited tries. If time allows you to write your answers in a word processing program and cut and paste them into the answer box, we highly recommend doing that to help cut down on writing errors.

REALITY ☑

We cannot emphasize enough that you need to work on perfecting your writing skills during your college career. Nothing screams "I am uneducated" like multiple writing errors.

Two-Way Videoconferencing Interviews

Today, forty-two percent of companies use video interviews compared to ten percent in 2012 (Chen, 2020). Skype, WhatsApp, Zoom and other software are used for videoconferencing. These programs allow for an in-person, face-to-face experience through technology. An interviewer can compare your facial expressions to the enthusiasm in your voice to check your perceived personality and character. You are seen from the waist up or even tighter depending on your distance from the camera. Unlike the phone interview, you will be able to see the face of the person speaking with you, which provides a more conversational, interpersonal experience.

Videoconferencing interviews have advantages as well as drawbacks. The advantages are that your interviewers can see what you look like. You can sell your nonverbal qualities that are omitted from nonvisual interviews. The drawbacks are that your visual presentation is now a critical component of your evaluation. The video is similar to appearing on television, with you as the director, camera operator, set designer, sound and lighting technician, wardrobe supervisor, and makeup artist (Chen, 2020).

Preparing for an On-Camera Experience

On-camera experiences mean there are many decisions you must make to put yourself ahead of other applicants. Here are some guidelines to get you started.

Appearance. This is essential just as with an in-person interview. Please read ahead in this chapter for specific tips. In addition, when you are sending images through the internet, avoid the color red and any busy fabric patterns. They don't transfer well, especially on smaller screens.

REALITY ☑

Please! Wear the entire suit! We had a student interview in a terrific suit, but a problem with his audio connection developed. He stood up to adjust it on his computer and gave us quite a view of his boxer shorts, which were not visible when he was seated.

Device choice and location. You'll need to decide whether you are using a computer or a phone. When you interview on a phone, there are black bars that show on either side of you and need to be accounted for in framing your image. You need to find a way to secure the phone. Holding it makes for awkward angles and an inability to hold your image steady. Whether using a computer or a phone, be sure to locate it on the same level as your face. If a device is too low, we are looking up your nose. If it is too high, we are looking down your shirt. Typically, you need to put your laptop on a stack of books to get it up to natural eye level. An interviewer expects to see your eyes clearly. Voice quality will be better with a dedicated microphone.

Set design. Consider creating a professional-looking background. A student dorm or apartment doesn't make a good set design, nor does a family living room. A plain background is ok, but if you can add a plant or a neat bookcase it can often set you apart from the other candidates who don't think about a background. Keep distracting elements out of the background. We interviewed someone whose background appeared to include a dead brown holiday tree. Another had a busy poster from a movie. In both cases we couldn't concentrate on the interview because we were trying to make sense of what we were looking at! Visual focus needs to be on you, some strategically placed professional items, and nothing else.

REALITY ☑

While revising this chapter, we interviewed three candidates. One was in a classroom with the computer pointed up to reveal old-fashioned ceiling tiles. Another had a plain white background. The third was at a desk in front of a very neat bookshelf and filing cabinet with a well-placed plant on top. There was a big difference in the sense of professionalism we got from each of the candidates.

Computer connection. Check your computer connection prior to the interview. Then check it again. And again. Make sure there is no static, that the audio levels are even, and that you aren't overamplified. Make sure there are no glitches in the video. We are in a rural location with sketchy internet. Our students must make sure to use a wired Ethernet connection instead of WiFi. Even then, they sometimes discover they need an alternate location to avoid technical problems. If there is a login, make sure yours is professional; eliminate funny nicknames, etc.

Lighting. This is incredibly important. You need three-point lighting to be effective—two light sources coming from the front sides and one from the back so that you are evenly lighted. If you only have back lighting, it is difficult to see your facial features. Never sit in front of a window or glass door if you want to be seen. If light is only on one side, then half of your face will be shadowed. Lighting is particularly important for people with darker complexions. You want the interviewer to be able to see all parts of your face.

Body placement. Don't be too close or too far away from the camera. Ideally, you should have your face and part of your chest in the shot (but never cleavage). Make sure the top of your head doesn't get cut off either. Additionally, look behind you. Where you are in location to the art on the wall is important. We once interviewed someone in front of a vertical picture of the Eiffel Tower—which was coming out of the top of her head. All she needed to do was move to one side.

Eye contact and body language. You must make eye contact with the interviewer. To do that, you must look into the camera of your device. Your instinct will be to look at the interviewer instead but that will look to them as though you are looking down. Try taping a pair of eyes to your computer camera as a reminder. Nervous gestures are amplified in close-up range. Keep your hands away from your face. Sit up straight and refrain from nervous rocking motions (absolutely no swivel chairs!).

Eliminate distractions. Dogs barking? Kids crying? Messy rooms? No. Hire a babysitter, make Fido comfy in another room, and clean up!

Practice. There is no excuse not to do this. Do a test run with a friend or family member so you can check color, sound, and your expressions. Practice makes this technical process go as smoothly as possible.

Moving On

So you've completed your interview through technology. Awesome! Sometimes this is all there is. If so, wonderful. You either got the job or you are back in job search mode. Often, however, you get invited to an on-site interview. In that case, there are a whole new set of experiences for which to prepare.

Preparing for the On-Site Interview

Once you receive an interview confirmation, there are a number of things you can do to plan for a successful, prompt arrival. You also need to research information to help you prepare psychologically. An on-site interview requires advance planning. Many people just take off with no thought as to what comes next. Big mistake.

Getting to the Site Preparations

Researching for the trip. Make sure you have the proper business address and directions for exactly where you need to go once you locate the building. If the business is a long distance from your location, or in a traffic-congested city, use a GPS system to guide you or use Google Maps, MapQuest, or a street map for directions.

Make sure to print a copy of the directions or save them to your phone before you leave. Satellites fail occasionally; there is no sense inviting Murphy's Law to your interview experience.

Plan where you are going to park your car. Remember to take the phone number of your contact with you in case you have an unexpected complication. Don't hesitate to ask for travel specifics when you have the initial interview conversation via email or phone. It is much better to research the trip exhaustively than to get lost.

Preparing for the trip. Some companies take care of the travel planning for you. Other companies expect you to book your own flight and hotel. Some companies reimburse these expenses; others don't. There is nothing wrong with asking "What is the procedure for travel arrangements?"

Double check your appointments and instructions. If it has been a few days or weeks since the original appointment was scheduled, it is a good idea to phone or email your contact a day before the scheduled interview to confirm the details of your appointment. Being flexible and adapting to change is important; corporate or personal emergencies arise. You may be asked to come back another day, or you may be assigned to another person who will conduct the interview. In both cases, display a calm, professional response to the situation. If you are thrust into an unanticipated situation despite all your preparation, the difficult situation gives you a chance to exhibit a skill useful to the potential employer—adaptability.

Mental Preparations

Ask questions of your contact person. A good question to ask the contact person is whether you will be interviewing with an individual or a group. Ask for the name(s) of the people with whom you will be interviewing. Look for the individual(s) on the company website ahead of time. The website gives you a familiarity with how they look and possibly provides information regarding their titles and responsibilities. It is useful to remember that names don't always reveal a person's gender. There are a few first names shared equally between men and women. You don't want to look shocked when you meet a woman after mistakenly assuming you would be interviewing with a man. In today's world, many people identify as nonbinary, so be prepared to simply use the person's name until you know their preferred pronouns.

Prepare yourself mentally. Anything can happen during a job interview, and it is wise to be prepared for the unexpected. A colleague told us about her friend, who had an unusual interview experience. The first question in the interview was would she drive the two of them to lunch. The interviewee was horrified because the condition of her car was less than presentable, with fast-food wrappers and other garbage strewn around the seats and floor. What would the interviewer's perception of the candidate be after that short ride? Although you wouldn't expect an interviewer to see the inside of your car, anything can happen, and you must be prepared. It is just as reasonable to anticipate that an interviewer might walk you to your car after the interview because it's the end of the workday, or the person wants to use the time to ask you a few more questions.

Even if your self-confidence is not high, you'll want to demonstrate competence and assurance. Think about the positive aspects of yourself; don't dwell on negatives or insecurities (Dehne, 2010). For some people, it is helpful to use positive affirmations on a daily basis as you are job hunting and surround yourself with supportive people as you move through the difficult task of seeking employment.

Positive affirmations are specific statements to focus your attention and to eliminate negative thoughts and feelings (Bishop, 2019). Repeating the affirmations trains you to be confident and upbeat in the interview. Listed below are five examples. You can Google positive affirmations for job interviews for more ideas.

- I am calm and confident; job interviews are easy.
- I am perfect for this position; I am their ideal candidate.
- I love job interviews, and my energy is contagious.
- I impress interviewers; I stand out above the rest.
- I am an excellent candidate, and I exude capability.

Finally, remember that you are "on" the entire time you are present at the interview site. From the moment you step out of your car, people may be watching you from windows. The same scenario is true during your departure. Until you are safely out of sight, you should appear to be a responsible, professional potential employee. You can collapse later.

Review the job ad and your résumé/qualifications. Employers describe specific programs or skills in a job ad, and you need to match those exact skills with your experience. Employers may ask you to complete a skills assessment or a talent assessment test. Eighty-two percent of companies conduct preemployment assessment tests (Zojceska, 2019). Tests can range from aptitude tests to general knowledge tests to job tasks tests to personality assessments to specific skills assessments. Companies may also ask you to participate in a job simulation exercise, such as a mock sales call or a presentation to a group. Simulations measure whether candidates can perform tasks associated with the job (Doyle, 2020a). If the job requires physical ability, the simulation would assess strength and endurance.

REALITY ☑

One of our alums interviewed to be a news anchor.
While she was there, they gave her a ten-question quiz including
"who is the current prime minister in Britain?"
"what is the capital of California?" and
"what does GNP stand for in business?"

Plan your attire and accessories. Employers notice every detail about you from the instant they meet you. You need to plan carefully to manage your personal brand. You can find specific information about attire and accessories in the next section.

Making a Great Impression

After thorough preparation, you are ready to embark on the actual interview. A **first impression** is extremely important in making an interviewer feel comfortable with you. Think back to chapter 2 on perception. Many interviewers decide in the first few seconds whether you seem competent, whether they like you, and whether you are a good fit with their company. The way you look when the interviewer first sees you, the way you move as you enter the room, the first words out of your mouth, and how you shake an interviewer's hand all contribute to making a great impression.

You must choose your personal attire (**artifacts**) carefully. For example, Aaron walks into an interview with an advertising agency in a crisply pressed, jet-black suit. He has a silver dress shirt and gray silk tie; his shoes are highly polished. His belt is black leather with a silver tip. Aaron's appearance establishes him as a person of potential interest when he introduces himself to the interviewer.

Lee Anne is not aware of how important artifact choices are, however. Although she can afford much more expensive clothing than Aaron, she has made some unwise choices for her interview. She chooses a flowery, casual, wrinkled dress. Her shoes have open toes and heels because it is August. The tattoo around her ankle is visible, and her legs are bare.

Aaron visually communicates success and confidence. There is nothing in his appearance an interviewer could interpret as objectionable. He sticks to the basic principles of the dress code for an advertising position. He realizes, however, if he were interviewing in a more traditional corporation, he should wear his dark suit with a white shirt rather than silver and should choose a more conservative tie. Lee Anne is clueless regarding the image her clothing projects. A flowery dress is simply too casual. Her visible tattoo gives the employer personal information about her personality that could be interpreted in a negative manner. (It is quite possible that Aaron has a tattoo, but it is covered by his suit and not visible to the interviewer.) Artifact choices should reinforce the idea you are ready to start the job.

REALITY ☑

Someday tattoos may be a nonissue, but there are still plenty of people and industries that are put off by a visible tattoo. Play it safe when you can; don't give anyone personal information they can use to discriminate against you.

The best way to make clothing decisions for an interview is to analyze the company thoroughly and dress accordingly. You may not be able to afford expensive, well-tailored clothing or gold and sterling silver jewelry, but you can choose colors and fabrics that make you look good. Employees in various corporate departments have a specific look, and you should try to find out what it is prior to an interview. In certain cases, the dress code is casual, and you may look out of place in a tailored suit. It is best to research the dress code for each company with which you secure an interview and to select a comfortable, appropriate outfit plus accessories that state "I belong on this team!"

A basic guideline is to dress for a position one or two steps above the position you are applying for. You can almost never go wrong with a suit. It is easy to remove the jacket and tie or blazer if you realize you are overdressed. But if you are underdressed, there is nothing you can do. People expect you to look like you are on an interview.

It's not a bad idea to become comfortable wearing dress clothing while you are still in school. Although the thought of occasionally dressing up for class may seem awkward at first, the ease with which you move, sit, and stand in corporate attire will be enhanced if you have some practice before graduation. If finances are tight, be resourceful. You can build your professional look slowly while in college. Ask for interview attire for holiday and birthday gifts. You can begin accumulating items such as shoes, jewelry, ties, scarves, and belts that still fit even if you gain or lose a little weight. Don't rule out shopping at high end thrift stores either. Occasionally, you can find a brand new or gently used designer suit for $20 or less!

Clothing needs to complement your body type. Here are a few of the fundamental rules for the conservative interviewing process.

DOs

- One earring per ear (no earrings for men).
- One ring per hand.
- Polished dress shoes.
- Plain, conservative tie (no cartoon characters!).
- Briefcase or bag to carry extra résumés and essentials.
- Always remove the X threads (tacking stitches) from the back of your coat or jacket (they are there only to keep the jacket from wrinkling in transit to the store; vents should be free to open).

DON'Ts

- No open-toe or open-heel shoes.
- No sleeveless outfits (women), no short-sleeved shirts (men).
- No gaudy or noticeable makeup.
- No work boots/sneakers.

Once the interviewer sees you, you have made your first impression. But his or her perception of you doesn't stop there. Your handshake will add or detract from the first impression. A firm handshake sends the nonverbal message of confidence—a personal quality desired by most interviewers. Wiping sweaty hands on your pants or fumbling with papers so you can extend your hand for a handshake sends a message of incompetence as well as a lack of professional interpersonal experience.

> Be aware in today's germy culture, some people simply don't shake hands. If you extend a hand and are rebuffed, don't take it personally. Gracefully move on and continue the interview.

There are a number of connotations related to gender with handshakes (Thibodeaux, 2018). People with a limp shake may be regarded as timid. The length of the handshake can be interpreted as showing power—longer handshakes may be perceived as dominance. Practice with friends and family and ask for feedback. Learn to adjust your handshake based on specific interactions. If someone grasps your hand firmly, you can increase your grip.

Standing tall will make you act more in charge and can help you stay ahead of the competition (Grant, 2011). Expansive postures such as standing tall, sitting straight, and keeping shoulders back will help you perform better in the interview because you will answer with more authority and more confidence. Use postures, gestures, and expressions that show active listening, energy, and understanding (Thibodeaux, 2018). Make eye contact, and smile. Leaning forward occasionally conveys enthusiasm; leaning back has the opposite effect. Engaging in these nonverbal behaviors has the double benefit of keeping you alert and aware while making a good impression on the interviewer.

> Women often need to practice these postures because they have been taught to round their shoulders and minimize the space they use. They need to break these habits to look confident.

Hiring mangers judge whether a candidate has hard skills—the-specific skills and knowledge needed to perform a job (Doyle, 2020b). Hard skills are quantifiable and easily evaluated; for example, a hard skill for someone in information technology is computer programming. Hard skills can be learned through education, training programs, and certifications. Hiring managers also look for soft skills—interpersonal skills such as listening, open-mindedness, friendliness, and empathy. The best predictors of future job success are often the most difficult to measure (Vozza, 2020). Soft skills are critical to success, particularly with today's focus on service and teamwork. Hiring managers look for interpersonal and relational skills.

The ability to communicate effectively and interact well with colleagues and clients is essential in all industries.

REALITY ☑

Prepare a list of your soft skills. Compare your list to the job description for the position for which you are interviewing.

Soft skills are transferable across jobs; candidates with excellent soft skills are adaptable. Hard skills can be taught; people who possess soft skills are perceived as having valuable and unique qualities. Companies look for the following soft skills (Lucas, 2019).

- Effective communication
- Teamwork
- Creative thinking
- Generating and accepting feedback
- Confidence
- Flexibility
- Resourcefulness

A study by Adobe found that communication was the soft skill most frequently sought by hiring managers followed by creativity and collaboration (Vozza, 2020). Almost 75% of job postings list communication as a necessary skill and 50% list creativity. A good conversation during the interview is a strong indicator that you have the soft skills needed to excel in the position. Companies need people who converse effectively, put people at ease, make connections, and create an environment that promotes productivity. If you respond to questions clearly and concisely, providing solid examples in a way that paints a picture, you will be viewed as someone with good soft skills. Also be aware of your eye contact and body language. If asked about a problem you solved, explain your thinking process. You can describe the situation, talk about the action you took and why, and the outcome, sharing how your soft skills contributed to the result.

The requirements for making a good first impression vary from one corporation to the next as well as from one culture to another. For instance, in U.S. culture, we exchange business cards after a meeting is completed. In some cultures, however, people exchange business cards as you meet someone for the first time. If you don't know the customs of the culture of an interviewer, you could eliminate yourself from consideration in the first few moments of an encounter. If you do any business travel or have the potential to meet people from another culture, you should research the other culture carefully to determine what you need to do to make a positive first impression.

REALITY ☑

People notice manners and etiquette. Do you hold a door for others? Push your chair in when you leave a table? Do you have wildly inappropriate gestures like habitually wiping your nose with the back of your hand? Do you know how to use a napkin at lunch? We talk more about etiquette in chapter 11.

The word *culture* also applies to the various departments and management levels within a company. Each department possesses a customary way of conducting business, using time, verbal jargon, and appearance. As you walk through different departments and floors of a building, you should observe a slightly different "look" in the people employed in each unit. Being aware of corporate culture and its variations assists you in making better decisions regarding which part of the company meets your future goals and needs.

You have a professional outfit, briefcase or bag, and a smile on your face. Walk in with good posture and emit as much confidence as you possibly can!

Answering Questions Effectively

Now that you have made a good first impression, you need to follow through by sounding intelligent and professional as you speak. You must be aware of your nonverbals such as volume, rate, and inflection. Some people speak very loudly or very quickly when they are nervous, which can be annoying to others and could lower their perceptions of your credibility, experience, and competence. In addition to paying attention to how you speak, you should consider what you will say. Practice your answers to potential questions for coherency and uniqueness. The more you practice creating an engaging answer to various questions, the better prepared you are to articulate excellent responses in an interview.

It is essential that your answers to various questions demonstrate that you have a basic understanding of the company and the position you are seeking. Research is imperative. Let's say you are interviewing for a job at a famous ice-cream company and you ask, "So what varieties of ice cream do you manufacture?" or "How many employees are in your company?" The immediate impression is that you aren't prepared. An interviewer would obviously think, "If you can't take the time to look up simple facts on our website, why should I consider you for this job? You are wasting my time."

Another area to research is the type of interview and the questions to expect. In a traditional interview, you might be asked to tell the interviewer about yourself or to list challenges you have faced (see examples below). The other type of interview is **behavioral interviewing**, Behavioral interviewing is a common professional tool defined as follows:

> a job interviewing technique whereby the applicant is asked to describe past behavior in order to determine whether she is suitable for a position. For example, an interviewer may ask 'Tell me

> about a time when you dealt with a disruptive customer." (Business Dictionary, 2020)

Behavioral interviewing focuses on the specific actions taken by the interviewee in the past based on the assumption that past performance can be a good predictor of future performance (Doyle, 2019b). Instead of asking how you would behave, the interviewer asks how you did behave. Recruiters value behavioral interviews as an employment tool because applicants showcase their oral communication skills, interpersonal skills, critical-thinking skills, leadership skills, and teamwork skills (Moody, Stewart, and Bolt-Lee, 2002). To be successful at behavioral interviewing, candidates must be prepared to use personal stories to demonstrate their competence for the job in a meaningful and memorable way.

You must tell a compelling one- to two-minute personal story as you answer questions. We define *story* as an answer that has *characters*, a *plot*, a *climax*, and a *resolution*. If you answer the question, "What is your greatest strength?" with "I'm very calm under pressure; I can really get the job done; I don't sweat the small stuff," you haven't said anything. The interviewer will recognize these clichés but never remember your name. There is no way you can make a good impression with that simplistic answer.

Instead, let's consider a behavioral response to the same question. When the interviewer asks Veronica that question, she answers with a one-minute story. "Well, I'm very calm under pressure. For example, when I was working at the ice-cream shop, a customer received a cone that had a hole in it. It was a small hole in the bottom, but the ice cream began to drip through it, because it was a hot day. The woman was so irate that the ice cream had dripped on her suit, she came up to me and threw the ice cream in my face. I had to stand there in front of other customers and handle the situation without losing my cool. My first reaction was to get really angry and say something I would have regretted, but I bit my tongue, wiped off my face, and said very nicely, "Is something wrong?" And with that, all of the other customers turned their heads and stared at her. Once the focus was on her rather than on her actions, she stormed out of the ice-cream shop. While I was disappointed I couldn't make her happy, at least the other customers complimented me on the way I handled the situation."

Note that this is a one- to two-minute behavioral answer. It meets all of the criteria of storytelling in that it has characters, a plot, a climax, and a resolution. It paints a visual picture the interviewer is not likely to forget. Plus, it answers the question creatively. This type of answer makes Veronica memorable to the interviewer and much more likely to be remembered when the discussion regarding final candidates for the position takes place.

Ethical Encounter

An interviewer looks at one of the employment sources on your résumé and asks you to describe a situation you thought represented your best accomplishment during employment. Unfortunately, the source they ask you about is a company where you actually accomplished nothing and even hated being there. Therefore, you decide to invent a situation to answer the question rather than admit the truth. What are some of the potential risks in telling a story like this?

Be prepared to answer basic questions like the ones listed below in a standard interview.

- Why should we hire you?
- What is your greatest strength?
- What is your greatest weakness?
- What accomplishment has given you the greatest satisfaction?
- What motivates you to put forth your greatest effort?
- Why do you want to work for our company?

However, as more and more interviewers are looking for behavioral interview answers, you may find that you are asked questions that lead you directly to a story, such as:

- Tell me how you handled your last conflict.
- Tell me about a time when you had to work on a team.
- Tell me about the last time you had to handle a really stressful situation.

The appendix provides an extensive list of additional interview questions.

The STAR interview technique provides a template for responding to inquiries about your competence for the job. STAR stands for **S**ituation, ***T***ask, **A**ction, **R**esult. The interviewer might ask you, for example, to describe a time when you dealt with conflict. You would then describe a situation (providing the context), your task (responsibility), the action you took, and the result (outcome).

As you create your answers to these questions while preparing for an interview, always keep your interviewer in mind—just as you think about your audience in public speaking. You shape your answers for the interviewer. If asked "Why do you want to work for our company?" and you reply "Because I really need a job," "Because I will learn a lot here," or "Because I find this company to be prestigious," you are not thinking about your audience. Your answer focuses on you. A better answer reveals personal, skill-based information that makes you useful to the company. It is important to articulate how your greatest strength can benefit the corporation. A personal story about your dependability and how that quality will benefit the employer works to your advantage.

REALITY ☑

Employers don't often care about what you will learn as an employee. Don't frame your answers as what they can do for you. Frame it so that they can clearly see what you can do for them. They want to think that they are getting something when they hire you.

As you get ready to create your stories, it is helpful to prepare a list of your skills and personality traits (refer to the statements you made about yourself in chapter 2). Skills are competencies you've learned, such as computer programs, problem solving, or speaking another language. Personality traits are desirable qualities you possess, such as being dependable, energetic, and detail oriented. Once you have developed your list of skills and personality traits, you can then create the stories to highlight them. Good stories will make you stand out as conversational and professional.

Sometimes the interviewer is looking for the ability to think creatively. In this situation, an interviewer may ask a **brainteaser**—an open-ended hypothetical question that tests the problem-solving ability of a potential employee and necessitates a factual, logical, descriptive answer. Brainteasers are common in interviews for creative jobs. William Poundstone (2003) gives the following example of a brainteaser: "How much does the ice in a hockey rink weigh?" He notes: "Why use logic puzzles, riddles, and impossible questions? The goal . . . is to assess a general problem-solving ability rather than a specific competency" (p. 20). Non-computer-related industries such as those that deal with the public or the law also use brainteasers. The goal of this type of interview question is to test your experience with problem solving as well as your ability to remain calm under pressure. Many brainteasers do not have a correct answer. Your verbal ability to piece together logical thoughts in an impromptu manner is important. The brainteaser is somewhat different from the expectations for behavioral interviewing. The details and sequential logic in your answer to the brainteaser need to impress the interviewer.

One hiring manager described asking unusual questions to learn from the interviewee's reactions and answers whether there would be a good fit with the company (Zupek, 2010). One question was: "If you were a candy bar, what kind would you be?" The interviewee thought for about three seconds, smiled, and said, "I'd be a Caramello because they're awesome and hard to find, but when you find them you get a happy feeling inside." The answer shows a lot of self-confidence. Keep in mind, though, not everyone would like that answer. Another person might answer, "I'd be a Hershey bar. I'm not trendy. I'm simple, straightforward, and have a history of consistent quality. What you see is what you get." Which answer do you like best?

Another situation you should be prepared to handle is the stress interview. In a **stress interview**, the employer will test you to your limits. We had an accounting major who went to an interview for a financial-planning position. The interviewer looked at her and said, "OK, Heather, here is a stack of travel brochures. I'll be back in 20 minutes, and I expect you to have a persuasive presentation ready for me concerning where I should go on vacation." He exited the room. When he got back and heard her presentation, he immediately launched into his questions. She was not allowed to use any material twice for her answers to 16 questions. When he asked her what her greatest weakness was, she paused for a brief moment, and he badgered her with, "What's the matter Heather, do you think you are perfect?" In this situation, the employer is trying to see how she will hold up under stress. Although this may seem unfair, a job as a financial planner entails dealing with very unhappy customers when the stock market goes down, and the employer needs to know if the employee can handle the pressure.

Another student who had a degree in broadcasting interviewed for a video-editing position. When the student arrived at the studio, they handed him video clips from a breaking story aired earlier the same day. He had 30 minutes to cut his own version of the story for the station. He received no training or explanation of the company's equipment in the editing suite. He finished creating his version of the story within the time limit. The supervisor thanked him for his time and said the senior producer would contact him after screening the applicant's video. No further questions were asked. The interview was over.

A third example of a stressful interview situation can occur when you are interviewed with other applicants. There are interviews where all applicants are brought into the same room and asked to answer questions in front of one another. We know of two people who have reported being asked to answer the question, "Why should we hire you instead of the specific person on your left."

Never say you are the best or that you are better than someone else. You don't know that. Instead try, "I really don't know what her qualifications are, but I can . . ."

Thinking about the three scenarios just described, it is important to find out what the interview norm is in your professional field. Are you likely to run into stress interviews? Make sure you can do what you say you can do on your résumé, because you may be tested. For example, if you state that you are bilingual, it is reasonable to assume that the person interviewing you could conduct the interview in the language listed on your résumé. Any hesitation on your part in performing a task or answering a question may give the interviewer a bad impression. Be prepared and remain as relaxed as possible to handle whatever the interviewer throws at you.

Asking Effective Questions

Part of an effective interview is being prepared to ask good questions. You will meet many people on the day of your interview who will ask you if you have any questions, and if you sit there silently or say "no," you will not be perceived as an engaged and inquisitive candidate.

There are a number of questions that you can ask; feel free to ask the same questions more than once if you interview with different people. Following are some questions that will make you appear intelligent and engaged.

- Why did the last employee leave this job?
- What are you seeking in the ideal candidate for this position?
- How would you describe your management style?
- What do you like best about working for this organization?
- What would you like to see happen six to twelve months after you hire a new person for this position?
- What is your vision for the department over the next two to three years?
- Are there any weaknesses in the department you're working on improving?
- How is performance measured and reviewed?
- What's the single most important challenge facing your staff/organization right now?

Obviously, there are many more questions that you can create. You want to be fully prepared to ask questions based on your research about the company and its employees. And you want to make sure this is the right opportunity for professional growth. Solid preparation will eliminate the dead space when someone asks you, "And what questions can we answer for you?" Never make the mistake of not asking a question. It makes you look unprepared and uninterested. Ask!

Illegal Interview Questions

There are a number of **illegal interview questions**. The Equal Employment Opportunity Act prohibits employers from asking discriminatory questions. Both federal and state laws cover discriminatory employment practices. It is illegal to ask questions based on age, race/ethnicity, gender, sexual orientation, country of origin, religion, disability, marital/family status, and pregnancy (Martin, 2018). The following questions are all illegal.

- What is your maiden name?
- What religious holidays do you observe?
- How old are you?
- Do you have children?
- Do you drink socially?
- Do you have any disabilities?
- Have you ever filed a worker's compensation claim?
- Are you comfortable working for a woman?
- Do you have any serious illnesses?

What is illegal and what is "troublesome" is sometimes difficult to ascertain. For example, "Have you ever been arrested?" or "Do you have a bank account?" or "Can you work weekends or nights?" may not be illegal in some states but could be problematic.

Interviewers sometimes ask illegal questions (they may or may not be unaware that their question is discriminatory). You'll need to decide ahead of time what you will do if an employer asks you an illegal question. If an interviewer asks an illegal question, you are in a difficult situation. You can point out that it is an illegal question, sidestep the question, or simply answer it. None of those three choices yields particularly good results. While you can prepare yourself for the possibility of an illegal question, the best procedure may depend on the specific situation—meaning you may need to decide what you want to do when the question arises.

Communicating After the Interview

It is essential that you use the utmost caution when writing to a prospective employer. Be absolutely sure to get the correct spelling of the interviewer's name and title while you are at the interview. You will need this information—and it ***must*** be accurate—to send a handwritten note after the interview. One misspelling in a thank-you note or email will reveal additional information about your abilities. Handwritten notes are more personal and may be more appropriate for some employment opportunities. If you decide to write an email thank-you (for example, after interviewing with a technology company), proofread carefully. Do not rely on spell-check programs alone—if you have mistakenly typed the wrong word but it is a word found in the dictionary, spell-check will not identify the error (for example, "principal" instead of "principle"). One hiring manager said follow-up behavior can tip the balance (Zupek, 2010). If he is undecided about a candidate but then receives an email thanking him for the interview, he then perceives the candidate as motivated, tactful, and professional. We agree!

Keep the thank-you note brief. It is not an opportunity to do a hard sell. Thank them for the experience and end the note.

As a student, you may not think about the implications of someone agreeing to give you a reference or to helping you make a professional connection. Rather than just providing a critical assessment of your skills, the person is putting his or her reputation on the line. Inappropriate or unprofessional behavior on your part reflects poorly on the person recommending you. Many professors and professionals are extremely cautious about giving recommendations because they have been burned by students and other colleagues. A recommendation is a transaction involving mutual respect. If Professor Yip gives Dominick a contact person, Dominick is obligated to contact that person and to let Professor Yip know he has followed through. Additionally, it is respectful to keep Professor Yip informed throughout the process, since she put her reputation on the line to help Dominick. A thank-you note to Professor Yip would also be in order. Networking is important; make sure you respond appropriately to someone's efforts on your behalf—keep expanding potential networks rather than constricting them through poor behavior.

Ethical Encounter

A professor gives you a contact for an interview and agrees to be your reference. You attend the interview and discover that the position isn't of interest to you, so you give perfunctory answers so the interview ends quickly. You don't thank the interviewer for her time or tell your professor about the meeting. What you don't know is that the business contact is a former student of your professor. What scenarios can develop from this sequence of events?

Final Thoughts

Remember that job-related communication is a package deal. Strong written materials will help you secure a job interview. But once you walk into a corporate environment, the employment pendulum swings away from your writing to your verbal and nonverbal communication skills and style. Potential employers remember everything you do and say. Practice and improve your written and oral skills while you are still in school. Remember to concentrate on your vocal technique at all times during phone interviews. Electronic interviews focus on only a portion of the communication package. Vocal technique and use of paralanguage become your selling points. It is important to develop your oral communication skills as soon as possible to make them effective. Sell your ability during an interview in a warm and friendly manner. Personal stories are an engaging way to keep the interviewer interested in your message. Your professional future depends on consistent communication skills and style. Don't underestimate the importance of soft skills. Excellent verbal, nonverbal and written skills allow colleagues to enjoy working with you daily.

Key Terms

- Artifact
- Behavioral interviewing
- Brainteaser
- First impression
- Illegal interview questions
- Interviewing
- Phone interview
- Skype interview
- Stress interview

Exercises

1. Schedule an appointment with a human resource person at a company to conduct an informative interview. What do they look for in selecting a person for a position? What legal issues do they face during the interview process? How many areas within the company hire entry-level personnel?
2. Pair students and have them interview each other in a timed format before the class. Classmates should critique the strengths and weaknesses of everyone at the end of the round.
3. Depending on the technical facilities available on campus, schedule a phone or a Skype interview with a classmate.
4. Each student should take a turn at the front of the class to respond to a typical interview question and to give a two-minute answer to a behavioral interview question.
5. Do a one-minute audio recording of an interview question. Play the recording for your classmates. Have them critique your vocalics and your answer.

CHAPTER
FIVE

Basic Skills for the First Week

Goals

- Explain the concepts of impression management and branding
- Assess your use of impression management and personal branding
- Explain the concept of stereotyping
- Analyze problems with stereotyping in the workplace
- Explain the concept of self-disclosure
- Analyze the effectiveness of your own use of self-disclosure
- Differentiate among the six listening styles
- Assess the implications of different listening styles in the workplace
- Explain the difference between fact and inference
- Examine your skill in attributing meaning
- Describe a good conversationalist

The anticipation of working at a new job site can be both exciting as well as somewhat nerve wracking. It is quite common to question whether your experience is substantial enough to handle the job, whether your personality blends with corporate goals, and whether your technical skills are strong enough to handle the workload. As unsettling as your intrapersonal thoughts may be, the reality of landing a job is that other people enjoyed meeting you and thought your résumé and skills fit the position they were trying to fill quite well. They selected you to assist them in advancing their business goals. Now, it is up to you to convince them that they made the right choice by hiring you.

The first week of employment is a time where you meet new colleagues, discover numerous workplace procedures, and figure out your actual workload as well as the communication structure of the company. There is a ton of new information to absorb rapidly. Therefore, it's important to listen carefully to the instructions you receive and to observe keenly the activities unfolding around you, so you blend in professionally. How you conduct yourself in the early days of employment can make or break the first impression others form regarding your ability, credibility, and potential for advancement within the organization.

ETHICAL ENCOUNTER

A colleague states that it is fine to do personal business on company time.

Should you use your office computer for private, social communication? What about to research a personal purchase on Amazon?

IMPRESSION MANAGEMENT AND BRANDING

As you prepare for your first day of work, try to recall what colleagues were wearing when you went for the interview. You want to make sure that you dress appropriately. You'll be meeting new people daily, and they will form first impressions about you based on how you look and how you behave. **Impression management** is the active process of projecting an image that correlates with how you want people to see you. Think about the clothes you wear or your behaviors in class. Everything you do or say projects an image of who you are. To manage your impression of competence in the business world, focus on career speech, impeccable writing, a classic wardrobe, and appropriate poise and movement to project professionalism. The term was introduced by Irving Goffman (1959) in his discussion of behavior as a performance. "It is apparent that care will be great in situations where important consequences for the performer will occur as a result of his [or her] conduct" (p. 225). We pay attention to our appearance and our behavior; we perform to manage the impression we make on others. Impression management is a personal commitment to excellence in verbal and nonverbal communication, whether the situation entails a formal presentation or a casual conversation with a colleague.

Impression management is a concept taught in communication theory classes, but businesses use this concept as well. The corporate world labels this concept as "**brand**" or "**branding**." Brands come in three categories: **corporate**, **project,** or **personal**. First, every business, school or university, political party, and religious establishment creates a brand for itself to communicate to the public and manage its image. Second, companies brand their products through their promotion, advertising, marketing, product's name, and physical appearance. Third, individuals themselves have brands. Celebrities, politicians, corporate executives, religious leaders, and everyday citizens brand themselves with their appearance, verbal ability, and ability to be noticed by others. It is useful to recognize the concept of branding so you can successfully brand yourself as well. Daily efforts to project a competent image can result in positive social and professional rewards. Everyone you meet and work with is doing exactly the same thing. Decisions you make about what to wear to an event, the language appropriate for a specific audience, or the type of thank-you note to send affect the impression of professionalism you project.

REALITY ☑

What is your personal brand? Would your professors/supervisors/peers agree? Are you happy with it? What skills/personal qualities would you change as you get ready for the work force? List three things you could start doing immediately to improve your brand.

People form first impressions in seconds. Your colleagues make judgments about you, just as you make judgments about them. As a new employee, it is extremely important to keep an open mind initially about everyone you meet and everything you see. Time is your ally in making appropriate judgments about colleagues and corporate policies. Absorbing and analyzing stimuli prior to communication will enhance the accuracy of your assessments and make you more effective in the workplace. Projecting a consistent image and behaving professionally helps others perceive you as someone with whom they want to work.

One of our students introduced us to the concept of a **personal representative**. Her mother warned her in her early teens that she would never really get to know the inner feelings or true nature of anyone she met in life. Her mother was a wise woman. All you will

---

REALITY ☑

When starting a new job in an environment that has been working well and the employees all know each other, it is key for you not to "stir the pot" during your first week. One of our former students offers the following advice.

- Watch your mouth—you do not know people's preferences, so don't use inappropriate language.
- Use your "vault"—if someone tells you something (positive or negative) about someone else in the office or you hear gossip about others, keep it to yourself.
- Don't immediately reinvent their corporate wheel—let the employees there show you what they have been doing whether you agree with it or not, and do it their way. When you have been with a company for a while, then you can provide other ideas or different ways of achieving a goal.
- Respect everyone—whether it's a vice president or the person who cleans the bathroom. You don't know interoffice relationships or friendships. Disrespecting the wrong person could put you in a negative light with someone you haven't even spoken to yet.
- Know and respect the rules—some places have unions that don't allow you to turn on a TV. Just because someone else does something doesn't mean their behavior is acceptable.
- Ask questions—if you need something or don't know how to do something, ask. Don't waste time; find out how to do your job as efficiently as possible.

—Stephen Daily
Four-time Emmy Award Winning Sports Television Director

---

ever be entitled to know about others is what they allow you to know about them. As you meet colleagues, each of you is encountering the other's personal representative; everyone uses impression management. Remember that accurate judgments of others take time to develop fully.

Business is a team effort, and it takes time to understand colleagues and corporate policy. Your communication and behavior must reflect consistent professional standards of conduct. The business environment is not a social club. Your job is to earn the salary you are paid while making money for the employer by improving the company's image.

So how do you do all this? As you walk into the building on your first day, you will be making a number of perceptual choices as you meet people and evaluate the corporate environment. Think of the job as a new beginning with new colleagues, corporate procedures, and an opportunity to advance your career.

Stereotyping

Stereotyping is the act of labeling or treating people with similar characteristics as though they all exhibit the same values, judgments, and behavior. We also label others for the artifacts they wear and use in their personal space. We use perceptual judgments constantly to decide whom we think we will like as well as what we would like to see in a corporate environment or do as an activity. We often base our perceptual decisions on experiences acquired in the past rather than clearly seeing the reality of the present. Therefore, it is important to put on the brakes to such automatic categorization in the workplace. A rush to judgment of another person or situation can prove fatal during a career.

We experience sensory stimuli daily and categorize the stimuli by comparing them to what we already believe is true. Stereotyping develops from information we choose to hear and remember from our family, peers, religious establishments, teachers, community, and entertainment media. Because stereotyping ignores the possibility of individual uniqueness, it can be problematic, especially in the workplace. For example, thirty years ago society stereotyped men who wore earrings as homosexual. Then, a transition period occurred during which people interpreted earrings as a statement of sexual preference depending on whether the man wore the earring in the left or the right ear. Today men wear earrings without anyone automatically stereotyping them as gay or assuming an indication of sexual preference. Over time, societal attitudes change. It would be wise to allow time before you make personal attitude adjustments.

Stereotyping is something many of us do without thinking. Since we organize stimuli during the perceptual process, stereotyping is a quick and easy way to group and analyze external information. However, we have choices when it comes to assigning meaning to stimuli based on previous stereotypes. While stereotypes allow us to organize information quickly, they can also limit our ability to assess people and situations clearly. A lack of objectivity could easily lead to communication misunderstandings in a diverse workforce. Once you clearly recognize your stereotypical perceptual issues, you become better equipped to communicate effectively with business colleagues and global clients.

Think carefully about yourself for a minute and think about the attributes you are most likely to notice about others. How do you think people might stereotype you on the first day of the job? Is your voice commanding or breathy—what are the stereotypes? Do you project an air of confidence or mousiness as you meet someone or enter a space? Stereotypical thinking exists, and you want to do everything possible to present the best personal image to new colleagues. You manage the impression they form of you.

People will stereotype you the minute they meet you. Dress and act your best at all times.

In some businesses, your supervisor will escort you around the office and introduce you to a number of employees. In other workplaces, your coworker may show you to your office and expect you to get to work with little fanfare. Thus, you need to figure out tasks on your own and complete the assignments handed to you. It's also possible that a portion of your first day will involve a visit to human resources to go over paperwork and corporate procedures as well as receive your security badge. Whether someone else introduces you or you end up introducing yourself, you know that meeting coworkers is the first item on the agenda the very first day. You don't want anyone to stereotype you negatively because of your appearance or behavior. As you anticipate the routine on your first day, you also need to anticipate what you are going to say as conversations begin.

Beware the stereotypes you make of others. Categorizing people can be useful to guide your behavior but only if the categorization is accurate—don't make assumptions.

Self-Disclosure

You enter the office space that you will share with a coworker. How do you get to know one another? Most people begin with a brief introduction: exchange names, nice to meet you, and so on. Additional information about an office mate is not necessary initially since you are there to do a job. However, social events like lunch and continuous days of working together allow for a greater exchange of background information between colleagues. **Self-disclosure** is the act of voluntarily giving personal information to another person. You need to disclose information about yourself in order to give others a feeling for who you are. Revealing information about your background and philosophy of life can strengthen interpersonal relationships. However, effective disclosure of personal information is done slowly and over a long period of time.

Common self-disclosures are obvious—name, prior work experience, etc. Sometimes it is hard to know what is appropriate. Some initial self-disclosures are appropriate or inappropriate depending on the region of the country in which one lives. For example, when I (KSY) moved to Arkansas, I was in the car with a colleague and her 7-year-old daughter. The daughter looked at me and asked, "What church do you go to?" I waited for the mother to correct her daughter for asking an inappropriate question. From my perspective, the question was too intimate for initial self-disclosure. Silence reigned, however. The mother was actually waiting for me to answer the question since in that region of the country, at that time, "What church do you go to?" was usually the second question asked of strangers, immediately after asking "What is your name?" The silence was extremely awkward because both of us were waiting for the other person to speak. A moment like this is a simple reminder of how self-disclosure can vary from one region of the country to another and why it is important to maintain an open mind in all spontaneous communication.

Digital media is making self-disclosure issues more challenging. Technology offers a platform for individuals to openly share personal information rarely discussed in a professional setting. Technology provides a fast path to discover a new colleague's background. Employers, HR, and colleagues can check social networking sites instantly to discover religious, cultural, and political backgrounds, as well as hobbies, likes, and dislikes. Therefore, it is important to review the material on every social networking site to make sure it matches the impression you are trying to create professionally.

One way to gauge the appropriateness of self-disclosure is by interpreting the nonverbal behavior of your conversation partner. People may demonstrate discomfort with your self-disclosure through their vocalizations, their silence, lowering eye contact with you, or a sudden shift of subject matter. When this nonverbal/verbal change occurs during a conversation, you need to be perceptive enough to stop your content disclosure immediately. If you are in a position where someone is disclosing information and expecting you to disclose similar details, you may find it necessary to respond in a very calm manner with something like, "I'm not prepared to talk about that right now. Can we please change the subject?" This is a reasonable way to let the other person know he or she has overstepped the bounds of appropriate discussion without closing off further communication. People have different tolerances for what constitutes an appropriate topic for daily conversation. If you have not yet reached the same comfort level for disclosure of a specific content area as your colleague, communicate how you feel while leaving the door open for the relationship to continue.

Please remember that some disclosures must happen for collegial relationships to grow. Some people find it difficult to disclose anything personal or philosophical in a social/business setting. It is extremely difficult, however, to build a working relationship with colleagues who never self-disclose how or why they solve problems or reach conclusions the way they do. Business conversations should always remain professional. It is important to remember that gender research supports the general conclusion that men tend to self-disclose much less than women do (Ivy and Backlund, 2012). Men and women need to solve problems and develop business strategies with the same degree of mental energy, but their levels of disclosure about how they reach conclusions may vary. How you decide to work verbally/nonverbally with a colleague of the opposite gender is a decision only you can make. The consequences of your verbal choices sit on your shoulders.

Ethical Encounter

A colleague shares personal information with you during lunch. The information demonstrates behavior that is against corporate policy. Do you share the information with your boss to gain favor?

Communication privacy management theory ties in directly to self-disclosure and sharing information. Once you disclose or share information with another person, it is now co-owned and can no longer be controlled. The only way to truly keep information a secret is to keep it to yourself. In the ethical encounter box above, your colleague chose to disclose and co-own the information with you. This can be quite a burden if someone shares this type of information. You will have plenty of instances throughout your career where you will need to make decisions about what to do with sensitive information that is shared with you.

The more intimate the information you choose to share, the greater the trust you must have in another person. While intimate self-disclosure can make personal working relationships closer, it also makes you vulnerable should the other person choose to violate your confidence. You should weigh the personal risks before sharing sensitive information with anyone. Unfortunately, we learn the lesson of what is an acceptable risk with life experience. There are moments when you may get burned by others, but it's a risk you must take when you feel someone is worth knowing at work or socially. Trust in anyone involves risk. If someone violates your trust, you will at least know that you were willing to participate in open, honest communication. Although withholding certain information may be prudent in numerous circumstances, silence does not lead to close relationships.

Observation

In a business setting, you are responsible for figuring out what you are supposed to do. Listening carefully to what is going on around you and observing how the office works are critical skills in becoming a professional person. For example, your exposure to memos, emails, and in-house documents will be immediate. You should read every piece of printed information that crosses your desk or computer screen carefully. A careful examination of the material alerts you to rules, regulations, writing styles, document formats, and procedures throughout the company.

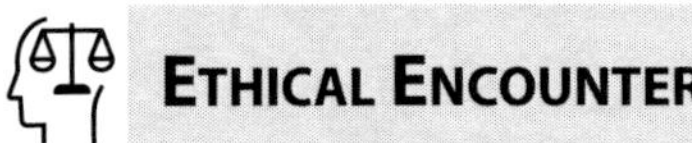

Ethical Encounter

Should you share internal policies that were discussed in a closed meeting with members of your family? Your significant other?

After your first day at work, you should read the corporate information given to you by human resources as well as all corporate policy procedures. Your understanding of these manuals will save you the embarrassment of making mistakes when communicating at work. Reasonable questions to clarify a specific statement or procedure are fine, but they have hired you as an experienced professional, and your colleagues and supervisors are not there to be your Google, Siri, Bixby, or Alexis. They expect you to work and problem solve at their level from your first day forward. Try hard to find the information you need before you bother someone for assistance.

Carry a small professional notebook during the first week to jot down instructions and procedures to remember. There is nothing worse than telling a new employee information only to have them come back and ask you about it a day later. Most managers are happy to assist you the first time; they will be annoyed the second time; by the third time, they will be wondering whether to terminate you.

Listening

Make sure to listen carefully when people introduce themselves to you or give you instructions. You don't want to ask them to repeat themselves nor do you want to struggle to remember names later. Colleagues simply assume you have retention skills. Therefore, if you have any question(s) about what you've heard, ask for clarification immediately. Confirmation of a name or point is better than a mistake later or admitting you have a faulty memory.

A majority of people are born with the ability to hear, but listening is an acquired skill. **Hearing** is a passive action; it is simply the process of sound hitting your eardrums. Think back to chapter 2 on perception. We talked about the concept of selective attention in response to the multitude of sounds that constantly bombard us. We hear everything, but we only pay attention to specific sounds based on personal need and preference. Initially, you need to treat every sound as important and strive to decode the messages accurately.

Chances are you really had a difficult time remembering the names of everyone you met on the initial office tour. This is because you were not actively listening to the names as people introduced themselves. **Listening** is an active process where you selectively attend to and assign meaning to sounds. If we analyzed every sound within earshot, we'd be overwhelmed. However, business situations require you to listen with a focus that may not be as necessary in many other aspects of your personal life. Once we focus on which sounds are critically important in our worklife, we can process information better and respond appropriately. The names of people you work with are important, and you should make a concerted effort to retain the information without having to ask again. One method to solidify the information is to repeat the name immediately: "It's really nice to meet you, Xiamara."

Being an effective listener is a skill that takes practice. Some of us develop this skill to a much finer degree than others do. Because every interpersonal business relationship is unique and because each communication situation has different listening requirements, we need to learn multiple listening styles in order to be a strong communicator. A review of listening and feedback styles should assist you in interpreting what you hear as well as understanding which responses are appropriate in daily communication.

Listening/Feedback Styles

Many communicators learn only one listening/ feedback style and use it consistently, but this rigidity doesn't allow for the uniqueness of situations. As you progress through various corporate situations, flexibility and the willingness to adapt to new information will help you become an effective listener and stronger professional. There are six different listening/feedback styles. Some of them are more useful than others, but each one serves a purpose. The six styles are judgmental, questioning, directive, empathetic, interpreting, and active. We will illustrate each of the stylistic choices with the following scenario. Frank approaches his colleagues and says: "I can't believe my performance review states that I need to improve my problem-solving skills and that I am not as team oriented as I should be."

Judgmental listening/feedback means a listener makes a judgment about both the content and the speaker. Judith, who is a judgmental listener, tells Frank: "Well, I told you that you needed to present better analysis of the research in our meetings." This response makes Judith sound superior because she "knew it all along." It also implies that Frank was negligent in not knowing what to do to make a good impression.

Questioning is another listening/feedback style. The listener asks probing questions of the speaker that are not necessarily supportive questions. They sometimes have a hint of accusation in their tone. Frank's office mate is a questioning listener and asks, "Why didn't you show up on time at our last meeting and present some research to back up your argument?" While he is inviting more conversation, he is also adding a confrontational edge to the communication. He is implying that Frank did something wrong. This leads Frank to reply defensively.

Both questioning and judgmental listening/feedback styles put down the other person without lending any support. They are not typically useful in the workplace.

Directive listening/feedback means a listener tells the speaker what to do. Giovanni tells Frank: "Well, the first thing you need to do is present an original solution to a discussion. Then you need to . . ." As a directive listener, Giovanni tries to solve the problem by giving advice.

Empathetic listening/feedback means a listener gives the speaker an emotional form of support. Sarah says, "Oh, Frank, I'm so sorry. You must feel awful. Is there anything I can do?" Sarah, an empathetic listener, tries to comfort Frank.

Directive and empathetic listening can be useful depending on the needs of the speaker. If you want to be emotionally comforted, empathetic feedback is great, while directive feedback feels like the person isn't listening. If you want to solve the problem, directive feedback is terrific, while empathetic feedback sounds condescending.

Did you think Giovanni's and Sarah's responses were stereotypical? We intentionally chose to use a male for directive listening and a female for empathetic listening because, in general, women are more likely to be empathetic listeners while men are more likely to be directive listeners (Fixmer-Oraiz and Wood, 2019).

The **interpreting** style of listening/feedback means a listener tries to offer another explanation of what happened. This style can be very useful in helping the speaker to think of other possible explanations for an event or a better analysis of the problem. Svetlana tells Frank, "Maybe your supervisor made a mistake. Did you think about going in to ask for specific examples of how you can meet their image of a better problem solver?" As an interpretive listener, Svetlana helps Frank explore other possibilities for his dilemma.

Active listening/feedback means a listener offers supportive questions and is clearly willing to listen. The listener tries to encourage more communication, using paraphrasing to ensure understanding. There are two useful types of paraphrasing. You may use a content-level paraphrase or a relationship-level paraphrase. A **content paraphrase** summarizes the message the other person states. The **relationship paraphrase** checks on the emotional state of the speaker.

Content paraphrase: "Oh wow, I'm sorry, so are you saying you might lose your job if you don't improve immediately?"

Relationship (emotional) paraphrase: "Oh my, you sound really upset. Would you like to talk about what happened?"

The active listener may use either or both of these styles if they are appropriate. In many situations, you may not need either. Active listening helps the speaker emotionally process his/her reaction to a situation or talk through ways to solve a problem. It doesn't superimpose a plan. The active listener acts as a sounding board and allows the speaker to discover the best solution for the dilemma themselves.

In addition to becoming more effective as an employee by consistently using the appropriate listening/feedback style, listening can also challenge you ethically. Let's say you are returning from lunch and while walking back to your office you pass a supervisor's door. The supervisor is talking on the phone and saying that a vice president of the company just ordered that the VP's daughter be hired to fill a job opening in your department. You were never supposed to hear this conversation. Sadly, someone you know applied for the position and even interviewed well for the job. The person you know has been out of work and is well qualified to work in your department, but she will be bypassed because of the inside hire. This situation is now an ethical challenge for you because you can't admit you overheard a private conversation, and you can't tell the person you know she is not getting the job due to a business confidentiality policy. Staying confidential isn't easy, and it can become a challenge, but it is necessary if you want to brand yourself as a professional.

The digital age has everyone talking, but sadly few people are listening and problem solving. If you promote yourself as a good listener, you may feel overburdened at times, but you will be unique in a crowded field of people who only want to be heard.

Retention is a key part of listening. By remembering information that others mention, you can polish your interpersonal skills. For example, a colleague once mentioned that she had family who lived on the coast in the Carolinas. The next time we heard about a Category 1 hurricane barreling in that direction, we were able to ask her how her family was doing. Doing so conveyed that we cared about her.

Implications of Styles

Communication misunderstandings occur when people don't receive the feedback style they are expecting. Think about how defensive you might get if you weren't expecting a questioning or judgmental response from a colleague after raising a question. If you are looking for help, sympathy, or an active listener to help you out, a questioning or judgmental listener will make you feel worse or angry. At this point, reasonable communication stops or an argument may begin. Careful analysis of your colleagues will help you decide whom to ask when you have a serious question or concern. Approaching those who have a feedback response style that is comfortable for you will often be the best choice. In other situations, however, the person whose style differs from yours may be the most informed about a specific topic. If that is the case, be prepared *not* to react to their style but to listen to the content of the response.

The point above highlights the necessity to analyze yourself as well as your colleagues. If you really want a listener to give you a pity party, you will choose someone with an empathetic style. If that person changes course and begins directing you instead, you may feel the person is not really listening to what you are saying. In this situation, you already feel emotionally drained, and if the listener begins to give you directives, you may resent someone telling you what to do. All you really wanted from a listener was momentary sympathy. You expected one response but received another. Your analysis regarding collegial styles may have been accurate, but each communication situation differs. The customarily empathic person may feel strongly about a particular topic and become directive. Being aware of such a possibility will help you be flexible if the feedback style isn't quite what you expected.

Improving Listening Skills

There are some easy ways to improve your listening skills. When you are in a business meeting, maintain good posture, make eye contact with the speaker, and take lots of notes. Note taking keeps you focused on the message as you write. You can also record the meeting on your mobile device if such a recording is permitted. Make sure that you are knowledgeable about the material to be covered in a meeting and be prepared to discuss it (review and analyze everything on the agenda). Knowing the discussion material makes listening easier. Of course, it is easier to concentrate during a meeting if the speaker is an excellent communicator and highlights the most important points—but not all businesspeople are good presenters. A poor presentation does not mean you can nod off or demonstrate a lack of interest in the subject, however. Active listening can help you overcome a variety of shortcomings in any presentation.

Take notes! Fewer and fewer students are taking notes in college classes. It's possible this habit stems from the student's ability to look things up quickly on the internet or because some instructors post slides with the information they covered during a presentation. Businesses do not typically work this way. When the boss explains how to do something, you need to take notes! Errors are not permitted in most of the corporate world.

The diverse workforce provides interesting challenges. When colleagues from countries other than the United States speak English, they may have an unusual inflection pattern influenced by their native language. Be aware of cultural uses of language, sound substitutions, and possible grammar variations as you listen to spoken language. You can perform tasks incorrectly if you fail to listen actively to a supervisor, client, or colleague who comes from a different cultural background. These communication situations are quite challenging for many people, but you can easily overcome them with active listening.

Fact versus Inference

As you are listening to coworkers and bosses and trying to assign meaning to perceived events, it is imperative to realize the difference between factual statements and inferential statements. Once again, listening is the key to responding properly. **Facts** are observable phenomena. Observation reveals the existence of, say, the office furniture around you: a desk, a chair, and a lamp. **Inferences** are conclusions we draw about the facts we observe. For instance, if the furniture in your workspace is brand new, you might infer that you are an important part of the organization and a valued addition to the company. On the other hand, if your furniture is old and tired in appearance, you might infer that you are an afterthought or the company is in financial trouble. We draw conclusions about our surroundings automatically. When you begin to interact with others and get a truer sense of your value to the company, you will realize your inferences are right or wrong. Thus, if we act as though a perception is fact when it is actually inference, we can create numerous communication problems for ourselves.

Confusing fact with inference directly relates to the interpretation step of the perceptual process. Be aware that emotional reactions to past and present experiences also affect our inferences. We may infer meaning based on how we feel rather than on what we actually see. A conclusion based on feeling may be incorrect. Let's say you are supposed to meet your office mate at a local restaurant around 5:00 P.M. You show up a little early and are surprised to find your office mate hugging an attractive person, and you notice empty cocktail glasses on the table. You feel like you are intruding on their space and are very uncomfortable. Your office mate sees you hesitate and waves for you to join them. The expression on your face makes it clear that they need to explain the situation. The attractive person turns out to be a cousin who happened to be having dinner at the same restaurant, and they were sharing a cocktail before you arrived. Your emotional reaction of being an unwelcome third party affected your inferences about an office mate's personal life.

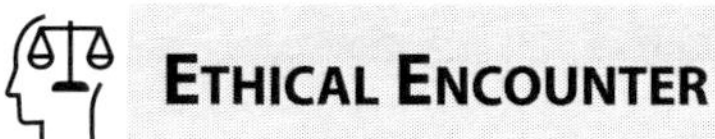

Ethical Encounter

What if the colleague is married and this had, in fact, been a romantic encounter with someone else? What do you do?

Attributing Meaning

When we witness the behaviors of others, we try to make sense of those behaviors and assign meaning to them. **Attribution** happens when we create meaning for behaviors. It is very likely that from observation alone we can never know for sure what behaviors mean, but we often feel confident about our interpretations. The process of attributing meaning to people, events, and circumstances can easily result in miscommunication.

For example, Laquaan sees Tina talking on her office phone as he walks past the door. Tina glances at him and quickly turns away without responding and lowers her voice. He feels ignored and interprets her action as a snub. She normally waves to everyone as they pass her door and often says, "Hello." Laquaan immediately thinks Tina is hiding something from him because her behavior is unusual. An emotional reaction to the encounter clouds his judgment. "Fine," he thinks and proceeds down the hallway. He assumes Tina intentionally ignored him, but is his assumption correct?

Laquaan has choices as he analyzes the situation. He can act as though his assumption is fact. Or, he can question his assumption immediately. He may also brainstorm other reasons that would explain Tina's action. Or, he can be more direct and active by checking his perceptions (see the section on perception checking in chapter 2). Laquaan would benefit from attributing reasons other than ignoring him to Tina's actions or doing a perception check immediately. The decisions you make about business colleagues and their behavior should always be factual. Assumptions can make you appear odd, ridiculous, or arrogant. It is best to analyze communication and/or behavior prior to responding to it. Everyone who experiences your poor communication will remember your error in judgment and lack of value as a colleague.

The Art of Conversation

Conversation is an interpersonal exchange demonstrating your ability to be engaging with others while asking appropriate questions of them as well as responding to their inquiries of you. Good conversation involves intense listening to messages and their intent in spontaneous dialogue. The spontaneous nature of conversation on a variety of topics appears to be a relic of past generations in today's overabundance of one-liners, emails, tweets, and focus on self rather than another person. Therefore, possessing the skills necessary for conducting a stimulating, social conversation is an excellent way to stand out in the business world.

Have you ever been in the presence of people who ramble on constantly? You hear about what she is doing. What he is thinking. Where she is going on vacation. How much he is spending on meals. Why her job is horrible and she deserves better. During the time you are with this person, does he/she ever ask how you are doing or feeling about anything? If not, this experience cannot be called a conversation. It is simply a monologue. This communicator does not want your response to any of the issues raised during the monologue. This person is a **spewer**. There is no exchange of ideas—only a one-sided stream of statements.

A true conversation allows both participants to share facts, opinions, or feelings on a wide range of topics. A conversation usually begins with a thoughtful question from one person followed by a reasoned response from another person. Your ability to listen carefully while someone is responding to a question is crucial in making a conversation successful. Throughout the other person's response, you should locate an idea (fact, philosophy, word choice, etc.) that allows you to follow up with a logical question/statement/comment on the same topic. This process allows both participants to fully explore an idea. The topic of a conversation usually changes during the time spent sharing ideas/thoughts while at the same time demonstrating a respect for the other person's point of view.

To do this effectively, focus on the positive! Your colleague says, "My trip to Costa Rica was amazing. I did not want to return to work today!" Your response should not be "I know! Seriously! Mondays are awful and now we have a pile of up backlogged projects. Did you know that blah blah blah happened while you were away?" Instead try, "That's wonderful! We all deserve a vacation once in a while. What was the most interesting thing you saw while you were there?" Also, do not try to "one up" them. When you share a com-

---

REALITY ☑

What are some appropriate follow-up questions/comments if your colleague says:

- I am so incredibly tired today. My little one was up all night.
- I just had a wonderful lunch with Supervisor Clevitski.

---

plaint or an injustice and someone tells you how they have it so much worse, they are not involved in a conversation—it is a competition instead.

Conversational style is definitely enhanced when both participants use storytelling to color real-life experiences and make their response to questions interesting to hear. The ability to listen to what another person is saying and then find an appropriate verbal/nonverbal response allows conversation to seem effortless for both participants. This effortless, enjoyable quality of time spent talking to others is becoming an art form worthy of mastering to stand out in today's workplace.

Daily conversations often focus on mundane topics such as sports, weather, and traffic. Today's workforce is expected to know a little bit about a wide range of issues/ideas. Most workplace discussions involve work-related themes. Coworkers may talk in depth about topics like new technology, economic growth, diversity, global acquisitions, current news items, and competitive start-up companies. However, you may find yourself in a position to enter into social discussions with colleagues as well. These social discussions may involve time management issues related to family and work, hobbies and outside activities, current books you've read, or personal interests.

Think back to the previous discussion about listening. If you can incorporate active listening skills into a conversation, you will excel in making a great impression on someone. Many people want to talk about themselves; personal monologues are not conversations. If you have the opportunity to talk to your boss or other important people in the company, there are a couple of strategies that will help to make you memorable. These strategies include your ability to listen attentively, ask thoughtful questions to engage others, and allow others to respond. When other individuals walk away from a conversation with a positive feeling about the experience, you make a tremendous professional impression. You must also be able to project sincerity throughout a conversation with your use of language and tone of voice. Simply nodding your head while zoning out will not help you make a positive impression.

While it may sound silly, if you know you are going to have an opportunity for social conversation at a business gathering or happy hour, you should plan a couple of good questions to engage people in conversation. If you've been paying attention in the workplace, you should have picked up a few clues about what is important to other people or what their interests are. Even a simple, open-ended question such as, "So, how do you spend your free time?" can open up a conversational avenue that allows another person to talk for quite a while about something that is important to them.

Be aware that most people in today's society have so much going on in their lives that quite often they don't care about other people's stories. Therefore, it is helpful to recognize the difference between someone seeking a brief response to a statement and someone attempting to engage you in a conversation. One of the best ways to ingratiate yourself with someone else is to demonstrate that you care, to listen actively, and to engage him or her in further conversation. So few people do it that the person you are conversing with will recognize the interpersonal experience as a unique situation.

Interpersonal conversations take time, which is one reason why people are uncomfortable having a productive conversation with someone else. People sometimes try to start a conversation with you when you are not interested or lack the time to respond. When you have a timetable to follow, make an opening statement such as, "I have a meeting in five minutes, but I can talk to you until then." This tells someone up front that your time is limited, but you are willing to chat. In other words, think before you speak and establish ground rules for time when they are necessary to maintain your personal schedule. It is important to be honest with your commitment of time as well as your listening and response skills for an interpersonal discussion to be called a conversation. Satisfying conversations should end with both participants appreciating the experience—feeling as though they were listened to and given appropriate responses.

Technology in the First Week

You may be tempted to leave your personal phone on as you go to work the first day rather than silence it. However, you may not make a good impression with an employer if you take personal calls while at work. You'll have to learn company policies immediately. It is usually safe to turn your personal device off and check it only when you are on a break or during lunch.

Tell your family you can't talk until the end of the day—and turn your phone off. It's time to focus on your career.

Basic guidelines about using cell phones at work include turning the ringer off, keeping calls short, speaking quietly, and respecting the personal space of your colleagues. Fixating on your phone distracts you from doing your work and may annoy coworkers (McKay, 2019). Let voice mail pick up your calls. Check messages during a break and respond only if urgent. Find a private place to make that call. Be certain that no one can overhear your conversation. We are amazed at people who conduct personal business on their cell phones and give personal identification information (like a bank account number) or financial information over the phone when colleagues are within earshot. Respect the privacy of your colleagues, and do not take your cell phone into the restroom. Cell phones can be an essential tool in meetings for taking notes or checking the internet for an answer to an issue raised in the meeting. Do not, however, use your cell phone for personal reasons while in a meeting.

Numerous corporate structures contain hidden microphones as well as cameras in elevators, hallways, lobbies, offices, and bathrooms. They use this hidden technology to protect the company and its employees during an emergency situation. A business is a public space, and the employer is trying to keep you safe rather than spy on you, but security will hear your conversations. Use caution if you choose to conduct personal conversations while at your work site. Show consideration for the people around you, and if your conversations will be overheard, make sure the language is appropriate.

Attitude

A positive attitude is a mindset that helps you see and recognize opportunities. Your attitude will help or hurt you as you progress in the business world. A positive attitude means positive thinking and optimism. Kate Lorenz (2010) believes in the concept that attitude is a critical factor in becoming a successful worker. She recommends developing and maintaining the following beliefs.

1. **I am in charge of my destiny.**
   If you spend your entire career waiting for something exciting to come to you, you will be waiting a long time. Successful professionals go out and make good things happen. So commit yourself to thinking about your career in an entirely different way. You will make it to the top, and you are in charge of making it happen.
2. **No task is too small to do well.**
   You never know when you are going to be noticed. One public relations executive in Chicago said that her first task in the PR department of a ballet company was reorganizing the supply closet. She tackled the project with gusto and was immediately noticed for her hard work and attention to detail. No task is menial; take pride in your work—all of it.
3. **It's not just what I know, but who I know.**
   Successful workers understand the importance of networking, both in and out of the office. Proactively establish professional contacts: invite a colleague to lunch; go to the afterwork happy hour; join your professional association. Do your part to establish a networking path for your future.
4. **Failure will help pave the way to my success.**
   While it seems like some people never experience setbacks, the truth is everyone fails from time to time. The difference between successful and unsuccessful people is how they deal with failure. Those who find success are the ones who learn from mistakes and move on.
5. **My opportunity monitor is never turned off.**
   There will be days when you are content with the status quo—but remember that successful workers are always on the lookout for opportunities to improve. Keep your eyes, ears, and your mind open to new opportunities. You never know when you will discover the one that will change the course of your career!

Attitude is commonly cited as a reason not to hire someone, promote someone, or extend their employment. Professionals control their verbal and nonverbal communication constantly as they mingle with colleagues in corporate settings and during social events. You are always visible to others and being judged by them when performing tasks or responding to situations. Critical thinking about your actions prior to speaking, writing, or moving can generate the perception that you have a great attitude and belong in an organization. Maintaining a positive attitude at work makes you an extremely valuable employee.

Final Thoughts

Your first job is the beginning of your financial future, so take it seriously. Obtaining a job requires you to manage the impression you make on others at all times. Advancing in your career is hard work, so think about possible errors in stereotyping others, attributing meaning incorrectly, or how you can use self-disclosure to your advantage as you develop a professional brand. Listening and observation skills provide you with essential information to analyze prior to responding to any message. Awareness of the six choices in feedback styles gives you flexibility as you interact with your colleagues. Practicing conversational skills will put you ahead of your peers who have not mastered that ability.

Mistakes normally occur when you fail to think about the consequences of what you are saying or doing or when you don't differentiate between fact and inference. Acknowledge a mistake if you make one and learn from your error. People will appreciate your ability to move forward gracefully. Improving all of the basic skills discussed in this chapter will allow you to reach the personal goals you've set for yourself in life. It's hard work, but doable.

A job is a privilege rather than a rite of passage—whether it is the culmination of a high school/university education, a second career choice, or a new position. A new job is a wonderful opportunity to showcase your skills in a corporate setting. Networking opportunities for a lifelong career start with the first job. Excellent performance leads to career advancement. Therefore, choose to be positive and successful, and make the person who gave you that initial career opportunity proud they did so.

Key Terms

- Active listening style
- Attribution
- Brand
- Communication misunderstanding
- Content paraphrase
- Conversation
- Directive listening style
- Empathetic listening style
- Fact
- Hearing
- Impression management
- Inference
- Interpreting listening style
- Judgmental listening style
- Listening
- Personal representative
- Questioning listening style
- Relationship paraphrase
- Self-disclosure
- Stereotyping

Exercises

1. Analyze your personal "brand."
2. Analyze the image and language of a political spot and describe the facts versus inferences used in the spot.
3. Discuss your listening style. How can you improve?
4. Describe the extent of self-disclosure with which you are comfortable when talking with people you do not know well. Discuss the positive and negative aspects of your choice.
5. Describe a time when someone disclosed information inappropriately in the workplace.
6. Discuss the most recent use of stereotyping in language and where you heard/saw it. Do you use stereotyping in your own communication?
7. Name two of your favorite media sites. Do you consider these sites factual or inferential? Why?

CHAPTER
SIX

Writing Skills and Technology for the First Week and Beyond

Goals

- List and employ basic writing skills
- Describe how the appearance of written materials is important in the workplace
- Identify and avoid common writing errors
- Create various types of written communication: email, texting, thank-you notes, invitations, letters, memos, formal task reports
- Use various types of technology: slides, web conferencing, social networking sites

So now you are employed. Writing becomes a significant portion of your professional life. If eventually you are lucky enough to have an executive assistant or office professional to edit your work, consider yourself a very fortunate person. Typically, anyone in an entry-level position is solely responsible for all of his or her written communication. Personal credibility (chapter 2) is revealed each time you correspond with anyone as a corporate employee. Mistakes in written correspondence can affect your future as an employable person.

In college, your emails and texts aren't always judged for their writing strength, but this scenario changes in the workplace. A majority of business professionals notice when you make simple spelling and/or grammatical errors even while emailing or texting. Some colleagues overlook these errors assuming that you are busy and in a hurry. But other individuals will immediately come to the conclusion that you either don't know how to write or lack attention to detail. This negative conclusion affects their perception of you as a responsible business professional.

> Edit and proofread absolutely everything. You do not want to be the student who sent us a note regarding their "abstinence." (rather than their "absence").

The degree to which you edit your written work is definitely a personal choice, but we recommend that you exercise care and diligence with written communication to establish yourself as a competent person. Quality writing can set you apart from other colleagues. It makes the most sense to be overly cautious when writing, editing, and distributing completed assignments and thoughts, since written documents are kept for legal reasons, copied, placed in files, forwarded to others, and so on. In addition, the appearance (layout and font choices) of written material is sometimes as important as its structure.

Basic Writing Skills

Mastering basic writing skills is a simple way to set yourself apart from peers. Make sure you understand the process. Most of our students think that their first draft is the final piece of work.

Terms

DRAFT

You should head all working documents clearly with the word "Draft." This alerts colleagues to the fact your communication is a work in progress and that feedback is expected. Once they return their comments, rewrite the document, remove the word "draft," and forward the completed document.

EDIT

Everything you send to colleagues and clients alike should be free of typos and grammatical errors; it should be punctuated correctly. This statement also applies to every team project that contains your name. Therefore, read every report for accuracy prior to its release. Your entire team looks bad when written errors appear in a final report. If you left the final proofreading to others, you don't get to complain or apologize to a superior after the release of the report.

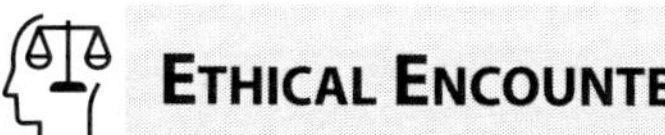

ETHICAL ENCOUNTER

Any time there is a team report, the coordinator must give the others a chance to read it and make changes. It is unethical to submit work with someone's name on it who was never given a chance to review it.

Editing doesn't end with correct grammar and punctuation. Look at sentence structure and whether you can tighten the writing. The following was an actual email.

> **From:** Professor X
> **Sent:** Thursday, September 19, 2019 11:28 AM
> **To:** MUP-Absentee Reporting
> **Subject:** Absent student
> In Oral Com 1101-03, student A #0012345 has not attended class since Sept. 4. Thank you.
>
> **From:** MUP-Absentee Reporting
> **To:** Professor X
> **Subject:** RE: Absent student
> With much appreciation for the detailed reporting. I am amid Absentee-Reporting efforts currently, and will reach out. I will inform back of anything that can be determined.
> Staff Member Y

A more effective reply would have been: "Thank you. I will follow up and get back to you."

RESEARCH

Factual information contained in a document must be accurate. Computers make double-checking facts and various sources much easier, so take the time to complete this task for all supporting material mentioned in the final document. Corporate files are usually available to you on a secure corporate intranet site. It is also possible that some business information may need to be researched in storage areas where paper files are located.

READ

Every document that crosses your desk and computer screen needs to be read and remembered. In most cases, you should save or copy important material for future reference. Your ability to keep up with the volume of information you receive is an incredible challenge, but you must do it. Good record keeping will help you remember or locate trends, legal issues, policy changes, and the dates they occurred. It can also be useful to remember the writing styles of important people around you so you can communicate with them electronically in their own style. Time assists you in building this personalized communication skill. When you receive the minutes of a business meeting, review them for accuracy. If you notice an error in the minutes, contact the session's recording secretary to have them corrected. Minutes of business meetings are legal documents and need to be accurate to protect your reputation as well as your department's reputation. As a participant in a meeting, you are just as responsible for accuracy in the minutes as the recording secretary, so be diligent as you review the material.

Nonverbal Appearance

As you create business materials, try to envision the nonverbal message they send to colleagues and clients. The layout and design, quality of paper, binding, and visual quality of each item will communicate your attention to detail. This statement also applies to PowerPoint and other computer-generated graphics. A superior presentation encourages people to read carefully and think favorably of the material in addition to analyzing its content more carefully. When business materials appear to be sloppy, the content itself becomes questionable, and the desire to read it wanes significantly. Here are some simple tips to send a nonverbal message that communicates competence.

- Use 20–25% cotton bond paper for important documents.
- Make sure to print material so that the watermark is facing toward you and is upright.
- Be sure that all holes are punched exactly alike so that pages line up if the document is put in a binder.
- If you are stapling, be sure to tap papers well, so they align perfectly.
- Make sure the fonts are consistent and legible.
- Use serif fonts for printed documents and sans-serif fonts for digital communication. Times New Roman and Georgia for serif fonts and Arial for sans-serif are recommended.
- Generate tabs for dividers on a computer.
- Proofread to eliminate typos and/or grammatical errors.
- In general, single-space sentences within paragraphs; double space between the paragraphs.
- If you are binding a document, set the left-hand margin at 1.5 inches.
- Cover designs should be simple and professional.
- Clip art is generally not used in professional design.

While some of these suggestions may seem picky, they will contribute to your overall professional image. Solid visual design attracts the eye to any document you create.

REALITY ☑

Glance at the cover pages your classmates have prepared when an assignment is due. Is your cover page better or worse than the competition?

Common Writing Errors

As your written communication with colleagues and clients begins, you want the messages you send to be concise and clear—and flawless. Employers expect educated employees to have solid writing skills. There are companies who give spelling tests to anyone applying for work in specific career areas, as well as for professional internal advancement. The idea of a corporate spelling test may seem startling, but these tests allow companies to make sure they are hiring the right person for the job. You can avoid common writing errors with proper attention to detail.

- If your document incorporates information from outside sources, cite the origin of absolutely everything you include and make certain the citation is accurate.
- Number all pages.
- Use headings and subheadings in your writing.
- Do not strand a heading at the bottom of a page with no text following—bump it to the next page.
- Use a preview and review if appropriate in the document.
- Professional reports normally look better with tab dividers, which should be printed (use your computer to format such projects).
- Watch for stylistic shifts when assembling group writing (i.e. team projects) and reformat material for a uniform writing style and visual presentation.
- Be careful with spell-check. Spell-check will catch typos, but it will not save you from using "there" instead of "their." In addition, look carefully at the options for changing a typo. The correct spelling for the word you intended may not be the first choice displayed. Do not automatically choose "change." Remember that many word processing programs don't spell-check items that are in all caps.

REALITY ☑

When someone misspells "definitely," the auto correct almost always chooses "defiantly"! Make sure you aren't *defiantly* going to the meeting instead of *definitely* going to the meeting.

- Eliminate the word "very" from your writing—and ***never*** use "very, very."
- "Nowadays" should never appear in your business writing.

- "A lot" is two words (not alot).
- Join two complete sentences with a conjunction, preceded by a comma. "The dog ran, and the cat sat. The rat jumped, but he did not bite."
- Many compound adjectives are hyphenated before a noun but not after a verb: "My hard-hearted boss would not give me a raise" but "My boss is too hard hearted to give me a raise."
- When in doubt, look it up.
- Do not use contractions in formal writing. "Don't" should be "do not."
- Create dashes by typing *two* hyphens with no space before or after the hyphens. Software programs such as Microsoft Word automatically convert two hyphens into an em dash—see what I mean? You can also create special characters using the insert feature in your software program.
- Refrain from using all caps in emails; all caps mean you are shouting.
- Use active rather than passive voice. "Raoul studied the reports carefully" vs. "The reports were studied by Raoul."
- Eliminate redundancy: "Cannot wait to hear from you" describes your anticipation; "Cannot wait to hear back from you" is redundant.
- Never begin a sentence with "Meaning."
- Make sure to use "myself" sparingly and seldomly. It is almost always wrong. "I, myself, think . . ." or "Joe and myself are on the same page" are both wrong. "I did it by myself" is fine.

Ethical Encounter

The supervisor asks you to prepare a speech she can deliver to a community organization. You decide to use a few ideas from an article you've read. Your deadline is approaching, and you don't have time to find the article to cite the sources. You write the speech without attributing the ideas to the source. What are the possible consequences?

- Make sure that you read all of your written material out loud. This will help you find punctuation errors, possible grammatical errors, and even improper word choices.
- Above all, edit numerous times, proofread numerous times, and have someone else look over the document for errors.

It always pays to review written work prior to sending it or handing it to a colleague or client. Your writing style and its accuracy make an instant impression on the reader. People are confident in your professional writing abilities until you give them evidence that their perception of this basic skill is incorrect.

Types of Writing in the Workplace

There are various forms of writing in corporate life. You can master each of them quickly as you become more familiar with the requirements of the job.

Email

Emails should be brief. If you find that you are writing a message beyond a screen length, then it is time to pick up the phone instead. Always select the best channel for every message. Emails are great for scheduling meetings and appointments, following up on issues requiring a brief response, alerting someone to a situation, participating in webinars, etc. An email message is usually brief.

> Always put a day in the email. You may write "are you free tomorrow" on Tuesday evening, but the recipient reading the message on Wednesday morning could think you are referring to Thursday! "Are you free tomorrow (Wednesday)?" eliminates possible confusion.

When you compose an initial email, you should always include a salutation. "Dear Dr. Young" or "Good morning, Dr. Young" are both appropriate depending on the person and the level of formality. Among colleagues you might even use "Hi Sue!" but by all means include a greeting. A closing is also good form. Please note that when a supervisor responds, they may simply answer your question. As a new employee, greetings and closings put you ahead of the competition.

Keep in mind, emails are an easy channel in which to make writing errors. Your typing speed while writing, responding, and sending messages makes this channel of communication extremely vulnerable to spelling and grammatical errors. Many email programs don't spell-check well. If you consider yourself a poor speller, we suggest writing your email message in a word processing program first (and remember that spell-check is only one tool, not a panacea), and then cut and paste the message into your email. While this extra step will add a few seconds to your response time, it is worth the effort to ensure the message is accurate. As an aside, timely responses are a definite plus, but it is also a good idea to take time to compose an appropriate response. Rather than hitting "reply" (or "reply all") immediately, make sure the response is accurate in both content and composition.

REALITY ☑

See what the default reply style is of the computer email program. One of your authors found out the hard way that a new email system was set to "reply all" as the default when she sent a message to the sender that went out to everyone at the university.

In addition, make sure that you understand when to use a CC (carbon copy) and a BCC (blind carbon copy). If a message is intended for Janice, but her boss Derice needs to be kept informed, then you address the email to Janice with Derice in the CC line. This says: "Hey this note is for Janice, but Derice you might want to know what is going on." Not every message needs to be cc'd to a long list of people. Only cc people if they truly need to know what's going on. In some organizations, employees will cc everyone up the chain of command on small details. This is simply annoying and time consuming for those who don't need the information.

A BCC is used when you don't want the receiver to know that you have supplied another person(s) with access to the email or you want to maintain confidentiality of others you placed in the loop. So, I might send a reprimand to a subordinate with a BCC to my supervisor. In this way my supervisor knows what I've said, but the subordinate does not know that anyone else got the message. This can backfire occasionally because if someone finds out, the action can be interpreted as "underhanded" or "nontransparent." The intended recipient can only discover what you've done if someone on the BCC list leaks the information. This situation alerts you to the fact that confidentiality was broken by someone on the BCC list.

A more reasonable use of a BCC would be to keep secret who is getting the message. So if I have to send out a delinquency notice to a number of students, I can send the notice to myself and BCC everyone who needs to get a copy. Then all they see is me as a sender and receiver. My note would begin, "If you are receiving this note, it is because . . ." rather than have any names on it. This maintains student privacy. A final time that a BCC is appreciated is when you have an enormous list of recipients. If a note is being sent to all chairs, I don't need to see three inches of email address before I can scroll to the message.

REALITY ☑

Why is it called a carbon copy? In the days before computers, copiers, and email, when you wanted multiple people to have a copy of something, you had to insert carbon paper between pieces of regular paper. When you typed on the first page, the carbon replicated the typing on the page underneath (of course, any mistakes were also transferred, which meant retyping everything or correcting each copy). Fortunately that technology is long gone, but the name sticks.

Emotional reactions to particular words can occasionally overtake you while reading email. Consider what could happen if you were in a bad mood when you opened a critical email. Your mood could influence your perception of the tone of the message. It's an easy mistake to make, which is why you should read every email you receive with an open mind and apply the same standard of mental discipline and clarity to your written response as you do to analyzing the message. Since paralanguage is missing in the written word, we often transfer our own emotional state into the words we read. Returning to our example of reading an email when you are in a bad mood, what is your first response? Many of us start typing a reply without thinking—we are simply reacting. It is crucial that employees stop, think, and save difficult emails until they have time to think critically. Your communication needs to be thoughtful and professional at all times. Move the email to a folder and reply later. If it helps "blow off steam," draft a reply but make certain you do not send it.

REALITY ☑

How many things can you find wrong with the following email?

Dr. Young,

I know that you hate excuses, but I am going to give you one as to why I couldn't complete the chapter 1 reading for tomorrow.

I had my mother order my Com book about a week ago through her amazon account because she has prime and I do not. This guaranteed that my book would be here by Tuesday. However, I came to find out that when it was ordered, it was shipped to my address in Anytown rather than my address in Universitytown. I didn't see this as a big deal because I thought I could go to the library and use the book on reserves. I went on Tuesday to do the reading and there was no book there and the woman behind the counter said that it was most likely because someone had it out and I should come back tomorrow, which would be today. When I did, I spoke to COM Student A who works in the library, who can verify my story, and we found out that the book is not on reserves yet because her boss has not gotten through all the books that need to be put into reserves. Long story short, I don't have a book or any resource to go off of and I honestly don't know what to do. I apologize because I know that there are many things that I should have done differently, but I cannot reverse.

Thank you,
Student X

It is best to set difficult correspondence aside briefly prior to responding. Wait a few minutes, hours, or even a day if time is not an issue. Then, go back and read the original email again. Occasionally you may want someone else to help you interpret an upsetting email prior to your responding. There is nothing wrong in seeking clarity for any message rather than making a foolish mistake. See if a colleague perceives the same tone as you do in the material. If you drafted an initial response, can you reword it? What are the consequences of sending what you wrote? It is useful to anticipate a response to your words before you send them rather than after they are sent.

REALITY ☑

The following is an actual student email. Read it out loud with an inquisitive tone—then read it with an angry tone. Could the reader interpret it either way? What could be changed to help convey the paralanguage?

Dr. Young,

I talked to Randi today about our journal pitch project. She told me that we were docked 5 points because our journals were not actual journal articles. I have a question/complaint about this. When you verbally told us the assignment someone asked where to get the articles. You replied Ebsco Host was perfectly fine. To find our articles I used Ebsco Host. I clicked on the business section and searched for cover letters. So, I guess my question/complaint is: since I used the program you told me to I assumed all the articles on that program were acceptable. Was this a wrong assumption? And if it was, how do I tell the difference between a journal article and a nonacceptable article?

Tracy

Luckily for the student in the reality check above, I knew that she had a sincere request. But it is truly amazing how much negative tone can be read into that email based on some of the word choices.

Email can occasionally create an ethical dilemma. Once in a while people do not pay attention to the contact list on correspondence. You could receive information not intended for you because the sender hits "reply all" rather than "reply." This is another extremely difficult situation to handle professionally because you are now aware of information not intended for you. What should you do in this instance?

Keep emails short, on topic, and worded professionally. If you want to complain with your friend about work or share the details of a fantastic date last night, do so on your own time, your own device, and your personal email account.

Texting

Technology has helped make businesses more efficient. Texting is an effective tool because of its speed and its reach (SimpleTexting, 2019). About 95% of texts are read within three minutes. The average response time to a text message is approximately 90 seconds compared to an average of 90 minutes for an email. Faster sharing of information with clients and colleagues makes decision making easier and work more efficient. Texts enable contact with the 4.68 billion people around the world with cell phones. However, regular use can also lead to abuse. Texts should be used only when they are the best medium for a particular message.

While texts may feel casual, professional text messages should be formal and include your name and an appropriate salutation (SimpleTexting, 2019). Having established a relationship with a client or colleague, ask what medium of communication is preferred. Secure permission before sending a text—a text should never be the first contact with a business associate (Gottsman, 2016). Texts should be sent only during regular business hours and should be convenient for the recipient. Confine texts to work-related topics that can be easily understood in a short message. Complex information that requires explanation should be handled with an email or a phone call. A brief text asking for the most convenient time to call facilitates more complex communication. Do not text confidential information. Emojis and abbreviations should not appear in professional texts. Spelling and punctuation are important. People sometimes do not want to be the first to close communication. When the goal has been reached, end the text exchange with a clear departure such as a thank-you. Do not extend the contact beyond the exchange of essential information.

Keep a careful record of the professionals with whom you are texting. We had a candidate for a job who was texting our search chair to coordinate a meeting place. The candidate wrapped up the information and signed off. Ten minutes later the chair received a "63." Confused, they said nothing. The candidate wrote "oops, wrong person." But it was evident that the candidate was talking to someone else about our proposed salary. It was awkward to say the least.

Thank-You Notes

Thank-you notes are a terrific way to stand out professionally and in your personal life. Too many people no longer bother sending a thank-you note for anything. Social manners are changing, but recognizing the efforts of others remains a way to make an impression. While an electronic thank-you note may be socially acceptable, it is far less personal than a handwritten one. If your handwriting is not legible, you may need to practice cursive writing to improve the technique. A handwritten note says that you took additional personal time to demonstrate your gratitude to someone for thoughtfulness. Since so few individuals use handwritten notes anymore, your effort is likely to impress the receiver.

Don't hesitate to combine a thank you note with the CC email function we talked about previously. Often if we send a quick note of thanks to someone electronically, we CC their supervisor. It is a professional way to recognize the recipient. The CC courtesy reminds a supervisor that their employee is doing excellent work.

Invitations

You should print invitations if they are formal, or you can create them through email or electronic services if they are casual. Electronic invitations are becoming an acceptable social practice for the digital generation. However, invitations should always include the **purpose, date, day, time**, and **place** at the very least. For example:

All Employees
are invited to join in a celebration
for the retirement of

John Jones

Friday, Dec. 6, 2020 at 4:00 p.m.
in the North Board Room

Don't forget the rules for time. Mornings and afternoons are denoted by lower case letters and periods after each, so it is 9:00 a.m. and 10:00 p.m.

Some invitations make the mistake of giving only the numerical date on an invitation rather than including the day of the week. This means that recipients whose primary organization of their schedules is by day of the week must consult a calendar to learn the day. Occasionally, people respond positively to an invitation without being aware that the day of the week for the event conflicts with their schedule. Stating the day in addition to the date is a simple way to reinforce the timing of your event so that people can respond accurately.

Letters

Employees generally print business letters on corporate letterhead. These letters are legal documents. Your company probably has a template you can use for corporate or general correspondence, or you may need to construct your own format (in some cases following legal requirements).

The format of business letters has changed over the years. Currently, most business sites recommend using the flush left block format. Purdue's online writing lab advises that business letters include the following elements (OWL, n.d.).

- The date
- Your address (we add our business email as well)
- The person and address you are writing to
- Salutation ("Dear Mr./Ms." or "To Whom it May Concern" followed by a colon. The name of a person is preferred)
- The paragraphs of the letter
- A closing ("Sincerely" or "Regards" followed by a comma)
- Your name
- Type the word "enclosures" if you include other documents

April 1, 2020

218 Allen
Department of Communication and Theatre
Mansfield University
Mansfield, PA 16933
kyoung@mansfield.edu

Penelope Longfellow, President
Early Retirement Planning, Inc.
345 Water Street
Anytown, PA 16901

Dear President Longfellow:

I would like to discuss my current financial planning with you to make sure I am doing everything I can to have a stable retirement. There are a couple of future dates that I am considering for retirement, and your advice would be extremely helpful. My daily schedule is open after 1:00 p.m. so you can select a meeting time at your convenience. I have listed my email address above. I look forward to hearing from you.

(If I had more to say, my second paragraph would start here with additional spacing before and after, as shown.)

Sincerely,

Kathryn Sue Young

Kathryn Sue Young

Note that there are spaces between the sections above. You will need four lines of space between your closing and your typed name so that you have enough room to sign your name. We recommend a pen with black ink for your signature because it can be photocopied; blue ink often does not photocopy well.

Memo Writing

Employees use a memo to make an announcement, remind colleagues of an event or policy change, report the results of a meeting, or share other information. Memos typically contain four parts:

(1) the person to whom the memo is addressed, (2) the person from whom it was sent, (3) what it is about (this is labeled RE: or Subject), and (4) the date. Be sure to put your initials immediately after your name. You don't sign a memo, but you should initial it. The initials make it legal and identifiable. Finally, make sure to tab all items so that the information in each of the four lines begins at the same place (see arrow below) A basic memo looks like this:

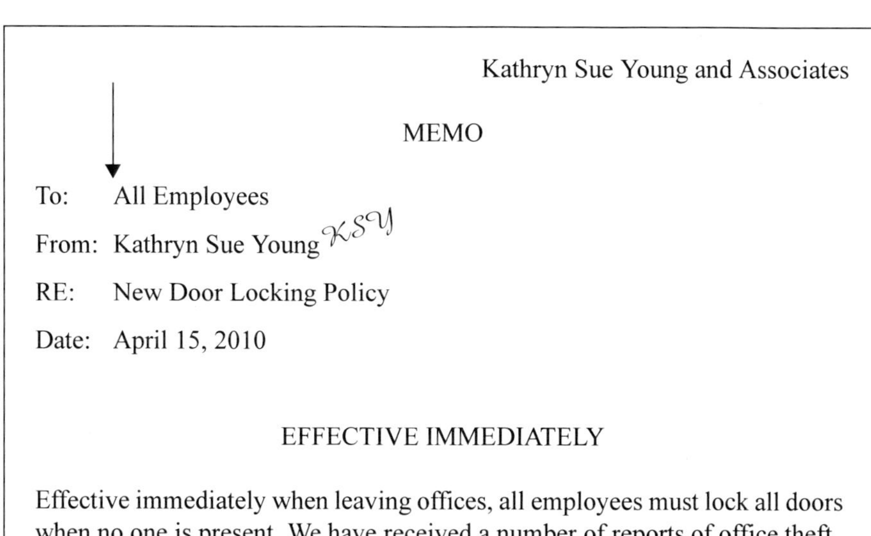

Kathryn Sue Young and Associates

MEMO

To: All Employees

From: Kathryn Sue Young KSY

RE: New Door Locking Policy

Date: April 15, 2010

EFFECTIVE IMMEDIATELY

Effective immediately when leaving offices, all employees must lock all doors when no one is present. We have received a number of reports of office theft in the building recently. Please lock your office door when leaving, even if you plan to be back momentarily. We appreciate your cooperation.

Most companies have a memo template as part of their corporate software package. This electronic convenience ensures that all internal and external memos have the same "look." You should only have to type the content of a memo onto the template prior to sending it.

Self-protective memos are pieces of correspondence to supervisors that document opinions, policy violations, uncomfortable situations, etc. Anytime you feel as though someone else should know that something happened, you want to write one of these memos. They provide a paper trail of a specific event. I (KSY) can still remember the first such memo I had to write. I was a graduate student teaching oral communication at Penn State University, and one of my students gave a speech on three ways to kill someone. It was unsettling, unnerving, and downright creepy. It was important for me to let my supervisor know that something unusual had happened. Following university protocol, I sent a memo to my supervisor documenting what had happened and who was involved so that my supervisor could take appropriate action.

The self-protective paper-trail memo is also useful when you attend a meeting at which an outcome is questionable. Although you may not be able to say anything about a statement or policy when it's made, you can certainly send a simple clarification note to the person who presented the idea. You may not receive a response, but your memo has a date and time code that may be useful later should the communicator be challenged legally or try to blame you for the situation. A memo or note of this type is usually a personal decision discussed with no one. Typically, you would remove your copy from the workplace and store it in a safe place in case you need to retrieve it at a future date.

Formal Task Report

An employer may ask you to join a task group to solve a problem. Once you are finished, you typically turn in a report of your findings plus the group's recommendations for a solution.

As you develop this report, strategy is important (Young, Wood, Phillips, and Pedersen, 2021). Many task groups simply divide information-gathering tasks, and each group member writes a section of the report. However, your group should be aware that there are many inherent problems with this strategy.

- The writing skills of group members usually vary. You don't want some sections to be written well and others to be mediocre.
- Each person has his/her own writing style. When a manager reads the entire report, stylistic shifts can be annoying and distracting.
- Occasionally group members do not do their work. If a group member does not finish his/her section, then the rest of the group is required to complete that section to meet a deadline.
- If using the individually-written-section strategy, the entire report will require extensive editing to correct errors and to achieve a readable flow prior to submitting it. Unfortunately, most groups are pressed for time at the end of a project. There

is a tendency to rush the written report as the deadline approaches, which produces substandard results. You don't want this to happen after working tirelessly on a project. Therefore, it is useful for the team to establish a timeline for the entire writing process at the beginning of the project.

ETHICAL ENCOUNTER

The CEO praises your boss at the annual meeting for his report on proposed changes in your division. However, you wrote the report. It becomes evident that your boss removed your name and put her own on it. What do you do?

As one writer completes the rough draft, another person can begin the initial editing. Having two or three people involved in multiple revisions almost always guarantees a tighter, more professionally written report. After your group completes the report (and time permits), ask another colleague, who is not in the group, to proofread the document for errors or unclear wording.

This may sound like a lot of work—it is. If you became accustomed to turning in first drafts of your writing in school, then it is time to break the habit as you begin a working career. We have experienced too many groups who put numerous hours of work into their problem-solving projects only to hand in a sloppy draft as their final report. This error in judgment negates all of the group's hard work. The presentation of every written assignment either enhances or diminishes your professional credibility. It's essential to save enough time and effort to execute this portion of the task well.

ETHICAL ENCOUNTER

You take a colleague's ideas and present them in a report as your own. What are the potential consequences?

As you begin your report draft, there are a number of sections that may be useful to consider for inclusion (Young et al., 2021).

- A title page
- An executive summary
- Background of the problem
- Explanation of the criteria
- Explanation of the best solution and how it meets the criteria
- Presentation of the plan
- Argued defense
- Conclusion

TITLE PAGE

With any professional formatted report, include a title page.

- Title
- Group name or title of task force (if appropriate)
- Members' names
- Date
- Name of person receiving the report

EXECUTIVE SUMMARY

The executive summary usually contains the following items.

- A statement of the task
- A review of the problem-solving process
- The routing for the final report (who gets it)
- A preview of the proposal
- Acknowledgments (if appropriate)

Don't try to say too much in the executive summary. This should be a brief summary of the task. Your group may want to detail what it went through. Remember that *no one rewards you for the effort you made; you are rewarded only for the effectiveness of the final product.* Pay attention to the needs of the receiver who reads the report rather than justifying your own hard work. Your employer will judge your group through content, analysis, and conclusions in the document. The hours spent in meetings and doing research is only part of the task. Make sure to spend the time necessary to present a report worthy of a positive impression after all the group's hard work.

Consider your audience carefully, though. If they are hostile to your plan, you may need to present additional solid evidence to build the problem before you preview its solution. Your group will have to decide whether to include this evidence in the executive summary of your final report.

BACKGROUND

Include all of the evidence that a problem exists (with appendices as appropriate).

- Detailed description of the problem, supported with evidence including: statistics, research, expert and personal testimony, examples and illustrations
- Discussion of possible causes, supported with evidence
- Explanation of whether your group will deal with symptoms and/or causes
- Projection of what might happen if the problem is not addressed or need is not met

By the time the reader finishes reading this section, he/she should truly understand every facet of the problem.

CRITERIA

- Explain your criteria
- Define any terms
- Explain the order of importance of established criteria

PRESENTATION OF THE PLAN

Present your solution in complete detail (Young et al., 2021). Do not make the mistake of putting too little detail into your plan. If someone else is in charge of approving the plan, they are much more likely to do so if your presentation provides sufficient detail that they can take immediate action. If they have to do a lot of work to figure out the plan's logic, they probably won't make the effort.

Typically, you would include the following information.

- Who?
- Does what?
- For what reasons?
- With what resources?

- Under whose supervision?
- At what cost? To be provided by whom?
- Evaluated as follows

Remember that the receiver of the final report has *only* the report on which to base a judgment. If you present an inadequate report, the receiver will assume you are an inadequate group and incapable of problem solving.

THE ARGUED DEFENSE

Your group must be prepared to defend its solution against whatever arguments others might make (Young et al., 2021). Persuasive proposals succeed when the proposal identifies and refutes any arguments the audience may have. In this final step, your group must deal with the question: "What can be done to prepare the most persuasive case possible for acceptance of our proposal?" You should first assess the possible obstacles to adoption.

- Who might express opposition to the proposal?
- Who stands to lose?
- Who has offered a different solution about which they might feel defensive?

Be prepared to answer the following attacks.

- There is no need/problem.
- There is a problem, but the plan is unworkable.
- There is a problem and the plan is workable, but it will not solve the problem.
- The plan is needed, workable, and will solve the problem, but it will bring undesirable effects (too costly, violates legal or moral limitations, etc.).
- The reasoning is ineffective. The documentation is ineffective.

Next, it is important to determine what your supervisor wants. Unfortunately, the world is not always a place where honest people do honest work and are rewarded appropriately. To make an effective appeal, you will have to look at the personal interests of those who pass judgment. Here are some issues to consider.

- The decision maker may have a sphere of influence. Does your proposal weaken or strengthen his or her influence?

- The decision maker may not be prepared to take on more work. Does your operations plan provide for additional people to reduce the pressure?
- The decision maker may be concerned about how particular individuals are affected by changes. Does your proposal displace anyone? What influence do potentially displaced people have on the decision maker? Can you protect them?

In this section of your report, you should include the following.

- An assessment of possible obstacles to the adoption of the solution.
- An answer to every possible argument against the solution.
- A final argument restating your solution and how it solves the problem.

CONCLUSION

Include any summary material that reinforces your message.

Writing a formal or team report is a test of numerous analytical and writing skills. Each and every time you submit a business report, make sure the final document represents your finest work. Just as your writing improves the more you do it, your advancement within an organization improves as colleagues consistently receive quality work.

Technology and the Workplace

Perhaps generational differences are most evident in one's familiarity with technology. Today, four generations—Baby Boomers, Gen X, Millennials (or Gen Y) and Gen Z (or iGen) work together. Digital natives grew up with the internet, while previous generations have had to adapt to technological changes. Technology in the workplace brings new challenges for communication in part due to the speed at which decisions are made. You need to master each piece of new technology as it is made available to you by your employer. While Millennials and Gen Zs were raised with digital games and computers requiring accuracy using physical and visual speed, the modern workplace adds thinking, analyzing material, and writing to the communication mix. It's useful to remember generational communication styles in the professional world.

Slides

If you are creating a slide presentation (using PowerPoint, Google, Prezi and others), you want to be as professional as possible. You need to present materials clearly with the audience in mind rather than using inappropriate production tricks that diffuse your message. Your slides should always be informative and visually appealing rather than gimmicky and entertaining. As you design your slides, make sure not to exceed six words per line or six lines per slide. Also make sure that your letter color is in high contrast to your background color; use the same background for each slide for visual consistency.

Use a blank template slide for times when you don't need to refer to the slides. There will be nothing on the screen, but it won't go to black or white, which could be distracting for viewers.

Web Conferencing

Computer-based meetings give you the opportunity to share written and verbal information throughout a discussion. With web conferencing services you can speak to others and share documents. The material you generate (whether typed questions for general discussion, analysis of data as it is presented, slides created during a discussion, emails, etc.) is shared immediately with colleagues participating in the discussion. Avoid writing errors during this real-time experience to highlight your professionalism.

Electronic Document Preparation

Google Docs and other programs allow you to import, create, edit, and update documents in various file formats—combining text with formulas, lists, tables, and images. You need to be familiar with word processing and spreadsheet software. Learn as much as you can using these programs in school so you will be prepared for the professional world.

The ability to share documents while you are working on them with teammates makes group work both easier and harder.

A global team creates time zone frustration as deadlines approach. Remember that a 1:30 p.m. (EST) deadline is 10:30 a.m. in California, 5:30 a.m. *the next day* in Australia, and midnight the next day in India (yes, 10 and ***one-half*** hours ahead).

REALITY ☑

At what point do you leave the document open, and at what point do you close it to further changes? People who have access can delete, rearrange, or otherwise distort what has been created. You may want to have someone take control of additional edits at a certain point in time to protect the integrity of the document.

Individuals working together on a project have the ability to contribute their ideas and writing skills to a document from any geographic location. Written documents become more collaborative and collegial as participants use their creativity and editing skills to create a unified document prior to its release for management, clients, or the public. Because every member working on a project can perfect the final outcome, the completed document should have solid content, editing, and writing.

Documents come together faster when teams/employees can access the project around the clock on their computers. No individual working on a project using this technology can say he or she was left out of the process. Like all digital communication, however, information security is the major concern for businesses. Internal and external projects should be read/seen only by those individuals for whom they were designed. Develop a secure site for the team as work begins.

Social Networking

Historically, self-disclosure was primarily limited to face-to-face interpersonal communication. Today, millions of people self-disclose via the internet to a multitude of unknown receivers through Instagram, Twitter, discussion boards, blogs and texting. People currently post personal facts about themselves that were once reserved for close, lifelong friends. New media is shifting the traditional role of self-disclosure in interpersonal communication.

If there are people we want to research/track, we can quickly find them through the internet and discover their hopes, dreams, favorite movies, foods, songs, social activities, home address, pictures, etc. All of these insights into their character are posted by the people themselves, perhaps without reflecting on privacy issues. On many social-networking sites, a stranger can discover personal information about a colleague that traditionally would never have been revealed throughout a lifetime of working together. Your digital footprint needs to be constantly examined to make sure you don't mind if business associates or HR become aware of personal information.

Ethical Encounter

What do you do when your colleagues want to friend you, but you want to keep your personal life private and separate from work? Do you have an ethical obligation to friend a boss or colleague if they ask through a social-networking site? Can you keep your personal life separate from your work life? If you say yes, what ethical considerations will you need to consider with every future status update on social networking? What message does it send to have a locked account and deny your colleagues access?

The interview process today increasingly includes checking publicly available databases like Facebook. A recent graduate reported that she was told to pull up her Facebook site during a job interview. Fortunately for her, there was nothing compromising on it. We find, however, that most of our students aren't so prudent. Many students post pictures of questionable behavior, poses, and attire; list membership in groups that reveal a lot about their moral character; and use profanity, demeaning, and derogatory language in their posts. There have been many debates about privacy issues and the ethics of checking personal information via these sites, but the fact remains that employers have access to a significant amount of information about you. Personal sites usually include links/addresses of colleagues that could also be used for information about you.

The one social networking site that you want to use to your advantage as a business professional is LinkedIn. You can establish a professional presence there that can help you to get your first as well as subsequent jobs.

BENEFITS

Self-disclosing via technology can be used for positive purposes. For example, I (KSY) keep track of the accomplishments and career moves of former students through the use of Facebook. The technology gives me the opportunity to see how their education has benefited them throughout their lives. Encouraging posts keep me connected and show them I continue to care about them as alumni. However, I also choose to post very limited information about myself.

DANGERS

There are negative aspects to social networking as well. People mistakenly assume they are anonymous when they visit websites online, but every movement is collected in a database. Loading a webpage tracks information about you, as do purchases online and subscriptions to newsletters. Social media users publicly share private information. If your job is listed on Salary.com and your vacation preferences on Orbitz, both might affect your ability to negotiate a raise or apply for a loan (Bennett, 2010). Credit-card companies use social media to determine what advertisements are most effective for a social group or to determine if someone is likely to default on a loan. An insurance company discontinued sick leave benefits for a woman in Quebec after they found photos of her on Facebook that contradicted her stated medical condition. Even the IRS scours social-networking sites for people bragging about cheating on their taxes. Nothing goes unnoticed on the digital landscape.

Employers can check your Instagram page to see if you really missed work because you claimed you were ill. It would be easy for human resources to review the sites of employees periodically to see what colleagues are doing when they are out for an illness as well as to make sure they represent the company in a professional manner. This constant scrutiny of personal information may seem unreasonable, but it is available. Scrutiny of a person's character could affect future bonuses, promotions, and continuation of employment. As these examples demonstrate, the interplay of technology, self-disclosure, and interpersonal communication in the workplace is complicated. The technical revolution in communication means coworkers, teachers, law enforcement, family members, and religious acquaintances can assess your information instantly and make judgments about your character and what you are doing.

Have you ever made comments on a blog or written an email using language and expressions you would never use in person? Steve Johnson (2008), a critic for the *Chicago Tribune*, says "nothing exposes what lurks in the dark corners of our souls more effectively than a keyboard and the firewall of physical remove from whomever you're writing to or about." We recently read about someone who was fired from his job because the daughter of the employer read comments made about her father on a website of a young woman who was venting about how the boss was a jerk and kept her father at work so he couldn't attend her school event. The two daughters attended the same school. Freedom of interpersonal expression can have disastrous consequences. Technology and our willingness to disclose personal information on websites open doors to multiple avenues of checking our social interactions while not at work and judging our credibility.

REALITY ☑

No one seems to think twice about posting pictures of their children. However, we had a colleague (professor) who was threatened by a student who said that he would harm the professor's daughter when he received a bad grade. The world has changed drastically, and sometimes it is best to keep children protected by locking access to accounts.

GUIDELINES

There are some general guidelines to follow to help safeguard your reputation.

- Establish privacy settings so your posts on social-networking sites aren't accessible to the general public.
- Assume that all communication might become public.
- Don't use offensive language or refer to illegal behaviors on your sites.

- Do not post about work and colleagues on your social-networking sites.
- Never visit social-networking sites on company time unless it is required for your job.
- It is usually safe to assume that you can do personal business on technology that you own when you are not at work. However, if the company gives you a handheld device for communication as part of your job, use that device for business purposes only.

Some employees appear to be tied to their mobile technology similar to doctors "on call." Other employees do not have this connection to their employer because their position does not require constant connection to the company or because they choose to ignore work when they aren't there. Discussions about work/life balance—dividing one's energies between work and other important aspects of life—have increased with the growth of technology in the workplace. Technology has been characterized as both the cause of work/life imbalance and as one means of improving it. While mobile technology can intrude on homelife, it also frees employees to work from home rather than spending long hours in the office. Familiarize yourself with company policy about technology and when you are expected to be available.

Final Thoughts

Solid writing remains a critical skill for employment and professional advancement; business writing must be logical and factual—and inviting to read. It's unwise to think you won't write as much when you leave school; the reality is, you write more. The days of not paying attention to proofreading your work and how you express yourself end with employment. The ability to express yourself clearly, concisely, and quickly becomes a reflection of a company's credibility. You are a public relations vehicle for your employer both at work as well as in the community. Companies notice employees with effective written and verbal skills.

New technologies use different jargon to communicate rapidly with receivers. It will be necessary to adjust to the various written styles required by specific technologies and to the culture of the receiver. Multitasking is a required professional skill. You may be web conferencing with colleagues on different continents, emailing, and editing the report all at the same time. Technology advances the speed of information, analysis, and response time.

Read everything that crosses your desk or computer screen carefully and repeatedly to make sure you have stated your messages and responses clearly and informatively.

Key Terms

- Email
- Formal task reports
- Invitations
- Letters
- Memo writing
- Nonverbal message
- PowerPoint
- Texts
- Thank-you notes
- Web conferencing
- Writing skills

Exercises

1. Discuss your strengths and weaknesses when it comes to writing. How do you plan to improve weak areas?
2. Write a thank-you note in cursive.
3. Develop a sales pitch with slides that could be used in web conferencing.
4. Write a letter to your teacher stating why you deserve a good grade for the course.
5. Exchange your résumé with classmates and critique one another.
6. Bring an email you've written to class. Exchange the email with another student asking for advice on how to be a more effective communicator.
7. Write an invitation for a special event.
8. Write a memo regarding an emergency situation on campus or in the community.
9. Name two apps you use regularly for communication. Could they be used in a business environment? How?

CHAPTER
SEVEN

Teamwork and Your Career

Goals

- Distinguish between groups and teams
- Identify what new groups should do to get started
- Compare and contrast task and social elements of group work
- Differentiate among types of followers
- Effectively plan and run meetings

Many self-motivated individuals find it difficult to work in groups/teams. However, corporate organizational patterns often require employees to work together to solve problems and accomplish goals on a daily basis. It is important to recognize that colleagues—whose background and work experiences are unique—will bring valuable insights to numerous projects. Merging various personalities and skills in a cohesive working environment is critical for a successful business and for employee morale. We build trust incrementally with each day of working together. You gain trust in colleagues' skills and their execution of those skills as you observe their work and behavior over time—just as they learn to trust you. An open mind when working with others combined with a personal commitment to excellence will help you become a valued team member.

Distinguishing between Groups and Teams

Groups are composed of individuals with similar ideas or goals who come together to complete a task or solve a problem for a common organizational good. Some groups can achieve cohesiveness: a feeling that they belong together. This sense of cohesiveness while working together usually distinguishes a team from a standard work group.

Teams begin with colleagues or strangers assigned to work together. A team becomes cohesive as members work to accomplish the assigned task. This cohesiveness can be seen and felt by colleagues who aren't even part of the team. There are many facets to good team problem solving. You must work on a task while simultaneously dealing with the intricacies of interpersonal differences. Only when individuals blend effective task work with effective interpersonal skills do you have an ideally functioning team.

There are task groups in the workplace in which participants don't feel a sense of belonging, don't support a common goal, and don't worry about their interactions with each other. This situation does not represent people on a team. Some corporations use the team concept in the workplace successfully. By using the word "teams," corporations encourage a spirit of family, cohesiveness, and productivity. However, not every corporation promoting the team philosophy achieves their goal. Some employees never actively embrace the team concept even though they do their work. Colleagues must fully cooperate with one another throughout the duration of a task to achieve the team label. Forming a team is obviously an ideal goal for any small group working on a task, but personalities sometimes block cohesion.

An Effective Beginning

How do you become a team member? The first few minutes of interacting with a new group of people present the same challenges as a first impression in an interpersonal relationship. Colleagues may like or dislike each other based on their appearance, nonverbals, or preconceived notions about each other's work based on previous experiences at the company. Colleagues must become cohesive quickly and forget their personal differences in order to be effective and complete the assigned task. Bosses have little tolerance for pettiness between group members.

REALITY ☑

The pettiness you experienced in school groups doesn't disappear in the workplace—you are simply expected to be better at managing it.

For example, in your fifth week at work you are assigned to a task force to review the current policy of no personal business being conducted during work hours. The options are to recommend a modification of the existing policy or to continue the policy. You learn that Anthony, Nancy, Rafael, Sheng, and Lenora have also been assigned to the task force. You are disappointed to discover that Anthony is in your group. He didn't complete expected tasks on time when you worked with him on an earlier assignment. You've also noticed that he usually arrives at work late and leaves early. Even when Anthony is in the office, he is obstinate and argumentative. You are not looking forward to dealing with him as a member of the task force. You are somewhat thankful, however, that Lenora is in your group, since she expresses her opinions in a positive way and is passionate about her work.

You meet with your colleagues for the first time. Theoretically, a new group should do the following.

- Introduce themselves to one another
- State everyone's skills
- Discuss everyone's personal goals
- Assess everyone's needs

Introductions

Take a little time to introduce people. Just because colleagues work in the same company doesn't mean they know one another. If the leader begins with "I think we all know each other . . . ," don't be afraid to introduce yourself to someone you haven't met previously. On the other hand, if everyone has been working together for a while, don't waste time on an introduction.

Skills

Depending on the task assignment, an initial skills assessment might be necessary to determine who is best suited for the various tasks necessary to complete the project—for example: research, writing, editing, proofreading, critical thinking, and a visual and oral presentation. Once you know who possesses the best skills, the leader can assign members to the appropriate tasks. It is obviously self-defeating to randomly assign the final draft to someone who can't write well. Assess member skills immediately and quickly so the project can move forward with everyone contributing equally to complete the assignment.

At a practical level, however, most business groups skip these steps. When people have worked together a long time, they already know each individual's strengths. If you are the only one new in the group, volunteer information about your skills in case no one asks. Your reputation is important, so get assigned to a portion of the project that aligns with your skills.

Ethical Encounter

What are the ethical considerations of telling the group that you are strong at a specific skill when you really are weak?

Goals

Group members should reach a common understanding of the goals of each member. What does each person want out of the experience? An initial conversation about goals can save a lot of misunderstandings and hard feelings later. Sometimes we work on exciting projects, and everyone is committed to doing their best. Other times, the task may be "busywork"—everyone in the task group knows no one will ever look at their work and evaluate it. In that case, you may decide just to get the task done and not put a lot of effort into it. The clearer the members are about their goals, the more cohesive the group will be and the closer they will be to ideal team status. In our example about personal business during working hours, the team knows that whatever policy they devise becomes the new working policy—and everyone in the company will know who created it.

Doing a basic inventory of members' skills and goals is a good start, but it does not guarantee success. If a colleague fails to follow through with a commitment, his or her strengths become irrelevant. In your first meeting, everyone's commitment to the project is usually pretty high. But as time passes and other deadlines get in the way, you may see some colleagues skip meetings, come unprepared, or behave in a disinterested, harried, or belligerent manner during the meeting. Achieving maximum effort from each member is essential to building cohesiveness, morale and a professional report.

Members' Needs

Colleagues work together to accomplish tasks daily. Often managers encourage employees or coworkers to function as a team on various projects. In order for employees to morph into a team, though, additional interpersonal efforts need to happen. One of the ways to get people feeling as though they are a part of team is to inquire about and accommodate individual needs. For example, one member might need advance notice for meetings and assignments; another member does best with positive feedback; another member looks for praise for good work. Understanding individual needs is a first step to building morale through accommodating the needs of team members.

> Sometimes finding out what people need is as simple as asking a question in the break room. "Hey Sam, what did you find to be the most aggravating thing in your last committee?" or "Hi Laura, I'm running this group, and I was wondering if there is anything you were hoping a new chair would do?"

Some managers never bother to ascertain why employees don't seem to have "passion" for their job or the company. Supervisors feel that you are there to do a job, so just do it. They don't care if you need advance notice—you'll get it when you get it. They don't care if you are motivated by praise, and they simply won't give it.

They may sense employee morale is low, but they choose to ignore it if the work gets done. It is extremely difficult to establish the concept of teamwork in an office without good morale. Poor morale makes everyone's experience a miserable one. Solid leadership (see chapter 8) influences morale.

Typically, a group becomes a team when it is cohesive and enthusiastically tackles all assignments with passion. Team members feel they are a part of something valuable and possibly special. They are happy to be working with their colleagues. Do colleagues always agree? No. Is there occasional conflict? Yes. But everyone knows at the end of their time together that morale is high, and they've been working with other people who value their contributions. They've created a great outcome: new policy, report, restructuring scheme, and so on.

Responsible managers consider, talk about, and analyze each employee's needs to facilitate solid teamwork. It's easier to work interpersonally with colleagues when you understand their needs and quirks. Some people need a lot of encouragement; they need to hear people say they are doing a good job occasionally. Other people are self-directed and find comments like "good idea!" simply condescending. Some people need to be in charge. Others have a high need for organization. And others may simply want to goof off. The more you know about colleague's needs, the better you can communicate with them. If every group member chooses to interact effectively on an interpersonal level, your group will be well on the way toward a team feeling where personal motivation and morale remains high throughout the work assignment.

REALITY ☑

Take a minute to jot down what you find to be the most enjoyable or useful part of being in a group. How could you communicate this need to your fellow employees?

Another factor to consider in deciding whether to assess member needs is the amount of time available for the assigned task. If you are getting together to review a policy statement, you'll be done in a meeting or two. You are going to meet, discuss changes in the language of the policy, and make a recommendation. On the other hand, if you are part of a public relations team developing a campaign for a new client or you are in a group charged with determining how to expand your business, reaching a workable solution will take time. In more complex situations, communication is more effective when members consider colleagues' needs throughout the project. You can reach team status more rapidly when needs are respected and valued—or, at the very least, tolerated.

Motivation can come in many forms. Some people are internally motivated; others are motivated by a break in routine, getting some food, or sharing comments with other team members. It is important for team members to discuss motivational ideas and decide what methods might work for everyone. Those colleagues who think they are already motivated and won't benefit from this discussion are not being realistic. Teams can lack motivation to move forward at any point during a project's development for a variety of reasons. You should revisit the initial discussion regarding motivation whenever the project focus dips. The more people enjoy working together, the better the final report/conclusion is going to be.

Task versus Social Elements of Teamwork

As you begin any project, it is important to remember that teamwork involves task elements and social elements. **Task elements** relate directly to the project itself—setting up meetings, collecting research and analyzing it, and writing a final report. **Social elements** include the entire interpersonal experience—chatting with one another, asking if people are doing well, and joking around when appropriate. Some people are very social all of the time, and nothing gets accomplished. Other people are so task oriented they prefer to begin working as soon as they enter the room. They call the group to order immediately, get to the business of the day, and become annoyed when someone cracks a joke. Neither of these methods works well. In order to work effectively on a team, you need to have a reasonable mix of task and social elements.

In most group work environments, it makes sense to spend a little time initially working with social elements. There should be a brief time, maybe even five minutes, where people can say hello, talk about the latest news, tell a joke, gripe about something going on, or simply make some observations that are not work related. But the group should remember that once the initial greeting period is complete, the meeting will be called to order, and everyone should focus on the business agenda. Even though the traditional interpersonal method of working with others on-site is shifting into digital channels, the initial greeting period is still valuable whether in the office or virtual.

If the work session becomes intense, it may be useful to build a "time out" break into the meeting structure. The value of scheduled breaks and possible comic relief by some team members can assist the team in maintaining focus when discussions become intense or if a meeting runs longer than planned. A little laughter or off-target commentary sometimes provides needed stress relief. After the "time out," the business conversation continues.

As specific tasks (taking notes, research, analyzing data, etc.) are assigned to various team members, and you volunteer to do additional tasks during the meeting, your timely follow through is critical if you want to maintain personal credibility. We have worked with numerous colleagues who say that they will email answers to questions by a certain time but find nothing when we check our inbox at the promised time. If you set a time to deliver information, people will be counting on you; follow through on your commitment. Supervisors notice your ability to get things completed on time, and the punctual behavior will usually be rewarded with future advancement, a bonus, or retaining your position if the company restructures.

Ethical Encounter

A team member does not meet a deadline. You panic as team leader and begin to do the member's share of the work without informing the person of your decision. Should you contact your colleague to find out what is going on? Ignore the missed deadline completely? Rally other colleagues behind you and against the rogue team member? File a final report dropping the team member's name from the title page?

Teamwork can often be problematic. It takes skill and patience to solve problems and integrate personalities into a cohesive team. There are occasions when it will seem more difficult to accomplish a task by working in a group instead of working on your own. However, at many points in your career you will have to work in a group either in person or virtually. Learn the necessary skills to have a good team experience. Once you make effective choices and are committed to a team and the task, you should have a solid, rewarding experience.

In order to be successful as a team, you must find ways to trust, to encourage, and to motivate each other. Your interpersonal skills can make the difference between a successful team experience and a poor team experience. A more successful team experience leads to a more professional report.

Followership—The Employee's Role

A tremendous challenge to any new employee is to sort out which colleagues possess real passion and talent for their jobs. These individuals can usually inspire you to learn faster and work harder to achieve their level of happiness within corporate life. Not all employees are motivated, however, and you need to navigate your way around these individuals until you can determine why people do and say the things they do. Positive behavior is valued; negative behavior adversely affects your reputation and possibly your employment. It is important to be a good listener and observer of the business environment as you start your career and throughout your professional life. Treat colleagues with respect and maintain a good attitude toward them regardless of how you feel about them personally. Only time will reveal whether your initial perceptions of others are accurate.

Robert Kelley encourages followers (as well as leaders) to understand their communication styles in order to be effective. His research revealed that followers differ on two dimensions: (1) independent/critical thinking and (2) active engagement. The best **followers** are those who think for themselves and initiate action (Johnson and Hackman, 2018). Typical followers take direction and complete jobs after being told what is expected of them. The worst followers need constant supervision. Until you get a leadership position, what kind of follower do you want to be? How will you deal with other followers who do not share your positive goals?

Craig Johnson and Michael Hackman (2018) summarize the five categories of followers identified by Kelley.

- *Alienated followers* are disillusioned with leaders; they use their independent thinking to fight rather than to serve organizations.
- *Conformists* defer to authority; although committed to the organization, they rarely express their opinions.
- *Pragmatists* are moderately independent and engaged.
- *Passive followers* rely on direction and meet only minimal expectations.
- *Exemplary followers* are active, innovative, think critically, and exceed requirements.

Learning the skills possessed by exemplary followers allows you to reach the same level of success. It's a wise idea to surround yourself with exemplary people because their efforts encourage you to learn more and work harder.

Exemplary followers understand what is important in helping the organization reach its objectives and develop the skills required. They network throughout the organization by joining teams, reaching out to others in the organization, and working with leaders as partners. They anticipate ethical problems and work through issues that could pose a significant threat and put the organization at risk.

Ira Chaleff talks about courage—accepting a higher level of risk—as an important characteristic of followers. Being courageous is easier if followers remember that their allegiance is to the corporation rather than to the leader (Johnson and Hackman, 2018). Chaleff outlines five areas of courageous followership.

- Assume responsibility (be accountable, assess skills and attitudes, seek feedback)
- Serve (be organized, develop time-management skills, exercise good judgment, meet/exceed expectations)
- Challenge (ask questions, provide feedback, avoid groupthink, address abuses)
- Participate in transformation (control reactions to confrontation, create supportive environment, model empathy)

- Leave (have the courage to leave if the leader's behavior is unethical or clashes with the values of the group)

Leaders should develop the courage to listen to followers (invite creative challenges, accept support and criticism, develop a culture of communication).

Barbara Kellerman (2008) offers another characterization of followers in an organization. Analyze the varying approaches. You will find a great deal of information that will help you hone your skills in analyzing each situation.

- *Isolates* are completely detached. These followers are scarcely aware of what's going on. They don't care about, know about, or respond to their leaders in any way. Because of this, they passively support the status quo. They are most likely to be found in large companies where they can get away with acting this way.
- *Bystanders* observe but do not participate. These followers are free riders who deliberately stand aside and disengage from leaders as well as other members of the organization. They are perfectly aware of what is going on around them; they just choose not to take part in any of it.
- *Participants* are engaged in some way. These followers are interested enough to invest something (time or money usually) in their company, but not interested enough to go any further than that.
- *Activists* feel strongly one way or the other about their leaders and organizations and they act accordingly. These followers are eager, energetic, and engaged. They are heavily interested in people as well as processes, so they will work hard to either support or overturn their leaders depending on the situation.
- *Diehards* are prepared to go down for the cause—whether it's an individual, an idea, or both. These followers are either deeply devoted to or decidedly against their leader. They are rare and usually emerge in dire (or close to dire) situations.

Think about each of the styles discussed above. Chances are you have worked with all of them at one time or another or will encounter them during your career. In most organizations, there is a surreal mix of these types of followers. If you are fortunate, your group/team experience will include a few of the supportive followers and, thus, balance the others. But don't fool yourself into believing that when you get into the business world, everyone will be devoted to the company and share your passion for success. You'll find the same mix of personalities that you are experiencing right now in your classrooms.

John McCallum (2013) lists a number of skills needed to be a good follower. Assess yourself carefully against the following. Which skills do you have? Which skills require a significant amount of work to acquire?

- **Judgment.** Followers have an underlying obligation to follow directions ***if*** the direction is ethical and proper. Judgment is the ability to know when a directive is wrong versus one with which you disagree. Good judgment is equally important for both leaders and followers. Followers who display good judgment will often have a chance to become a leader. McCallum advises that good judgment comes from experience—and experience often comes from bad judgment.
- **Work ethic.** Good followers are good workers; they are diligent, motivated, committed, try hard, and pay attention to detail. The responsibility of leaders is to create an environment that promotes these qualities, while the responsibility of the follower is to be a good worker.
- **Competence.** The leader must make sure that the follower is competent for the task assigned. If the follower lacks the skills required for the task, the blame falls on the leader.
- **Honesty.** Good leaders welcome constructive feedback from their team members. The follower owes the leader a forthright assessment—particularly when the leader's agenda is flawed. If feedback is rejected and the flaws are serious enough, the follower should consider asking for guidance from the leader's superiors.
- **Courage.** It takes courage for followers to confront a leader about concerns with the leader's agenda. Churchill believed courage was the preeminent virtue because all others depend on it.
- **Discretion.** Followers owe their leaders and companies discretion; all employees have a duty of care. Talking about work

inappropriately is careless—it won't help and is likely to be harmful. You cannot be a good follower and be indiscreet.

- **Loyalty.** Good followers have a strong allegiance and commitment to what the organization is trying to do. The obligation of followers is to the company rather than to the leader. Loyalty to the company and its goals is particularly important when there are problems with a particular leader. Followers who are not loyal create problems between team members, compromise the achievement of goals, and waste everybody's time.
- **Ego management.** Success for good followers relates to performance and goal achievement not personal recognition and self promotion. Good followers keep their egos under control.

Most workers are a combination of the various categories discussed above. It's a good idea as you start your career to determine how you want to be perceived by other people and the type of employee (follower) you want to be. Enthusiasm is the best way to make an impression and be remembered by everyone. It takes many years of devotion and hard work to advance to the top within an organization. Therefore, you remain a follower for a long time because someone above you determines your fate. To be a good employee takes patience, passion for business and people, and the constant professional development of your communication skills.

Interpersonal Skills in Teams

Excellent interpersonal communication skills are the key to having others perceive you as a valuable team member. How you articulate a message verbally and in writing demonstrates your credibility and professionalism to others. The statements you make reveal your thoughtfulness, analytical ability, research ability, and comprehensive approach to completing a task well. Listen carefully to everything team members say. Think critically about the statements you hear; analyze them for accuracy.

This is another time to practice retaining what you heard. Take notes and pay attention so you can contribute later with confidence.

Members of the team examine your nonverbal reactions to the statements of others. Colleagues perceive you to be a professional by how you react to statements, jokes, memos, emails, and general conversation. Someone is always observing you to see if they can trust you or want to deal with you. You need to appear comfortable even when a conversation or action makes you uneasy. Your reaction to stressful situations can demonstrate ease and sophistication. Maintaining professional conduct at all times is essential.

Multitasking is a requirement. You need to be organized to save time and avoid mistakes in verbal and nonverbal communication. Team members will expect you to remember issues discussed and actions taken. Immediately file every piece of information from team meetings—whether physically or electronically. You must be able to access information easily without wasting time—and especially not the time of other members who already know the material.

Good team members analyze all actions in terms of the goals of the organization. Loyal employees use supportive language and behavior to reinforce the mission of the organization. An employee must assess various situations accurately and find the proper words to explain actions and policies. Audience analysis determines how you shape your communication. A closed meeting with colleagues provides greater freedom for raising challenges to proposed procedures than a discussion on the same topic in a community setting. A personal commitment to reshape communication to meet professional demands reflects your passion for a full-time career.

How you want colleagues to perceive your communication skills is totally within your control. You need to constantly improve your "value" to an employer, and you can do it quite easily by working to look and sound professional. While this may seem like a simple concept, it is not. The components of professionalism are endless—every gesture you make, your appearance, the way you speak, your written communication, your interpersonal skills, the efficient use of time, digital skills, perceived intelligence, perceived leadership potential, perceived responsibility, and multitasking ability.

Planning and Running Meetings

Much of a team's work is carried out in meetings where members develop strategy and coordinate assignments. Although such meetings are an everyday occurrence in the business world, you cannot take them lightly. We have all been the victim of a poorly run meeting. Preparation is the key to effective participation in team meetings.

Planning for Meetings

Planning is part of effective teamwork. One team member will be assigned the responsibility for coordinating the details for the meeting site in a conventional setting. In selecting a space, make sure it contains the technology your team needs. For instance, everyone should be comfortable in the meeting space. There should be space to set materials and equipment—a large table that allows you to display/arrange information for the meeting. You need to make sure the lighting is sufficient for everyone attending the meeting. Don't forget record keeping as you make these plans. It may be useful to have an alternative corporate site available to your team just in case the room you have reserved becomes unavailable.

As an individual member, make sure you are 100 percent prepared for whatever is on the agenda. You should have read the minutes of the previous meeting, so you can identify corrections and can vote to approve them. You should have reviewed the agenda, so you know the plan. Be sure you are prepared with a concise, accurate report for your portion of the task. You also need to have completed all of your assigned tasks. Team members get irritated quickly when individuals make excuses for their incomplete work. This shows great disrespect to your team members. You also have additional planning if you are meeting virtually, which we discuss a little later. There are often severe consequences for not being prepared.

Prepare an Agenda

Have you attended meetings where a team accomplished nothing? The leader began with "What are we doing today?"; no one remembered what had even been decided in the previous meeting. In other words, no one prepared for the scheduled meeting. An effective leader creates, distributes, and sticks to an agenda. A leader who is organized, prepared, and unwilling to waste time demonstrates respect for the other team members. You cannot waste anyone's time in business. Sticking to an agenda demonstrates respect. Occasionally a meeting may finish early, which allows members to leave to complete other tasks or remain and socialize with one another. A brief meeting is rare—but certainly appreciated and remembered.

A group meeting starts with a written agenda. The agenda can be formal or informal, depending on the team. Most agendas include the following items:

- a professional heading,
- a start time,
- correction and acceptance of previous minutes,
- announcements,
- reports from team members,
- unfinished business from previous meetings,
- new business items,
- ending time for the meeting.

Preparing an agenda takes a significant amount of time. You need to consult with group members for items you may have forgotten or items they know about but you don't. After you decide on the order of items, you need to make sure you have all the paperwork you need. Do participants need to review documents before you begin? Do you need handouts? Do you have all of the information in order to discuss each item. This takes time and planning.

Running Proper Meetings

You should always have a formal record of every decision the team makes. This record is called **minutes**. In order to keep proper records, the recorder of the day should indicate the date, a list of who attended the meeting, what time the meeting was called to order, a notation of every item discussed, who initiated the idea, and what decision was reached. The recorder should also keep a written record of every vote taken, unless the leader makes a request not to record it for a specific item. Minutes conclude with the phrase "Respectfully Submitted" and the recorder signs his or her name. If the recorder distributes the minutes electronically, a signed original copy is filed for the legal record.

A simple format can help to keep track of who said they would do what.

DRAFT **DRAFT**

DEPARTMENT OF COMMUNICATION MINUTES		
DATE:	**TIME:** 12:30–2:00 p.m.	**PLACE:** 312 SH
PRESENT: Young, Travis, Cho, Fitzpatrick, and Olsen		
TOPIC	**DISCUSSION**	**ACTION**
Senior Celebration	Young asked whether the department would like to continue the celebration at the end of the semester since attendance was down. Fitzpatrick listed the benefits. Olsen confirmed the benefits and suggested ways to increase attendance.	Travis agreed to make the arrangements. Green will send out the invites and emails.
Other topics		
Adjourn at 1:45		
Submitted by: Eva L. Green		

Ethical Encounter

There are instances when your notes and conversations from a group meeting are considered confidential. You must be careful to adhere to the agreements related to confidentiality that your team or organization establishes. You accidentally leave the notes from a closed meeting on your desk as you head to lunch. When you return, you discover a colleague was in your office to collect some material you had promised to pass along, and you think this person read your confidential notes. How should you handle this situation?

Some miscellaneous tips for record keeping include keeping a file folder of all agendas, all copies of the minutes, copies of all email correspondence, copies of all memos, and copies of any handouts from team members. You should also date all information that crosses your desk, so you know when you received it. A recorder's goal is to keep all information concerning a specific project in one file.

You write minutes in a formal style, with no abbreviations. Be sure that you spell and record all members' names correctly. In formal business, use only the last name of individuals in the record. Everyone should take responsibility for reviewing and editing minutes prior to voting to approve them. There are many formats for minutes that you can find on the internet, but businesses usually have a preferred style you should follow.

Meeting Dos and Don'ts

While there is no comprehensive list of what you should and should not do in a group meeting, we offer the following suggestions.

- Be on time.
- Stick to the topic and stay on task.
- Leave personal issues behind.
- Be prepared.
- Have handouts ready, if appropriate.
- Give an update of where you are on the project.
- Don't keep a critique to yourself because you think you will be unpopular if you mention a problem.
- Be positive when you ask questions of other members.
- Remember the difference between being critical of an idea and criticizing an idea or person.
- Use a proper, respectful tone when being critical of an idea.
- Be honest about what you can/can't do.
- Follow through on every assignment in a timely manner.
- If you are having difficulty, say so as early as possible, so other members can help you.

REALITY ☑

If you are done, ADJOURN! We have watched administrators literally panic because the meeting wrapped up twenty minutes early. They spent the time trying to get people to contribute on a meaningless topic. If you have covered the information, let people get on with their day.

Virtual Meetings

The need for virtual meetings and virtual teams in business is increasing rapidly. An employee's personal computing device can now serve as a meeting room. Participants can share documents, make visual presentations, and/or demonstrate products and services in a collaborative manner from their desktop. If we can simply flip a switch and meet electronically, we eliminate the time and expense of travel to bring people together. **Virtual teams** consist of dispersed individuals (whether geographically or within an organization) who use information technologies to collaborate and communicate to accomplish a specific goal. Employers are seeking individuals who are comfortable communicating on digital platforms with a diverse pool of colleagues from multiple cultures.

Organizations with team members from different countries need to foster a global mindset where people see themselves as part of an international network (Brokaw, 2017). Inter-cultural training promotes that mindset and the development of diversity-friendly attitudes. Many companies forget to consider the social skills required when communication and collaboration are done electronically—particularly when multiple cultures are involved. For virtual collaboration to work, team members must be self-reliant and able to overcome obstacles on their own. Virtual workers need to be more self-sufficient because the team leader may not be in a position to help.

Although employers are optimistic about personal self-motivation as they appoint employees to virtual teams, team members may not always work efficiently due to different cultural backgrounds, methods of communication, and individual perceptions on the best way to contribute to the teams' progress. Some cultures work on an assignment until the work is completed, ignoring other demands until the current task is resolved. Other cultures treat time differently. Become familiar with everyone's working style and expectations. Discuss differences and arrange a schedule that accommodates all members. Email is generally preferred for communication, but that will not always be the most effective method for every individual on the team.

Virtual meetings differ from face-to-face meetings, and there is a specific skill set that you will need to be successful. When you communicate with a virtual team, you need to remember time zone differences when communicating globally (recall the discussion in chapter 6). There are some situations when you can communicate during normal working hours; other times, a project may require transmitting messages around the clock to global team members. You may need to work a 12–16-hour shift and will have to allocate portions of the 24-hour day to personal or sleep breaks coordinated with the schedules of others on your virtual team.

There may be many different cultures within a virtual team, and culture can influence how people function within the team. The cultures in which we grew up shape our choices and decisions, while people evaluate our actions based on *their* cultures (Lamson, 2018). If we aren't aware of this fact, there may be misunderstandings based on cultural differences. Colleagues may be communicating with you in their second, third, or fourth language. Therefore, it is imperative to pay close attention to their use of English. Most educational institutions in countries other than the United States teach British English. This form of English uses a different spelling for some words in addition to differences in syntax and jargon. When a diverse virtual team generates a team document, it needs to be edited for a consistent style. The same statement applies to your own work when you generate material with colleagues in Spanish, French, or another language. Language is fluid, and unless you constantly update the nuances of a word's meaning it is quite possible to make a mistake in communicating a thought accurately. Working in a virtual team requires accuracy, understanding, and patience.

A good manager is knowledgeable about potential communication barriers prior to establishing a virtual team. Inform every team member regarding potential communication issues so everyone can recognize possible skill and cultural differences and smoothly pull their ideas and information together for a final report. This does not imply that team members can't solve communication issues as a project moves forward. They can, but some deadlines are easier to meet when a manager makes everyone aware of member differences initially. This saves time, avoids potential frustration within the team, and leads to a better result.

Don't forget the planning details. Make sure you are located at a site where you can connect to a virtual meeting with no background distractions and with a reliable internet connection. Technical glitches and power failures occur, but meetings go on as scheduled. Make sure you check all the technology ahead of time so you can participate fully.

Another wonderful feature of the virtual world is that you can participate in critical team meetings from home during an emergency or illness. You can access every secure file and program in your office computer off-site thanks to software and passwords. Employees can present information and participate in critical meetings even when they can't be at their desks. It is important to remember that electrical power and natural disasters can disrupt virtual communication unexpectedly. Plan in advance how to address such problems.

Final Thoughts

Teamwork and the numerous meetings that populate professional life are expansions of interpersonal communication. Teams bring numerous colleagues together temporarily to solve a problem—whether in the traditional face-to-face context or the virtual world. You need to work comfortably in both situations. The traditional face-to-face meetings and teams continue in community organizations, educational institutions, religious organizations, nonprofit organizations, political organizations, and business. Virtual meetings and teams continue to evolve in corporations who have the financial resources and need for instantaneous solutions to planning issues on a national or global scale. Each individual within a team possesses a specific expertise, personality, communication style, and work ethic. Cooperation and understanding are critical components for a productive team experience in which everyone works together to achieve an employer's goals.

Teams challenge every aspect of your communication skills and style because each group situation has unique components and requirements. Good communication is the glue binding colleagues together for a common goal. Once your oral and written skills have evolved and been tested by colleagues and employers in countless situations, the topic of the next chapter—leadership—becomes your next communication challenge.

Key Terms

Activists
Alienated followers
Bystanders
Conformists
Diehards
Exemplary followers
Followers
Groups
Isolates
Minutes
Participants
Passive followers
Pragmatists
Social elements
Task elements
Teams
Virtual meetings
Virtual teams

Exercises

1. Evaluate the other members of your blog group for their professionalism or lack of it.
2. Describe the type of follower you are. Can you change?
3. What challenges do you see in your ability to work in a virtual meeting? Participate in one if your school has the technical facilities to do so.
4. Analyze your multitasking skills. Practice typing a formal document while chatting with a friend on the phone for five minutes. Check for typing errors. Debrief with the friend about how much you understood the conversation.
5. Are you self-motivated? What have you accomplished to prove you are?
6. How have you resolved verbal disagreement with someone?
7. List the research tools you rely on to complete a paper or project. What are the strengths and weaknesses of each tool mentioned?

CHAPTER
EIGHT

Decision Making, Problem Solving, Management, and Leadership

Goals

- Explain and use the four types of decision making
- Differentiate among the four problem-solving methods
- Explain the steps of the reflective-thinking process
- Compare and contrast leadership and management
- Describe the traditional functions of management
- Describe the different leadership theories
- Explain the characteristics of good leaders
- Analyze your own leadership strengths

Problem-solving skills are highly desired in the corporate world. These skills allow you to analyze complex issues competently and to reach a reasonable solution. Every time you speak, write, or move, your brand demonstrates your analytical ability. Make sure to highlight your problem-solving skills to a potential employer during behavioral interviewing. Problem solvers use concrete personal examples to shape their accomplishments as proof of an excellent work history. For example, you coordinated a fundraiser for a community organization and collected over $50,000 for the first time in the group's history. In discussing the project, you articulate a brief background of the group, its existing problems, an analysis of organizational issues, your strategy to raise the money, a financial description of when and how the money raised was spent, and an overview of the end result for this organization. Your thorough answer demonstrates to a potential employer that you possess analytical skills in addition to the ability to complete a task. In other words, you produce results. Your working life should consistently produce positive results, reinforcing your value to an employer.

It takes time to find the appropriate solution to a problem. You must constantly observe, listen, remember, and reflect about the professional environment that surrounds you. How can you assist a business to work more efficiently? Whenever you can save an employer money and still meet productivity goals, you enhance your value to the company. The time it requires to solve a problem is worth every second of research and analysis because a company that performs efficiently usually survives financially against corporate competitors. Excellent skills not only keep a company in business but they also keep you employed.

Types of Decision Making

Decision making is the act of choosing the proper solution among available alternatives. We make decisions all the time—whether to go to restaurant A or B for lunch; whether to make 15 or 25 copies of a report; or whether to copy material immediately or put it off. Decisions become more difficult in our professional lives. We may need to decide who of our three subordinates should be promoted. There are many factors used in making decisions in the business world. The type of task, the organizational culture, and the characteristics of employees all play a part in determining the best decision-making method to use when resolving a potential problem.

Vote

A **vote** is when you tally how many people are for or against an idea. This is a simple form of decision making. Whichever side of an issue receives 51% of the vote is the winner. You might be asked if you are in favor of a certain policy or rule, which person you'd like to move into a position, or other similar types of basic decisions. Typically, when a vote is required, there is a lot of factual discussion and disclosure of the various sides of an issue before you take a vote. Companies also use a vote as a last resort when an instant decision is required and employees cannot come to an agreement. Or, a vote can be used informally to save time: Should we go to restaurant A or B? Let's take a vote.

Leader Mandate

In the **leader mandate** type of decision making, a leader makes all of the decisions. A good leader gathers information and input from everyone who will be affected by the action and makes an informed and rational decision. If the leader is power hungry and arrogant, he or she makes decisions without the input of others. If followers are happy with a leader's decisions—and the leader's communication is effective—employees will probably be satisfied with the leader mandate. For example, the military thrives on this type of decision making. However, if a leader is inept and unreasonable, employees may be extremely dissatisfied if they don't have input into a decision that affects them. This situation usually leads to low morale within an organization.

Compromise

A compromise decision happens when people working as a team negotiate a solution. **Compromise** consists of each side giving up a little of what it originally wanted. As negotiations occur in any work environment, compromise is taking place—especially between workers and management. Think about negotiating contracts. Each side comes in with unrealistic expectations, and then they begin the compromise process. For example, management offers employees a low deductible on their health care plan if they accept a $1 million lifetime cap on coverage. One of the hazards of any compromise is that no one is completely happy with the decision negotiated.

Consensus

Consensus happens when all parties involved discuss every aspect of a problem and arrive at a solution. The critical importance of a true consensus decision is that everyone is willing to stand behind the decision. They may not all be happy with it, but everyone agrees that the solution generated is indeed the best one. Consensus is reached through interpersonal persuasion, enlightening everyone with new information or new ways to look at old information, and further exploration of the issue.

The type of decision making needed to solve a problem varies with the complexity of the issue, the time available for reaching a decision, and the specific employees asked to participate in the process. You will probably experience each of these decision-making techniques during the course of your working career.

Problem-Solving Models

As with decision making, there are various methods for solving problems. The specifics of each issue dictate which problem-solving model would be most likely to generate an effective solution.

Brainstorming

Brainstorming isn't really a problem-solving model by itself, but it is an important part of any problem-solving activity. Groups typically use brainstorming to generate ideas. The key concept behind **brainstorming** is to generate as many thoughts as possible in the shortest amount of time. You appoint one person to jot down every verbal thought expressed. People quickly say what comes to mind, and others use what they hear to stimulate their own creative thinking and express more thoughts. Participants shouldn't evaluate or comment on any of the ideas generated during a brainstorming session. Ideas simply flow without interruption or evaluation.

Brainstorming is used to create lists of goals, solutions to problems, options for using technology, ideas to improve morale, etc. After you have generated a list of random ideas, evaluation begins. Everyone analyzes the potential of each idea to achieve the group's goal. The goal of many brainstorming sessions is to present the top three ideas to a supervisor with an explanation of why each of them can solve the problem. Brainstorming is a technique that can also be used as an integral component for any of the following models.

Nominal Group Technique

The **nominal group technique** is basically a ranking system. Group members individually rank a list of options, solutions, goals, etc. and then average the scores. For example, an outstanding employee of the year committee might use this model to make their final decision. Let's say there are 10 nominations. The committee looks at the list of names and whittles it down to the top 4 based on criteria they generated for the nomination process. Next, they interview each nominee. Once the interviews are complete, there is no discussion about the candidates to make the decision Instead, committee members rank the candidates numerically; then, they average the rankings to find the employee with the best score.

The advantages to this model are that each individual has a say in the decision, and there is no influence from a boss or supervisor, who may be a member of the team. The disadvantages of this model are that sometimes the best person doesn't win. For instance, look at the following totals.

Nominee 1:	1, 2, 1, 1, 1, 2, 1	=	1.285
Nominee 2:	2, 1, 2, 2, 2, 1, 2	=	1.7142
Nominee 3:	3, 3, 3, 3, 3, 4, 3	=	3.1428
Nominee 4:	4, 4, 4, 4, 4, 3, 4	=	3.8571

These totals make it very clear that Nominee 1 should win. However, consider the situation with the following scores.

Nominee 1:	1, 2, 3, 1, 1, 4, 4	=	2.2857
Nominee 2:	2, 3, 4, 3, 2, 1, 2	=	2.4285
Nominee 3:	4, 4, 1, 1, 3, 3, 1	=	2.4285
Nominee 4:	3, 1, 2, 4, 4, 2, 3	=	2.7142

Nominee 1 wins in both cases. In the first scenario, most members of the committee will be satisfied with the decision. Usually if our second choice ends up winning, we can live with it. In the second scenario, three of the committee members ranked the actual winner in the bottom half of the candidates. Notice how close the numbers are between Nominees 1, 2, and 3. Committee members can be very unhappy and angry when the numbers shake out like this. What you thought would be a fair, impartial method does not always produce a unified result.

Delphi Technique

Groups use the Delphi technique when they are not meeting face-to-face, when there are power players who try to manipulate others in the group, or when underlings would sense pressure to conform to powerful members in a group. Once the group discusses the problem or issue, the **Delphi technique** is implemented by having everyone write a reaction, an assessment, or fill out a questionnaire about the problem or issue. In some applications of this technique, respondents remain anonymous. They send their comments to a central person who synthesizes all the ideas and sends them back to the group for further review. Currently you can use an anonymous survey monkey or google docs to solicit this input allowing everyone to speak freely. This process can occur as many times as necessary until the group reaches its final decision.

REALITY ☑

We knew a new university president who met with chairs of the departments on campus. At the first meeting he asked if we were concerned about any issues. When everyone remained silent, he said, "You can trust me." However, the chairs had only just met him and were in a low morale environment. How could the Delphi Technique be used to get more out of this meeting?

The Reflective-Thinking Process

The reflective-thinking process is derived from John Dewey's (1910) classic work, *How We Think*, in which he described five basic steps in scientific reasoning. The reflective-thinking process has been adapted into a variety of problem-solving models. Gerald Phillips developed The Standard Agenda as a flexible, time-tested method for problem-solving discussion (Young, Wood, Phillips, and Pedersen, 2021). The Standard Agenda has six steps that take the group through the reflective-thinking process.

Reflective thinking is "systematic" and "orderly" thinking. You'll find that many professionals approach problem solving in this manner. Your teachers may have given you rubrics of their criteria for figuring out your grades. In the workplace, HR requires you to submit a rubric for interviewing individuals. Long gone are the days where you could simply look at résumés and determine whom to hire. Currently, you need to progress through the reflective-thinking process and submit each step of decision making for approval from HR before moving to the next step in the process.

The purpose of the **reflective-thinking process** is to keep problem solving fair, equal and systematic—as well as to keep communication moving forward. There are a few key steps that must be followed to allow a group to arrive at an optimal solution. Every group member must understand this procedure. They must also be flexible enough to work back and forth between the steps. The fact that reflective thinking is fair, equal, and systematic also helps if anyone questions your solution. The format that follows presents a reliable process for reaching a fair decision (Young et al., 2021).

REALITY ☑

Why did she get a raise and I didn't? Reflective thinking to the rescue. Simply point to the criteria and demonstrate how the individual asking the question did not meet the criteria well enough to warrant a raise. Discuss the criteria and the process only as it applies to the disgruntled person. No need to discuss the person who received the raise.

STEP 1: UNDERSTANDING THE CHARGE

Group members must understand the task. We have seen numerous groups, both at the student and professional level, attempt to problem solve an issue before they realize what it is they are supposed to accomplish.

Understanding the charge means being able to answer the following questions: What is the goal of the group? Who formed the

---

REALITY ☑

If you are a member of a search committee, what is your charge? Do you hire? Or do you simply make a recommendation? Does it make a difference to know that?

---

group and why? What resources are available to the group (including financial, material, technological, and human support)? When must the group make its final report? What form must the report take? Who gets the report?

STEP 2: UNDERSTANDING AND PHRASING THE QUESTION

Once group members understand their mission, it is time to define the problem. Often group members assume everyone understands the problem, but they may not. Some individuals come to group projects with varying opinions and thoughts based on past experiences with similar assignments; thus, they fail to approach the problem as a new entity.

During the phrasing phase, the group must determine exactly what issue requires a decision. To do this effectively, the members should establish a discussion question. You typically phrase discussion questions in the following manner: Who should do what about what? An effective discussion question could be: Which candidate in the pool will be the most effective to help us progress with company goals?

STEP 3: FACT-FINDING

During fact-finding, interactions must focus on (1) critical examination of the facts by all members, (2) whether the facts should alter the phrasing of the original discussion question, and (3) whether you have gathered enough information to proceed.

To be effective problem solvers, members must collect as much detailed data as possible. It is often difficult to determine when this step is actually finished. For our discussion question, the group would determine what requirements are necessary for a candidate in terms of their level of education, degrees earned, experience, the requirements for the position, and so forth.

STEP 4: ESTABLISHING CRITERIA

By now members are usually ready to jump to a solution, but there is one additional step. **Criteria** are the standards by which we judge people and things. Everyone uses criteria; you have standards by which you judge restaurants, movies, music, and so forth. Instructors have standards by which they judge speeches, assignments, papers, and exams. Instructors cannot just put a "B" on a paper because it "feels" like an above-average paper. Instead, they need to know what they are looking for and how they'll know it when they see it. Criteria tell us how we know a good solution when we see it.

The standard form for criteria is "Any solution must . . ." You would substitute words for "solution" as necessary. If we were hiring an entry-level PR person for our company, we would say, "In order to be hired, a candidate must . . ." and the group would develop a specific list of requirements such as:

- have an undergraduate degree in public relations;
- have experience writing news releases, designing flyers, and creating promotional and marketing campaigns;
- have a cover letter with no typographical or formatting errors;
- have a proven record of community service.

Note the difficulty with the last element—how do the committee members define "proven record?" The first three criteria are objective; the fourth is subjective, and you need to define it more clearly in order to proceed.

It's a good idea to generate the criteria you will use for accepting your first position. What does your list look like? It begins with "Any job must. . . ." Possible completions might be "offer a salary of 45K per year" or "be in an urban area." Jot down your specific criteria.

Do not move past the criteria step until you have defined and prioritized all criteria. A concrete definition of items is important so you have objective, concrete statements with which to work. Prioritization of the criteria is important in case you have more than one candidate who meets the same number of criteria. If two candidates meet two of the criteria above (Candidate A has the degree and experience but no community service, while Candidate B has community service and experience but no degree), you need to be able to determine which candidate is the better choice. Thus, you need to prioritize your criteria—in this case our company cannot hire anyone without an undergraduate degree, so that item is ranked first. We also cannot hire anyone without experience, making that our second criterion. However, lack of community service or a possible typo is not a deal breaker in this particular company, so we rank them lower.

STEP 5: DISCOVERING AND SELECTING SOLUTIONS

In this step, group members brainstorm a list of solutions and select the best one. Notice that we do not even mention the idea of solutions until this step. Groups must gather facts and establish criteria before they consider solutions. After the earlier steps have been completed, group members brainstorm solutions. Remember, participants should *generate*, not *evaluate* ideas while brainstorming. Suppose your group is solving a problem of low morale in the organization. You collect data and develop criteria for your solution (such as it can't cost over $200, or it needs to be able to be implemented immediately). In this situation, you would brainstorm possible solutions—such as having an employee appreciation lunch, giving out movie tickets to the most productive employee on a weekly basis, or having a rotating parking place reserved for someone who performs extraordinary work.

In the example we are using, there is nothing to brainstorm. Each candidate is a potential "solution" to the problem: a job opening. But note that we have not been allowed to access candidates' résumés until the work leading up to this step was completed.

Next, we systematically evaluate each individual against each of our criteria. It is often useful to create a matrix.

Solutions	Candidate A	Candidate B	Candidate C	Candidate D
Degree in PR				
Experience				
No typos				
Community service				

Ethical Encounter

How ethical is it to list the community service you did that was required as part of your fraternity/ sorority membership under its own résumé heading instead of indicating that it was required?

You could simply indicate "yes" or "no" in each of the boxes, but what about variations of degree? Most HR departments now require problem solvers to specify a point system. So your evaluation could look like this:

BS degree in PR
10 = yes
0 = no

Experience in PR
8 = ran a campaign for real-world clients
6 = ran a campaign for class assignment
4 = wrote several flyers, PSAs, newsletters, or press releases for a company
2 = wrote flyers, PSAs, newsletters or press releases for a class

No typos in paperwork
6 = none
3 = one or two
0 = more than two

Community service
5 = performed self-initiated community service
3 = performed community service while a member of a campus organization
0 = none

At this point, the group needs to discuss whether or not, and to what degree, each candidate matches each criterion. Criterion #1 is simple—candidates either have a degree or they don't. But criterion #2 has some gray areas to consider. Maybe you can't tell from the résumé whether the work was for business clients or for a class. Maybe there are multiple campaigns versus just one. Maybe one committee member perceives one thing after reading the candidate's paperwork while another member perceives something else. You will need to discuss these perceptions and facts in order to reach consensus on the candidate.

Once committee members score each candidate against the criteria, it should become evident which candidate is the best one to hire.

STEP 6: PREPARING AND PRESENTING THE FINAL REPORT

The last phase is reporting your findings. The report is prepared in the format requested by the person who formed the group. If submitting a written report, please refer to chapter 6. We discuss group presentations in chapter 9. In the case of a job hire, your final report is the recommendation to HR. They may or may not require an extensive report with all of your minutes of meetings, rankings of candidates, and other materials, but it's also possible they might require all of the material for legal reasons.

REALITY ☑

On the facing page is a sample grid for a search team at a university. A first column that contains applicant names was deleted from the visual. The second column (minimum requirements) is answered "yes" or "no." The minimum requirements include: an earned doctorate from a regionally accredited university; experience as a college or university faculty member; 5 years of administrative experience in positions of increasing responsibility; eligibility for tenure. The search team assigns a weight to each additional requirement (column 2) and preferred (column 3). You can see the importance of writing your cover letter to address the criteria in the job advertisement (as discussed in chapter 3). The search committee evaluating you will look for the information. If it isn't there, you will get a lower score.

When Does Reflective Thinking Yield a Bad Solution?

Do not be lulled into a false sense of security. The Standard Agenda helps people make the best decisions possible through systematic thinking. However, there are times when a group doesn't use The Standard Agenda effectively. The following are potential pitfalls when using The Standard Agenda.

- Members do not accurately assess the problem.
- Members do not gather all the necessary facts.
- Members do not accurately analyze the facts.
- Members fail to construct a good set of criteria.
- Members do not systematically apply the solutions to criteria.

	A	B	C	D	E	F	G	H	M	N
1	Department: Academic Affairs (M11-FT-2011)									
2	Position Title: Assoc. Provost & Dean of Arts & Sciences									
3	Minimum Requirement(s)	Additional Requirements							Preferred	
4		Demonstrated knowledge and understanding of postsecondary education, organizational, and governance structures	Demonstration of skills in decision-making, problem solving	Demonstration of excellent writing, technology, and management skills	Demonstrated commitment to diversity and affirmative action principles and outcomes	Demonstrated understanding of public liberal arts university mission and current issues in higher education	Demonstrated collaboration with a wide spectrum of university constituents	Active participation in appropriate professional associations	Experience in collective bargaining	Experience in a liberal arts environment
5	Assigned Weight:	5	4	5	3	5	5	1	3	5
6	Yes/No	*Use a scale of 0 - 5 (5 being the highest)								
7	No									
8	Yes	3	0	3	0	0	0	1	1	3
9	No									
10	Yes	2	2	0	3	3	3	1	3	3
11	Yes	3	2	2	0	0	2	1	0	0
12	No									
13	Yes	1	2	0	1	1	4	1	0	3
14	Yes	5	4	5	1	5	5	1	0	5
15	Yes	2	2	1	1	0	2	1	0	1
16	Yes	4	2	2	0	4	3	1	1	3
17	Yes	3	2	2	0	2	3	0	0	2
18	Yes	3	2	3	0	4	3	0	0	3
19	Yes	2	1	1	0	2	1	1	0	2
20	Yes	2	1	2	1	1	1	1	0	1
21	Yes	3	2	3	1	3	3	1	3	3
22	Yes	2	1	1	1	1	1	1	0	2
23	No									
24	No									
25	Yes	2	1	0	1	2	2	1	1	2
26	Yes	4	4	5	2	4	4	1	3	4
27	Yes	2	1	1	3	2	2	0	0	2
28	Yes	1	1	0	0	1	0	1	0	0

Many of these pitfalls occur in groups. We have seen people totally botch an analysis of the facts or a good set of criteria. Problem solving is time consuming and yet rewarding if everyone in the group fully participates in reaching a productive decision. The key to resolving any issue is to be as logical as possible in how you evaluate facts/candidates. It is important to be honest and fair in discussing how you plan to reach your decision before you establish criteria; once criteria are in place you must apply them fairly. Criteria should not be changed during the process of solving a problem. This is unethical except in instances when the problem solving cannot be completed based on the current criteria. Once evaluation begins, a solution is not far behind.

Managing and Leading

Leaders are associated with change, crisis, and innovation; managers are associated with organizational stability (Johnson and Hackman, 2018). Managers may also be leaders but often are not; similarly employees can take a leadership role without being in a managerial position. Leadership and management are both important activities in an organization. The outcomes of the two activities differ significantly. Management produces orderly results; leadership often leads to change. Leadership and management are both communication-based activities. "The higher the level of leadership, the higher the demand for communication competence" (p. 21).

Organizations flounder when employees are unaware of what is happening as policies shift, personnel changes, new technology replaces current technology, departments merge, unqualified personnel are promoted over more competent employees, the local press reports fraud within corporate accounting, and no one in the company communicates changes or the reasoning behind the changes. Each aspect of a company's daily operations needs to be assessed by a manager/leader and then analyzed to determine which employees need to be informed about decisions. Open communication creates a sense of belonging and encourages pride in a progressive organization.

The management concepts reviewed below continue to evolve with globalization, the influence of new technologies on interpersonal communication, and the influence of cultural differences on language and behaviors.

Management

Managers are the people in charge of getting things done. Management theories emerged at the turn of the nineteenth century; the perspectives were either discarded, revised, or updated as the workplace evolved. The first management theories were scientific. People like Frederick Taylor (the father of scientific management) believed there was only one way to do things and advocated a specific formula. Other theorists like Max Weber shifted Taylor's approach and advanced a bureaucratic theory of management. The corporate structure was a hierarchy, with workers reporting to people above them in the structure. In the mid-1950s theorists focused on the human element in managing people. Theorists next began examining contingencies and situations. They began to acknowledge that each individual is different, each situation is different, and those differences necessitate different management styles. Corporate structure and communication change so rapidly that anyone who becomes a manager needs to possess some basic tools—and good communication skills head the list of basic tools.

The list below includes some of the major theorists who have affected the field of business communication. Research their backgrounds and their theories about management. Share your findings with classmates and compare your impressions.

Frederick Taylor	Max Weber	Elton Mayo
Rensis Likert	Mary Parker Follet	Henri Fayol
Abraham Maslow	Douglas McGregor	Robert Blake and Jane Mouton
Joan Woodward	Peter Drucker	Peter Senge

REALITY ☑

While they aren't theorists, should influencers be considered in the study of leadership and organizational communication? What can you learn from Oprah, Richard Branson, Mark Zuckerberg, Michelle Obama or Daymond John? Who else would you list as an influencer?

Overview of Management Duties

Managers have a number of duties. They are responsible for seeing projects through to completion with the least amount of cost, the fewest number of employees, and in the least amount of time. They need to manage the use of company resources—both equipment and personnel—efficiently and effectively. Meeting the goals of the company requires managers to plan, staff, organize, lead, and regulate. Planning includes deciding the best course of action for a project and implementing contingency plans if something goes wrong. Staffing involves hiring and/or assigning the right people for a project and training them to do the necessary work in a timely manner. Organizing means deciding how to use people and time efficiently to complete a project. Leading a corporation includes communicating what the company needs, motivating employees, and building successful teams. Regulating requires the ability to monitor productivity and results and to discipline others when necessary. Do you see yourself enjoying these tasks? If so, management could be a realistic future goal.

Think about how communication skills impact each of the tasks mentioned above. How do you handle a crisis, build teams, control productivity and people, discipline, or train without good interpersonal skills? If you choose to move into a management position, you need to make sure that all of your communication skills are excellent. Many managers never expected they would be in the position of running a department, division, or company when their careers began. They were simply given the opportunity to serve in a responsible position by superiors who carefully observed their skills while working within the organization—and they liked what they saw. Other people allow you to advance your career as they assess your value.

Although you may feel invisible within an organization as an entry-level employee, you are not. Your attitude about work and the people around you is constantly visible. It is very important to perform professionally in every job you hold throughout your life. As a new employee or an established employee, your written work needs to be concise and clear. Your verbal responses to colleagues and clients need to be thoughtful and articulate; your nonverbal behavior needs to be appropriate at all times. You need to be a problem solver and find ways to make things work. Your attitude regarding change and the future should be optimistic. An employee with these professional qualities stands out in any organization. Superiors are likely to move someone with these communication skills into a management track quickly. If you want superiors to consider you for a management position, there is no established timeline on how long advancement can take. It is your responsibility to demonstrate professional skills and to project a professional image continuously.

Leadership

There has been an explosion of leadership theories. There are numerous leadership theories to be aware of as you enter the workplace. While studying all aspects of leadership can help you target areas in which to improve personal skills, there is no single step to becoming an effective leader.

Leadership ability is judged by others over time. Your interactions and behavior on the job will determine whether you are perceived as a leader. Some basic leadership theories will help you develop leadership skills.

Difference between Management and Leadership

The basic difference between a manager and a leader is that managers make sure the work gets done while **leaders** inspire others to accomplish the goals of the organization. Think about the numerous tasks a manager must accomplish each day: making sure people are at work and doing their jobs, performance evaluations, running meetings, establishing and maintaining schedules, and so on. They have to make sure that all of the jobs are executed properly, so the company runs smoothly and makes a profit. Leadership is a little more nebulous and subjective. It involves inspiring people in addition to creating a working environment that fosters contributions. A manager can assist you with your work, but a leader instills in you a desire to do your finest work at all times.

Can you be a good manager and not be a good leader? Absolutely. For example, Seth makes sure everyone is doing their job, processes all the paperwork, keeps the office organized, and meets deadlines. His division completes every assignment on time; employees get their jobs done. He talks to employees when something needs to be communicated. However, there is no vision for the future, no feeling of cohesiveness or belonging to the company. He does not share goals or dreams. Employees are not particularly inspired to work longer hours or to accomplish tasks differently. Seth manages employees well, and the work gets done. He does not, however, encourage or empower employees to excel.

Can you be a good leader and not be a good manager? Absolutely. For example, LaQuisha is perceived as a visionary. She consistently communicates to employees what is going well and what needs to be improved. She shares this information in a way that inspires them to work harder and to take pride in what they do. When she talks, employees listen. When employees talk to her, she gives them 100% of her attention. The morale in the division is high, and LaQuisha inspires everyone to do their jobs well. Her employees wake up each morning excited to go to work, and they take great pride in being a part of her division of the company. However, LaQuisha cannot keep up with her daily paperwork. Reports are often received late. Employees get to a meeting room, and essential elements are missing. The meeting can't begin until someone finds the necessary supplies and equipment. Valuable time is lost because of poor management skills.

In either scenario, workers may step in and cover the shortcomings of their bosses. However, it is far more likely that employees will step in and cover for LaQuisha's missing managerial skills (slipping her a reminder before the meeting about what needs to be done, reminding her of deadlines, etc.) because she inspires people to do more to make the company successful and to share in corporate success as a team member.

If you can develop managerial and leadership skills, you will be a valuable asset to any company. Very few business professionals have developed both of these skills extremely well. Management skills are easier to demonstrate than leadership skills because the perception of colleagues is a dominant component of leadership. You may perceive yourself as a leader, but the reality is that the perceptions of others will be more important in determining whether you are assigned a leadership position. You can only lead if others recognize your power and support you.

Examine the visual representation of management skills depicted in this graphic by F. John Reh (2019).

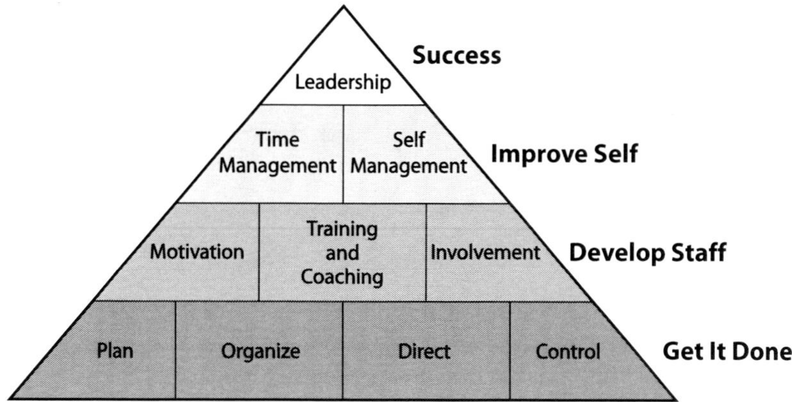

As you can see, leadership is possible after you truly master a number of other communication skills.

Do you think the order of improving self and developing staff should be switched? Explain your reasons why or why not.

Brief Overview of Leadership Theories

One of the first leadership theories, the **trait approach**, can be summarized in one phrase: leaders are born not made. The theory asserted that certain personality types will be leaders, others won't. Leadership characteristics cannot be learned. Good leaders are decisive, intelligent, and responsible; they take initiative and have excellent communication skills. The trait approach dealt exclusively with traits of the leader and did not consider the needs of followers.

Other theorists realized that there wasn't a "one model fits all" explanation of leadership. They suggested there were styles of leadership: authoritarian, democratic, and laissez-faire. The idea was that each style should be used in situations that required that type of leadership. **Authoritarian** leaders make decisions and make sure the group follows them. Today you might find the authoritarian leadership theory labeled as "directive leadership style." Authoritarian leaders are necessary when followers are not skilled or informed or lack maturity to complete a task.

REALITY ☑

Where are we likely to find authoritarian leaders?

Democratic leadership is quite different from authoritarian leadership. A democratic leader solicits information from followers, taking people's needs into consideration when making decisions. Today you might find democratic leadership labeled as "consultative leadership style" or "participative leadership style."

REALITY ☑

In which situations is the democratic leadership style most effective?

Laissez-faire leadership is a "hands off" style. In this model, a leader allows followers to govern themselves with very little input or direction. Today you might find laissez-faire leadership labeled as "delegative leadership style." Laissez-faire leadership works if the followers are highly skilled, informed and motivated. They don't need someone micromanaging them.

REALITY ☑

Identify laissez-faire leaders in business or politics.

As leadership theories evolved, theorists began to see the value in understanding the needs of the employees/followers that leaders were trying to inspire. Situational theories soon emerged where leaders were expected to take into account motivational theories that might inspire their followers to perform better. Leaders were expected to use different styles based on the specific situations before them.

In other words, the best leader for most discussion/task groups is going to be the one who is flexible. There are times when the leader needs to observe and listen while colleagues run with an idea. At other times, colleagues may be unmotivated, and the leader should move immediately into an authoritarian mode, directing people. A democratic approach works well most of the time in discussion/task groups because the leader is constantly soliciting ideas and synthesizing feedback. However, if your colleagues reach an impasse during a discussion, you may need to become authoritarian and tell everyone what they need to do so time isn't wasted. A laissez-faire leader might be extremely effective for motivated workers who know what they are doing. As a leader, you will need to finesse your skills so you can communicate appropriately to those around you. It is important to move out of your normal comfort zone when dealing with others, especially if you primarily rely on only one of these styles. As a leader, you need to be fair to everyone and use the appropriate leadership style for the situation. If you communicate caring about the success and well-being of others, you are more likely to lead an effective team.

Transactional Leadership and Transformational Leadership

James MacGregor Burns (1978) introduced a new perspective on leadership. He compared traditional leadership, which he called *transactional*, with a more complex and potent style that he called *transformational* (Johnson and Hackman, 2018). **Transactional leadership**, as implied by its label, involves exchanging rewards for desirable outcomes. The leader tells you what needs to be done and rewards you for doing it. The tricky part is that what each individual considers to be a reward will vary. Baby boomers typically enjoy monetary rewards whereas millennials prefer time off. In addition, specific colleagues within the same demographic prefer different things. Transactional leadership essentially maintains the status quo. Good performance is rewarded; poor performance is corrected.

Burns believed that **transformational leadership** was both empowering and inspirational, creating more than a mere exchange. Many researchers have studied leaders to identify common characteristics of transformational leadership. "The characteristics of transformational leaders identified by all of these researchers are strikingly similar. Five primary characteristics appear, in one form or another, in all of the classification systems dealing with extraordinary leaders" (Johnson and Hackman, 2018, p. 110). The five characteristics are:

- creative,
- interactive,
- visionary,
- empowering, and
- passionate.

Since transformational leadership can convert followers into leaders, these characteristics permeate transformed groups and organizations.

While exploring the concepts of leadership, you may encounter additional terms. All of the theories developed attempt to explain why some people are successful in motivating others to accomplish a task and other people are not. We feel strongly that exemplary communication skills are integral to any leadership style.

- Max Weber wrote about charisma and leaders in the early twentieth century (Johnson and Hackman, 2018). **Charismatic leadership** occurs when a leader has extraordinary talents, a radical vision for solving a crisis, and followers who perceive the leader's capabilities.
- **Transformational leaders** can communicate a vision to followers—a concise description of the direction in which a group or organization is headed. The vision attracts commitment and energizes people; it creates meaning for followers; it establishes a standard of excellence; and it bridges the present and future (Johnson and Hackman, 2018).
- **Servant leadership** is a new buzzword in leadership theory. A servant leader uses the same techniques outlined in transformational leadership. The difference is that the leader uses those techniques to serve followers.

If you walk around telling people you are a servant leader, then you probably aren't. Servant leadership, like credibility, is a receiver-oriented phenomenon. It is a title bestowed on a leader by followers. They decide if someone is a servant leader based on their experiences.

- **Facilitative leadership** involves gathering information from the team to create shared knowledge. However, when you ask for input, you should let your group know what you will do with it: Will you do what they determine is right as a group? Will you consider the information and then inform the group what you have decided based on their input? Being honest and up-front is important with facilitative leadership.
- **Compassionate leadership** has emerged as another leadership style. "To be great, leaders must have the necessary empathy to inspire understanding and knowledge in team members. Empathy is key. Empathy begins with taking an understanding of life from the experience and perception of another" (Campbell, 2018). Compassionate leaders are kind and caring.

Characteristics of Good Leaders

The following are some of the characteristics of effective leaders (Hasan, 2019).

- Good communicator
- Decision-making capabilities
- Ability to delegate and to empower others
- Creative and innovative
- Visionary
- Resilient
- Confident
- Inspirational
- Authentic
- Possessing emotional intelligence
- Empathetic
- Committed and passionate
- Accountable
- Honest
- Humble

How many of these characteristics do you possess? Since self-assessment is central to leadership development, you may want to look on the internet for self-assessment exercises related to leadership concepts to build your weaker skills. For example, motivation to lead (www.mindtools.com); locus of control, power profile, goal setting, and emotional IQ (www.queendom.com); type A/B personality (testyourselfpsychtests.com) to name just a few. Many of these sites offer a free "snapshot" report with no obligation to purchase the full results.

Peter Drucker, one of the most highly regarded experts on management principles, details the following traits for the ideal leader (Krames, 2008, p. 135).

- Possesses character and courage
- Creates a clear mission
- Instills loyalty
- Focuses on strength
- Does not fear strong subordinates
- Is consistent
- Develops tomorrow's leaders

Again, how do you measure up on this list of traits? What kind of activities or behaviors could you practice to enhance your skills? Can all of these skills be cultivated? At what age? Is there a limit to acquiring new skills? An individual can improve certain skills, which enhances confidence for a business career, but can a totally introverted individual who lacks self-confidence transform into a leader? There is no clear answer to the question, and opinions vary dramatically. However, if you feel you are missing some of the skills necessary for leadership, you can certainly work to improve any weakness. Identify the personal skills that need improvement, and then read about and develop strategies to strengthen deficiencies. Personal commitment and constant practice help you perfect your skills—and increase your potential for employment.

What Sets a Good Leader Apart from the Rest?

Have you experienced examples of poor leadership in the following areas: teaching, coaching, supervising, etc.? If so, let's look at some of the qualities that separate mediocre leaders from the truly inspirational ones.

Good leaders recognize the contributions of associates. Their recognition heightens commitment to group goals and maintains motivation to contribute ideas and time. Employee contributions deserve acknowledgement, and exceptional contributions merit special praise. Leaders can set an example for mutual supportiveness by being generous with praise that calls attention to the good work of various individuals. Sincere recognition shared with employees strengthens the sense of caring and pride in the organization. Respect for the contributions of others enhances self-respect (Young et al., 2021).

Excellent leaders are people who are not afraid to hire smart, articulate employees. Some individuals in corporate America are threatened by people who might outperform them. They will often choose a lesser qualified person to fill an opening or promotion. As noted above, Peter Drucker believed that good leaders don't fear strong subordinates. In our own department we were recently fortunate enough to hire a candidate who knows far more about communicating through modern technology channels than we do. She is an expert blogger and does research in interpersonal communication via various technology channels. We could feel threatened by her knowledge, but we don't. We are thrilled to have someone with those skills and knowledge join our department. Individuals who hire a lesser qualified candidate because they are insecure and want to be perceived as the most knowledgeable are actually quite foolish. Poor managers deflate morale and work quality.

Genuine caring about employees and the company is another essential quality for leaders. You'll know instantly when you visit companies with caring leaders. For example, they may take time to create an environment that communicates their attention to the needs of employees—providing a clean and safe working space; furnishing new technology and supplies to help employees be more productive; supplying extras (nap pods, breastfeeding stations, exercise areas, healthy snacks). One organization we know keeps a stock of organic granola bars and snacks in the break room for its employees and provides a yoga space for them to de-stress. Others provide on-site day care and meals. These types of perks may seem unrelated to the work of the organization, but they send a message to employees that they are the driving force of the enterprise.

Leaders can also promote a caring image by managing communication effectively: keeping employees informed about company policies and explaining the nuances, acknowledging achievement via a personal note or formal announcement, responding to questions and criticisms immediately and with a professional and receptive tone. Many of these items may seem “little,” but attention to detail keeps employees up-to-date and comfortable with a leader. So often, when change is taking place, employees are kept in the dark. Even a brief note—“We don’t have any new information this week, but we’ll update you as soon as possible”—can help keep employee morale high. Timely communication makes employees feel like the leader cares about them. It also minimizes rumors and lessens the chances that employees will become suspicious of the organization itself. A leader’s nonverbal communication should also promote caring, whether it is eye contact when communicating or the fact that they are the first people in the office in the morning and the last to leave at night. A leader sets the tone for everyone’s behavior.

Sadly, it is much easier to identify a poor leader than a good one. The early years of your working life should be spent observing the actions of others as well as listening to what is said and then analyzing the follow-through of everyone around you. Your early observation skills can assist you tremendously in figuring out how communication works or doesn’t work in various situations. Life experience makes you a better employee and a potential leader because you’ve analyzed the successes and mistakes of others to develop your own professional persona. If you have the opportunity to work with a remarkable leader, consider yourself fortunate—and let that person know you value the experience. It takes a lot of work and some special personal characteristics to be truly effective as a role model and motivational as a leader.

Final Thoughts

Decision making, problem solving, management, and leadership may seem like responsibilities for higher level positions as you begin your career. However, problem solving is an essential professional skill. You will develop problem-solving skills as you participate in groups assigned a task to help the organization function more effectively. The reflective-thinking process is one problem-solving model. If you can streamline a procedure, work effectively with difficult people, or recommend a new idea that makes money for the company, people will recognize you as a problem solver—perhaps even the “glue” holding the company together.

The more you work, the greater the opportunity to expand all of your skills—as long as you listen attentively, observe those around you, and evaluate your own performance honestly. Your observations will help you decide what leadership style works best in a specific situation. You will learn management skills such as time management, organization, and how to motivate others. Confidence in your abilities improves as you demonstrate your value to others.

It will take you a while to be promoted into a position of responsibility, so you can demonstrate your management and leadership skills. Until that moment occurs, you have the opportunity each day to project a positive attitude, a strong work ethic, excellent communication skills, knowledge of new technologies, an ethical approach to life, and an optimistic outlook about the future. After all, aren't these the qualities of good managers and leaders? It is easier to become a manager/leader if you exhibit to others that you already possess valuable skills as a novice in the organization. Project professionalism from the moment you begin a career, and your career path should be satisfactory and rewarding.

Key Terms

Authoritarian leadership
Brainstorming
Charismatic leadership
Compromise
Consensus
Criteria
Delphi technique
Democratic leadership
Facilitative leadership
Laissez-faire leadership
Leader mandate
Leaders
Managers
Nominal group technique
Reflective-thinking process
Servant leadership
Trait approach
Transactional leadership
Transformational leadership
Vote

Exercises

1. Describe the management style of someone in the workplace whom you admire.
2. Analyze an experience where you completed a project with consensus. How did you feel about the final decision?

3. Describe which problem-solving method you use a majority of the time.
4. How do you react to being told what to do by an authority figure? Why?
5. What do you perceive to be the greatest institutional problem at your school? Discuss pros and cons of each decision-making style in eliminating the problem.
6. Discuss a teacher who possesses the best management/leadership skills and why.

CHAPTER
NINE

Presentational Speaking

GOALS

- Understand the importance of selecting a purpose, topic, key, goal, and thesis
- Learn the importance of researching, organizing, and outlining
- List the parts of an informative presentation
- Differentiate among the persuasive structures
- Compare and contrast the different types of group presentations
- Identify effective elements of practice and delivery
- Construct an effective presentation

There is a good chance that you will be asked to make a presentation at some point during your career. Although you may have wondered why an oral communication course was necessary during your academic studies, you will use those skills daily throughout a professional career. Whenever you make a presentation, it is important to remember that your goal is to reach a target audience. For example, when speaking with business colleagues, you do not generally need to define specialized terms since the audience is familiar with the terminology. However, an audience of laypeople outside your organization would have a different set of communication expectations. Memorable speakers know their audience for the presentation—

whether subordinates, upper management, the board of trustees, or the general public. Business colleagues will pay close attention to the structure of a presentation. Time is valuable, so your ability to cover a topic efficiently, use technology effectively to enhance the presentation, and present the necessary information logically, concisely, and memorably is important. Each presentation is an opportunity to demonstrate that you are an invaluable asset to the organization.

Colleagues want to work with a professional person rather than someone who makes obvious mistakes in speaking and writing. These mistakes are easy to document and record in a performance evaluation. Poor performance restricts your career potential. If your goal at the outset of your career is to become a manager or run your own business, then you need to project a competent, polished image to colleagues.

Colleagues and staff see and hear your conversational style every day as you interact with them. Although some individuals consider the time spent with colleagues and clients as "social" conversation, every conversation contributes to how others ultimately perceive you. The personal qualities you project as you speak give others the opportunity to envision a future for you at a higher level in the company. For example, whenever you are given time to speak to your boss or supervisor, it is critical to be clear and concise in delivering your idea(s) while paying close attention to the time you were given for the meeting. If your boss gives you five minutes, make sure you can state your idea(s) in five minutes or less. Supervisors are quite busy, and they appreciate employees who do not waste their time. Therefore, organize your thoughts properly before talking to a superior.

As you advance in responsibility, you may have to present specific ideas and reports to one person (your boss), a few people (colleagues), or a group (a corporate division). The general purpose of a presentation is usually to inform or to persuade. There are some presentations that combine these two purposes. Therefore, it is useful to select an appropriate strategy for your remarks, so they are easily understood by the listener(s).

To design an effective business presentation, use the following procedure:

1. choose your general purpose: informative or persuasive;
2. confirm your topic;

3. prepare your key, goal, and thesis;
4. research, organize, and outline;
5. practice and delivery.

Choose Your Purpose

It is important for a speaker to consider carefully the purpose of the presentation. Is it informative or persuasive? For example, you may be explaining a new online payroll system to the rest of your colleagues. The purpose of the presentation would be **informative speaking** because you are simply providing information to everyone. **Persuasive speaking** occurs when your purpose (goal) is to get the audience to change an attitude, belief, value, or behavior. What if you need to submit a reorganization plan to the boss for making the division work more effectively? You have to persuade her that your plan is best for your division. Or, you may need to persuade colleagues to stop doing personal business on company time. If you are asked to convey information about a new policy, it may be more complicated to determine your purpose. Are you simply giving information about the policy, or are you expected to persuade employees to embrace it? Or is it a mixture of both? Knowing your purpose helps you shape your information in the most dynamic, effective way.

Confirm Your Topic

Normally, when someone asks you to speak, they also provide the topic. A supervisor may ask you to present an update on a current project at the weekly meeting or to teach colleagues about a new technical program. Basically, these are informative presentations. If you are a manager, there may be corporate news to share with colleagues weekly. No matter what the topic is, your first responsibility is to analyze two elements: (1) is the topic specific enough to present all of the information? and (2) will the information you select fit into the time constraints?

Time is of the utmost importance to every listener. Colleagues have numerous work-related duties and usually have a packed daily routine. Americans live in a monochronic culture where everything runs by the clock. Therefore, individuals are extremely fussy about deadlines and time limits. Professionals get intensely annoyed when someone abuses their time, which could have been spent addressing other demands. Make sure to narrow a topic enough to deliver all of the necessary information within the time limit.

REALITY ☑

Culture is changing; gone are the days of telling a personal story in a speech that is somewhat unrelated to the topic. Remember, a speech is about the needs of audience members—what relates to them and what is relevant to them. If you begin by telling a story about the birth of a child, your time in college, etc., the only reaction is #NobodyCares.

Prepare Your Key, Goal, and Thesis

If you have taken a basic oral communication or public speaking class, the organizational elements of key, goal, and thesis should sound familiar. These three elements help you focus so that the information in your presentation possesses continuity.

Key

The **key** is the connection among the main points in your presentation. Types of keys include: *steps, aspects, characteristics, parts, areas,* or *reasons*. Without an organizing, connective thread, your presentation is likely to wander and end up as "everything you ever wanted to know about x," or it will be so disjointed that people won't understand what you are talking about.

REALITY ☑

An exception to this rule would be if you are giving a "highlights" speech. For instance at the beginning of an academic year, a university president might begin the semester with a "For your information" presentation where includes numerous unrelated topics that are important for everyone to know.

For a polished informative presentation, you need a key. Once you know whether you are speaking about *steps* in a process, or *characteristics* of an environment, or *events* in a campaign, or *aspects* of a problem, it is easier to connect the main points. For example, let's say your human resources department just determined that there is not enough accountability in the question-asking process of interviewing. They have decided to add three new steps to the hiring procedure. Your key is "steps," and each of your main points will explain one of those steps.

Goal

The goal is what you want as an end result of the presentation. Remember that a presentation is about gaining a specific audience response. We like the following goal format for informative speaking:

> After my presentation, I want my employees/colleagues to understand that . . . (basic information).

In the human resources assignment example, the goal would be:

> After my presentation, I want my employees/colleagues to understand that there are three new steps in the hiring policy.

The **goal** includes the **general purpose** (an informative presentation) and the **specific purpose** (explaining the three steps). You are not persuading employees to embrace the policy; you are simply informing them about a new policy and how it works.

PREPARING THE GOAL FOR PERSUASIVE SPEAKING

Persuasion deals with changing the attitudes, beliefs, values or actions of audience members. As you plan your corporate persuasive presentation, whether it is interpersonal or in a public speaking setting, it is important that you clearly establish for yourself what you want to accomplish. Are you trying to convince (change an attitude, value, or belief), reinforce (strengthen an attitude, value, or belief) or actuate (change an action). We like the following formats:

> After my presentation, I want my employees/colleagues to believe that . . .

> After my presentation, I want my employees/colleagues to believe more strongly that . . .

> After my presentation, I want my employees/colleagues to . . .

Examples:

After my presentation, I want my employees/colleagues to **believe that** our security team is top notch. (Audience currently doesn't believe this)

After my presentation, I want my employees/colleagues to **believe more strongly that** management will retain employees in the United States while it expands global operations. (Audience currently believes this)

After my presentation, I want my employees/colleagues **to recycle all paper products and aluminum cans.** (Audience currently is receptive to the idea—no need to convince—but needs to be motivated to change behavior).

Thesis

The **thesis** for the informative speech includes the main points in the presentation. This would read:

After my presentation, I want my employees/colleagues to understand that the three new steps in the hiring policy are approval of phone interview questions, approval of on-site interview questions, and approval of conversational topics for meals.

Once you have your key, goals, and thesis for the informative speech you can begin to construct its outline.

Research, Organize, and Outline

By the time you are searching for a job, you should have had either high school or college classes that taught you how to gather appropriate research materials. We won't review that process here but urge you to use those skills to acquire the facts and information necessary to support your presentation. The most up-to-date information is important for credibility in a presentation.

You also should have learned how to organize your material into an outline. You should be familiar with the basic organizing scheme of dividing your topic into major ideas with supporting material; that each statement under any main point should support that point. If you don't understand how to do this, it is time to get some outside

Ethical Encounter

You are applying the final touches to a presentation due tomorrow. You realize that you did not write down an important citation. Can you just leave it out? Make it up? What should you do?

instruction. We will spend some time talking about basic speech structures for outlining a presentation. Whether you have five minutes or eight hours to present, this is a tried and true structure for presenting information.

The Informative Structure

Any informative speech consists of an introduction, body, and conclusion. Speakers often compose the body of the speech before writing the introduction and conclusion.

INTRODUCTION

The introduction should include all of the following.

- *Attention-getting device:* Prepare the audience to listen. Quotations, striking statements, current events, visual aids, or illustrations give momentum to your speech.
- *Relate to audience:* Audiences won't listen if they don't understand why the information is relevant to them.
- *Credibility:* Establish why you are the one who should be talking about this topic. If you have a title, this step is not necessary ("Here is Trevor Stravinsky, the Vice President of Finance, to give us an update on the budget situation.") If you don't have a relevant title and are introduced to give a training session or to run a seminar, state your credentials.
- *Preview:* Share your topic with the audience (reveal your main points). A simple statement such as "Today's presentation will cover X, Y, and Z" will suffice, but a clever transitional statement helps stimulate audience listening.

BODY

There are usually three or four main points with supporting material in this section. It is customary to state the most important point of the body first. Be sure you have effective transitions between each of the points.

CONCLUSION

The conclusion should include the following.

- *Review:* Remind the audience of the main points covered in the body of the speech.
- *Restate the relevance:* Reiterate why your information is important to your listeners.
- *Concluding statement:* Some business presentations require a formal concluding statement. On other occasions, simply thanking the audience for their attention may be sufficient.

This format should work for almost any informative presentation you would be asked to deliver in a business setting. The next section reviews persuasive formats.

> Remember to be flexible and adapt to the audience and occasion. For example, if you are the expert on your topic, there is no need to include a credibility statement.

The Persuasive Structure

There are a few basic persuasive structures—*statement of reasons, problem-solution,* and *Monroe's Motivated Sequence*—that you can employ depending on the purpose of your presentation. We will review each briefly.

STATEMENT OF REASONS

In a statement-of-reasons structure, a speaker reveals the persuasive claim at the beginning of the speech and then presents a number of reasons why the audience should accept it. Use this structure if you want to convince your audience to accept a claim. For example: "I want my employees to believe that it is in the company's best interest to freeze salary adjustments in order to: save jobs; benefit all employees over the long term; preserve current healthcare benefits."

Typically, the reasons are presented in order of strength. Each of the reasons needs to be fully documented with factual evidence. Each of these reasons would be a main point in the body of the speech.

PROBLEM-SOLUTION

A problem-solution structure is useful if you want to convince the audience someone should do something. In this structure, your main points are (1) the problem, (2) the solution, and (3) the advantages of the solution. For example, you are a manager at a company where employees are habitually late, and you want your administrator to believe that you require help to solve the problem. "I want my administrator to believe that employee lateness can be solved using a time clock system. (1) Employee lateness is costing the company time and money. (2) A time clock system would solve the lateness issue. (3) Time clocks are inexpensive and will result in more employee productivity."

This structure is essentially a policy claim. You want someone else to do something about the problem, and you are working hard to convince the administrator or administrative board that there is indeed a problem with an easy solution available. Your emphasis in this speech is convincing them the problem exists, and they can help solve it. In the next speech structure, Monroe's Motivated Sequence, the emphasis is on motivating your audience to embrace a solution—you want the employees/audience to do something immediately.

MONROE'S MOTIVATED SEQUENCE (MMS)

MMS is a five-part, action-oriented organizational pattern (German, 2017). This organizational pattern is appropriate when the audience is not opposed to your topic; audience members just lack the motivation to perform an action. You'll see that there is a similarity between this structure and the problem-solution structure. However, this structure is more complex than the previous ones because you are attempting to get the audience to take action rather than simply agree with you. You need to ignore the statement-of-reasons structure to be successful with MMS. You are no longer stating a claim and giving reasons why someone should do something. With MMS you must describe a problem the audience faces, and then motivate them to action.

I. Attention Step
(Use an effective attention-getting device here)

II. Need Statement

A. Make a definite, concise statement about the problem (avoid a circular argument).

B. Use one or more examples explaining and clarifying the problem. Be sure to include additional examples, statistical data, testimony, and other forms of support.

C. Show the extent and seriousness of the problem.

D. Make it clear that the problem affects the audience.

III. Satisfy the Need

A. State the action you want the audience to begin (or stop).

B. Explain your proposal thoroughly.

C. Demonstrate with reasoning how your proposed solution meets the need.

D. Refer to practical experience by supplying examples to prove the proposal has worked effectively where it has been tried.

E. Forestall opposition by anticipating and answering any objections that might be raised against this proposal.

IV. Visualize (choose 1 of the following)

A. Describe future conditions if the solution you propose is carried out.

B. Describe future conditions if your proposal is not carried out.

C. Use both the negative and positive potential results.

V. Request Action
(Tell the audience every detail they need to know in order to perform the action.)

Let's look at an example of a presentation using the MMS structure. For this example, the speaker is a manager whose goal is to motivate employees to save energy and reduce costs by powering down their computers at night and turning off lights when they leave their offices.

Attention step. You first need to get your audience's attention. The attention step in MMS is similar to the attention-getter in the informative speech. After hearing this step, the audience should say, "I want to listen!"

Showing the need. In this step you must convince the audience there is a problem that affects them. The first thing you do is state the problem; be clear and specific. To prove to your audience that this is indeed a problem, you will need to include lots of evidence in the form of supporting material. It is not enough just to say a problem exists—you must prove it. Obviously, some problems require more evidence than others. If you want to prove your audience is stressed, it might not take much convincing. However, if you want them to believe that energy is being wasted, you may need a lot more factual evidence and emotional appeal to accomplish your goal.

Be careful not to reveal your topic in this step. The idea is to convince your audience that they face an urgent problem (company costs are eating into profits). You will show them what to do about it in the next step (save energy). Note the problem is company costs. If you say the problem is that the employees don't power down computers, you are building a circular argument.

Don't forget to link the problem to your audience; they must believe immediately it is indeed their problem. Think about the commercials for starving children in the developing world. You know the problem exists, but how many of you send money to help? If you don't, chances are the reason you don't send money is that you don't feel connected to the problem. It is something that happens "over there" and doesn't affect you personally other than the fleeting emotion you may feel when you see the commercial. The commercial does not resonate sufficiently for you to take action.

So in this step, you would present the audience with data on the monthly cost of utility bills and how that cost affects their raises and company profits. They have to believe that this issue directly connects to them. If they think that the money is coming out of the CEO's pocket, they may not care as much.

Satisfying the need. You reveal your claim and tell the audience what it is you want them to do. There are five parts to this step.

- First, reveal the action you want them to perform in a clear and concise manner (power down computers at night and turn off lights as they leave the building).
- Second, you explain what it is you want them to do. In some speeches, you will need a lot of explanation. In others, you will not. For this speech, the explanation is simple.
- Third, explain how the action you want them to take solves the problem you outlined in the need step. You must use strong reasoning and factual support. You will have to provide calculations that show the overall savings their actions will have for their company.
- Fourth, present evidence that the solution has actually worked. You might use personal testimony, research studies, and citations by expert authorities to prove this point. What other companies have done this with success?
- Fifth, present information designed to meet anticipated objections. Keep in mind you can't persuade people if they are arguing with your claim in their minds. In this part of the satisfaction step, you need to refute any potential arguments the audience could be composing mentally. Here is where a thorough audience analysis comes in handy. You need to know *why* they aren't currently doing the action. They just don't think about it? Believe that it takes more energy to turn the computers and lights on and off than to leave them on? Each of these reasons necessitates a different angle. By the time you complete the satisfaction step, your audience should realize that executing your claim will solve the problem and that there are no obstacles to prevent them from doing so.

Visualization. In this step, you want to show the audience how their personal environment will be a better place if they perform the action you suggest. You can do this by describing how things will improve if they do the action, how things will worsen if they don't perform the action, or you can include elements of each. Show them the direct benefit they will enjoy by cooperating with the plan.

Requesting action. In this step, you motivate the audience to begin the action. You need to give them every detail they need in order to do so. You might give them a handout that prescribes the specific actions they should take. Or you can give audience members a Post-it® with the necessary information in an easy-to-read list and encourage them to attach it to their computer screen as a simple reminder. This section must end with a strong concluding statement.

Selecting a Structure for Miscellaneous Presentations

There are multiple situations where it may not be immediately clear whether you should use informative or persuasive structures. In these situations, always think about your purpose as you develop your remarks. Listed below are examples of presentations you might be asked to give.

BUSINESS PITCH

A business pitch might be informative, or you might use any of the three basic persuasive organizational strategies adapted for your purpose. For example, let's say you have to pitch an idea to the boss. Some textbooks have "pitch outlines," but what is the purpose of your pitch? If it is to convince the boss that the company is losing money through employee theft, then you may want a statement-of-reasons structure. If it is to propose a solution to that problem, but the boss doesn't know about it, you may want a problem-solution structure. Use the MMS when the pitch is being made to an audience that already embraces or has little opposition to the idea but needs motivation to act on it.

CRISIS COMMUNICATION

A crisis befalls your company. What structure do you use for your presentation? It depends on your audience and your purpose. Are you communicating to the employees or the public? Is it strictly informational (there will be no bonus checks this quarter) or persuasive (convincing the public to maintain confidence in your company after an environmental disaster, corporate scandal, etc.)? Once you know your purpose for communicating, you can select the appropriate structure and craft your presentation to fit the occasion.

COMMUNICATING GOOD/BAD NEWS

Are you simply informing audience members of a decision or event that impacts them in a positive or negative way, or do you need to go a step further and shape their reaction to the news?

TRAINING SPEECH

Is there only the element of giving information to an audience, or are you expected to persuade the audience to adopt the new software, incorporate a new procedure, and so forth? You may choose a mixture of the above structures.

COMMEMORATIVE SPEECH

You may have to give a commemorative speech for a retirement, a funeral, corporate anniversary, or another occasion. For such occasions, you will probably use a hybrid of an informative speech with elements of persuasion to reinforce the fundamental theme of the presentation. The audience already knows the person or company; they should be happy (in the case of celebration) or sad (in the case of death) or congratulatory (in the case of retirement). Decide on the most relevant points to highlight for the commemorative speech and then personalize your remarks. You need to present fascinating details about the person or company that connect and resonate with everyone in attendance. The creative use of language and examples in this type of speech make it memorable for the audience. A commemorative speech is challenging and quite different from other presentations you make as a professional.

Always remember that you may need to finesse whatever structure you select based on the specific situation. For instance, if we want our boss to make a change because morale is low, chances are good he already knows that, so we don't have to delve heavily into the need step of the MMS. However, if we gave that presentation to the president of our company, she may need to be convinced that low morale is a problem, so we would include that step. Sometimes your audience already knows about the problem, in which case you modify your problem-solution structure to simply mention the problem and then devote the bulk of your time to detailing a creative solution for the audience.

Structure and Organization of Group Presentations

Numerous group presentations rely on the presentational structures mentioned above. We will discuss four types of **group presentations**: symposium, roundtables, panels, and forums.

SYMPOSIUM

The symposium refers to a presentation where a select group of people is visible in front of an audience, and each person gives a portion of a prepared speech. This presentation should include an introduction, a conclusion, and transitions between the speakers. Each speech lasts approximately the same amount of time, and the transitions between speakers are seamless. The audience perceives a unified, factual, and well-rehearsed message. The information discussed earlier on informative and persuasive speech structures apply to a symposium presentation.

A group needs to shape the entire presentation with participants presenting a main point or section. In a group of five, one person might give the introduction, the next three people would each give information about a specific main point, and the fifth speaker would conclude the presentation. Dividing organizational responsibilities in this manner makes it easy for the audience to listen and comprehend content.

ROUNDTABLE

The roundtable discussion consists of a moderator and group members having an actual discussion. The moderator can be a group member or can be someone from outside the group. In a symposium, members prepare their remarks on a portion of a topic; in a roundtable, participants must be prepared to discuss every aspect of the topic. A roundtable discussion is similar to a polite, informal discussion among knowledgeable peers without an audience. This is a popular television format for journalists discussing topics of national interest (in this case, there is an audience, of course, but not in the studio. The audience is eavesdropping on the discussion). A roundtable discussion may be used for focus-group research where there is a set of prepared questions and a moderator who leads the discussion. Focus-group research is designed to obtain information from a group of people concerning their opinions or knowledge on a particular topic or product. They are commonly used for market research and for public opinion polls.

PANEL

A panel discussion is basically a roundtable discussion made up of expert panelists; the discussion takes place in front of an audience. Participants must be fully informed on the topic. The group uses a moderator to keep the discussion moving, usually with preplanned discussion points and within a specific time limit. Some panel discussions allow questions from the audience near the conclusion of a presentation.

FORUM

Forum discussions directly involve the audience. Any talk show that you see usually has a forum component—the host asks the audience for input or questions. You can combine a forum with any of the group presentations mentioned earlier. For example, you may find a presentation advertised as a symposium/forum, meaning there will be a prepared presentation given by multiple people followed by questions from the audience. Panel/forums do the same thing. Town hall meetings are one example of forums. Political campaigns use town hall meetings, as do numerous organizations and universities.

TIPS FOR GROUP PRESENTATIONS

There are numerous tips that can make your presentation outstanding.

- Every member should be in **professional attire and dressed in similar colors**. Dressing alike has definite psychological advantages because your group appears united. For example, notice how many political candidates use red, white, and blue in their attire to be perceived as patriotic. Be aware of your nonverbals throughout a group presentation. If every presenter is in front of the audience, it is essential that the nonverbal behavior of every member demonstrates attention riveted on the speaker. As soon as members doodle, talk to one another, or fidget, they compromise the credibility of the entire group for an audience. If presenters can't pay attention to their own colleagues, why should the audience?
- Be sure to **practice** the presentation as much as possible. Many groups have each member design a portion of a presentation. However, if you don't rehearse the presentation as a team, you may make the mistake of more than one member communicating identical information without additional insights. The audience notices the lack of organization immediately. Without rehearsal, the verbal and physical transitions from one member to the next may not look or sound polished. One per-

son may transition well to the next speaker, but another does not. Team members must always look and sound as though they worked together. It is extremely difficult to prepare separately and make a presentation look like a coordinated project. A post-analysis critique is essential after each rehearsal. If members just present their portion of the material and others say "great job," no one really listened critically for the flaws in the presentations. Self-criticism improves group confidence in the ultimate presentation before the audience. Just because you deliver information does not mean it will be received; you must practice so the audience receives your very best efforts.

- It is useful to **review and practice in the actual space** where the group will be presenting. Learn where the electrical outlets are located, the technology available to you, and the best way to use the space. Reviewing and rehearsing help you avoid mistakes during the actual presentation. Sometimes team members find they have differing definitions of professional attire due to their division's dress requirements. It is important to appear unified nonverbally. Business colleagues accept these nonverbal differences in attire, but the general public may wonder why one presenter is wearing khakis and a sport shirt, while the others are in suits and ties. Do your best to keep the attention of an audience on what you are saying and doing; eliminate distracting elements.
- Make sure to **check the research**. Preparation is critical for every presentation you make. As you research a topic, question all of the facts you gather and double check them to make sure they are accurate. Make sure your research is exhaustive; don't rely on notes you made months or years earlier. If you overlook new research that contradicts a point you are making, your presentation is compromised. The time you spend researching material and organizing it keeps you focused and calm. Confidence in the material you put together, both written and visual, gives you the psychological edge you need to speak eloquently—whether with colleagues, clients, bosses, or the general public.

Visual Aids

Visuals are an important part of good presentational speaking. Use a ***visual aid*** whenever you wish to clarify a concept or enhance the understanding of audience members. Some people need a visual to back up the auditory message they hear—they need to see what you are talking about to understand. Presentational platforms (PowerPoint, Prezi, Google Slides, etc.), DVDs, objects, and streaming video are some of the many choices available to help engage listeners. When choosing a visual, think about which concepts in your speech may be hard for the audience to understand without seeing something. A good general rule is to make sure your visuals do not take any more than 5 percent of your total speaking time.

REALITY ☑

Many people talk about designing a PowerPoint presentation. This is the wrong orientation. You design slides as a visual aid—only use them if they help to reinforce the content. A business presentation does not need to be a "slide show."

You should always rehearse all visual segments of a speech to make sure your oral transitions in and out of the visuals are as smooth as possible—as well as making sure you know how to use the technology itself. Nothing is worse than watching speakers attempt to use a piece of unfamiliar equipment—discovering too late that they do not know how to turn it on or how to load their information.

Practice and Delivery

Effective delivery of a presentation is an obstacle for some speakers. It takes patience, practice, and confidence to translate written words and thoughts into a personal vocal style. Your voice helps a prepared message resonate with listeners; excellent oral skills make you stand out professionally.

Practice

The old saying, "Practice makes perfect," is absolutely true. You should take the time to rehearse every presentation you make multiple times and with a timer. Articulating the words out loud help you to hear and correct awkward phrasing of words. The more you rehearse, the greater the chance that the words in your speech will flow easily when facing an audience. No one will ever know how long it took you to prepare a good presentation—nor do they care. The most effective presentations often appear effortless to an audience. In addition to practicing pronunciations and phrasing, you need the presentation to fit the time limit you are given. Therefore, time each practice session. An audience appreciates the fact you finished within the time limit, because they need to return to the daily demands of their schedule and do not want to walk out while you go overtime due to poor planning.

Our favorite student remark is "I don't know what happened to my presentation. I was so eloquent in my mind!" Practice out loud.

Remember, an audience of business professionals expects a polished presentation. There are no "do-overs" in the corporate world.

Delivery

There are three basic business delivery styles: impromptu, manuscript, and extemporaneous. The **impromptu** style (unprepared, "off the cuff") is used daily to communicate with colleagues. A great deal of business discourse doesn't require the sequential development of an idea or a detailed response to a question. However, conversations with fellow employees or supervisors occasionally require more detailed explanations or an overview of a procedure. These moments test your ability to mentally organize a logical response using a standard verbal outline: introduction, body, and conclusion. These detailed impromptu answers can be challenging if you aren't prepared to share your expertise confidently with others.

A **manuscript** style is self-explanatory. A presentation is read from a prepared script. Although some disciplines and professional areas use this style, it is not an engaging performance style for the audience. Professionals know how to read and would prefer to listen to presenters highlight and explain key points only. Audience members can take a copy of the presentation back to their offices to read or access it on their computers. Audiences want eye contact from a speaker and a chance to get a sense of their personality in a "live" or webinar situation; reading from a manuscript does not provide that immediacy. Politicians, news professionals, and corporate CEOs use a teleprompter to make the manuscript style acceptable. In these presentations, audiences do not object to a read speech because a teleprompter creates the illusion that a speaker is looking at them during the presentation. The technology makes reading a presentation more acceptable because it appears spontaneous.

The **extemporaneous** style is conversational speaking. It makes listeners feel as though they are important to you because you talk *to* them, not *at* them. Many presenters find this method of speaking slightly uncomfortable because they don't have a manuscript in front of them—only a few notes. The extemporaneous style requires the presenter to remain fully engaged with the topic and the delivery of the information to an audience throughout their performance. A topic outline or a few note cards becomes a guide for the entire speech. The speaker's mind and personality drive the material shared with listeners. An effective way to remain calm and vocally relaxed during an extemporaneous presentation is to imagine yourself holding a social conversation with the most influential, trusted person in your life—for example, a morning conversation over breakfast with your grandmother at the kitchen table. If you can think of a person in your life with whom you were emotionally comfortable while talking, this mental image can be useful during your professional career because it keeps your voice passionate and engaging.

A conversational speaking style is as natural and lively as you are when associating with family and friends. The important vocal qualities to use for stressing key words and ideas during a presentation are projection, articulation, rate, and inflection.

Projection is the physical energy behind your voice—it's used so you are heard in the back of the room; sometimes it's used to make a point. Fortunately, your voice is amplified through a microphone in the majority of business presentations, which eliminates the necessity of over projecting your voice and sounding forced. If an amplification system fails (which does happen) and you know how to project, you will be able to continue with your presentation without waiting for a technician to repair the malfunction. Transitioning smoothly after a failure in technology keeps the presentation moving and demonstrates clearly to an audience that you have experience in public performance.

If you are on a microphone, make sure not to over project. Simply use conversational speech.

Articulation is the proper formation and release of the sounds that make up a spoken language. Using "proper" speech should be the goal of all speakers. Many local dialects don't use properly articulated English sounds, or they modify those sounds. For example, many people drop word endings. Going fishing becomes "goin' fishin'." In other regional dialects, people drop the "t," "k," and "p" sounds. So, gift becomes "gif." A word like "fact" should actually be articulated as "fa-k-t," but some people drop the "t" sound and simply say "fak."

When you move into the business world, you may find that people will perceive you to be uneducated or incompetent if you use the local dialect from the region in which you were raised. For instance, some people from the town of Scranton, Pennsylvania, drop the "t" and say they are from "Scran-in." While that pronunciation is usually acceptable locally, people in other parts of the country would question why someone pronounces the name of their own hometown incorrectly. It is your job as a speaker to monitor your sounds and to correct any errors from your local dialect.

Proper articulation relates to proper ***pronunciation*** as well. Pronunciation is the accepted sound of a word according to the dictionary. A word like "get" is often pronounced "git." People say "you are taking me for granite" instead of "for granted." "Ask" in urban speech is pronounced "aks" or "axe." Some people refer to "shtrength" rather than "strength."

You may think a discussion of articulation and pronunciation is mundane; however, proper speech is critical to your personal brand and essential to make your message clear to a diverse audience. People who speak well stand out in everyday conversation.

Look up "Commonly mispronounced word list" on the internet. How many errors are you making?

Rate refers not only to the speed or slowness of articulation but also to the length of time the vowels within syllables are used to emphasize a point. Stretching a vowel sound catches the listener's attention because the sound of the word is suddenly unusual. Southern speech in the United States uses vowel blends within words, which most audiences find pleasing and charming.

Inflection is the pitch range of your voice. It adds aural interest to a presentation because the higher and lower pitches of voice can emphasize words and phrases in a subtle way. Some presenters attempt to control their presentation style so much that they sound monotonous and repetitive in everything they say. However, a conversational style gives you the opportunity to connect with an audience as a "real" person, even though the information you are delivering may be quite formal. Your voice is as unique as you are, so use its full potential to establish a professional identity as well as credibility.

FINAL THOUGHTS

Every audience deserves an informed, poised, enthusiastic, and organized speaker. A thorough understanding of the purpose for your presentation guides your research and selection of the most effective structure to achieve your goal. Three elements—key, goal, and thesis—keep you focused as you prepare. Basic structures for persuasive presentations include statement of reasons, problem-solution, and Monroe's Motivated Sequence.

Speaking in the professional world is somewhat relaxing because you know the material well through work experience and expertise. The audience is usually internal, so everyone knows something about the topic and is eager to hear what you have to say. Since the audience is somewhat knowledgeable on the topic, your research must be accurate and up-to-date. Preparation and practice are the key elements to giving a solid presentation, whether informative, persuasive, crisis, commemorative, roundtable, or forum.

Presentational speaking is an excellent way to demonstrate your value to an employer. Whether you are presenting information by yourself or with a group of colleagues, your verbal skills, perceived personality, ability to integrate technology into your presentation, and professional demeanor are on display—work to make them memorable.

Key Terms

- Business pitch
- Commemorative speech
- Crisis communication
- Extemporaneous
- Forum
- General Purpose
- Goal
- Group presentation
- Impromptu
- Inflection
- Informative speaking
- Key
- Manuscript
- Monroe's Motivated Sequence
- Panel
- Persuasive speaking
- Problem-solution
- Projection
- Rate
- Roundtable
- Specific Purpose
- Symposium
- Thesis
- Training speech

Exercises

1. Analyze moments you do and don't enjoy while preparing and giving a presentation. Why?
2. Give a one-minute business pitch for a product.
3. Write a eulogy for yourself.
4. Give a commemorative speech (three to four minutes) for a high-school classmate.
5. Do a five-minute group presentation with your blog colleagues. Use some additional technical platforms as part of the presentation.

CHAPTER
TEN

Potentially Threatening or Uncomfortable Communication

GOALS

- Describe the eight types of conflict
- Explain how conflict can be useful or destructive
- Describe the five conflict/resolution styles
- Analyze when each conflict resolution style would be effective
- Explain the steps of the collaborating style
- Analyze if sexual harassment is occurring in certain situations
- Explain the concept of a performance review

CONFLICT IN THE WORKPLACE

We have stressed the importance of interpersonal communication skills throughout this book. However, interpersonal communication doesn't always go smoothly despite excellent verbal and nonverbal skills. Conflict is inevitable—whether due to corporate policies, corporate culture, diversity in the workplace, or personality conflicts.

Conflict occurs any time there is a disagreement between two or more people. Stephen Littlejohn and Kathy Domenici (2007) list six types of conflict.

- Data conflicts
- Interest conflicts
- Relationship conflicts
- Value conflicts
- Structural conflicts
- Moral conflicts

More recently, we've seen two additional categories.

- Serial conflicts
- Meta conflicts

Data conflicts are caused by a lack of information, misinformation, different views on what is relevant, different interpretations of data, and different assessments of procedures. **Interest conflicts** are the result of perceived competition or differences in procedural or psychological interests. **Relationship conflicts** are caused by strong emotions, misperceptions or stereotypes, poor communication, or repeated negative behavior. **Value conflicts** result from different criteria for evaluating ideas or disagreement over beliefs. **Structural conflicts** are caused by destructive interactions, unequal distribution of resources, unequal power, physical hindrances to cooperation, and time constraints. **Moral conflicts** result from differences of worldview or ideology (value differences are one aspect of moral conflict, which is more persistent and difficult to manage). We suffer from **serial conflicts** when we have the same conflict over and over again without any resolution (how many times have I said X!). And, finally, **meta conflict** moves the disagreement beyond a particular issue to a disagreement over whether or how to engage in conflict.

What types of conflicts do you encounter the most in the workplace? In your relationships?

Disagreements can involve a policy, an approach to a problem, a scheduling issue, workload, use of technology, use of language, behavior, interpersonal differences, and so on. In a diverse working environment, employees see issues in totally different ways, including ways to resolve problems. While many people think conflict is undesirable or bad, it is actually essential to any growing relationship. What is important is how you resolve conflict when it occurs. If you resolve it effectively, then you actually experienced a conflict that made something better.

Ineffective conflict resolution involves yelling and screaming, manipulating, issuing ultimatums, silence, walking out of the room, or refusing to discuss issues. While such behavior may seem unimaginable, it does occur in corporate America. These negative strategies leave participants feeling angry, used, scared, and/or frustrated.

If a boss or coworker starts screaming—try to remove yourself from the situation immediately.

Effective conflict resolution is comprised of spirited discussion, active inquiry, listening skills, critical thinking, and problem solving. The goal is to find a solution to the disagreement without creating animosity in a working relationship. If you are afraid of conflict, chances are that you have experienced ineffective conflict resolution in the past. People who engage in effective conflict resolution tend to enjoy working through their differences to reach an acceptable resolution. A healthy working relationship between two people must involve an environment where participants can feel comfortable in resolving a disagreement. Each person wants to feel that his or her ideas have value and that there can be a mutual resolution—rather than one person winning and the other person feeling left out.

The potential for conflict exists everywhere in daily communication—from little things like how offices will be set up or who will make the coffee to larger issues like how to reduce expenditures in a financial deficit. You can choose to escalate or de-escalate most conflicts once you identify them. The decision is yours. When we use ineffective strategies, we escalate the conflict. For example, if you mouth off to a colleague or superior, you may escalate a conflict tenfold in addition to shortening your tenure with the company. What other choices do you have? Thinking carefully about how to respond to someone and choosing the right words and vocal tone are skills you need to develop and use to de-escalate a conflict.

Conflict-Resolution Styles

In any interpersonal relationship, conflict is inevitable. Some people have a very negative connotation for the word "conflict." Conflict itself, however, is not bad. It simply means disagreement. However, if you handle the conflict or disagreement poorly, the result will be negative feelings for both individuals. Ralph Kilmann and Kenneth Thomas developed an assessment to measure a person's behavior in conflict situations. The Thomas-Kilmann Instrument (TKI) has been used for over 40 years by human resource departments to open discussions on difficult issues and to facilitate learning about how approaches to handling conflict affect personal, group, and organizational dynamics (Kilmann, 2015). More than 8 million copies of the instrument have been published in 12 languages.

Kilmann and Thomas (1977) suggest there are five styles of handling conflict. The five styles vary in the amount of assertiveness and cooperation necessary to find a solution.

- **Competing** involves assertive and uncooperative behavior. People using this style pursue personal concerns at the expense of others. The style is power oriented. When competing goes too far, it becomes **bullying**.
- **Accommodating** involves unassertive and cooperative behavior—the opposite of competing.
- **Avoiding** is both unassertive and uncooperative. It can involve **withdrawing** and **delaying**.
- **Compromising** involves moderately assertive and moderately cooperative behavior. It falls between competing and accommodating.
- **Collaborating** involves both assertive and cooperative behavior. People explore an issue to uncover underlying needs and work together to solve the problem.

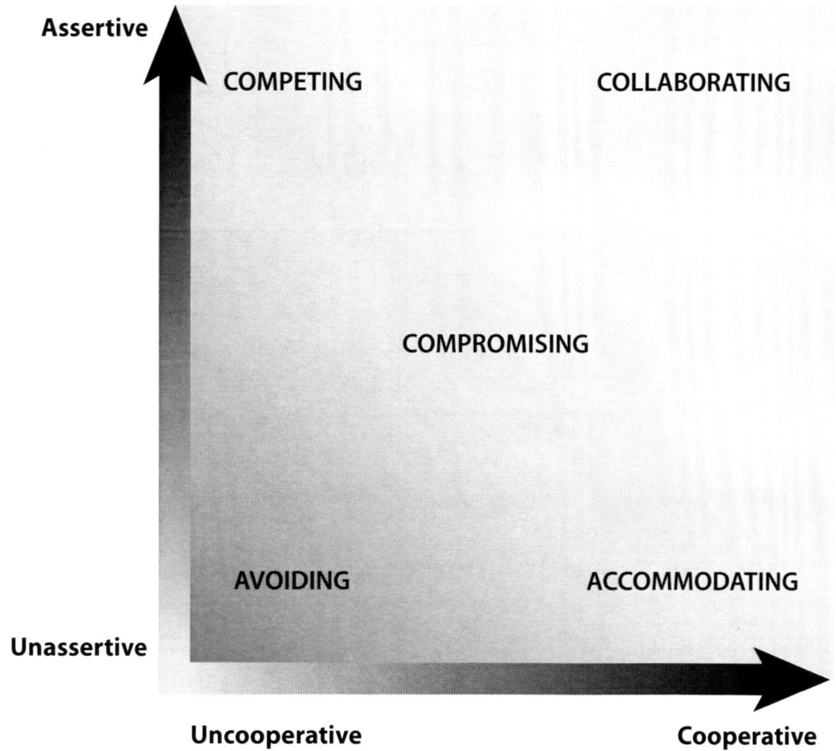

The figure illustrates where the five styles fall on the two continuums of assertiveness and cooperativeness.

The most effective communicators assess the conflict situation and apply the style or styles most likely to be effective in that particular context. You should become familiar with each style and use the one that best enables you to handle a specific disagreement. Learn to assess the needs of both parties involved in a disagreement, so you can use the style most likely to result in both parties having a positive experience.

Competing Style

When it is important to "win" the conflict at all costs, the competing style is appropriate. This style is effective when you truly believe in something or if a crisis situation calls for resolving the conflict immediately. For example, a supervisor in a department where two employees fight constantly and cannot resolve personal differences would assert her power and transfer one of the employees to another division. Other forms of handling the conflict would be ineffective given the history of the two employees. The competing style is generally ineffective for most interpersonal relationships. Competitive responses close the door to further discussion. Too often, competitors do not listen to others and have no regard for the thoughts or needs of "opponents."

Sometimes in the work environment, the competitive style can turn into the subcategory of bullying. **Bullying** occurs when a person must be right no matter what and uses coercion, manipulation, or intimidation to force compliance. This is an extremely difficult situation in business. If someone tells you to "choose your battles," they might be indicating that you are unreasonably aggressive. Be sure you don't turn into an interpersonal bully who has to win every argument at any cost. Colleagues tire quickly of working with someone who always has to be right.

On the positive side, two people who enjoy a spirited discussion of an issue could use the competitive mode of resolution. Both individuals may be asserting themselves, wanting to win the discussion, and they have fun while trying to convince each other of the correctness of their position. While some people enjoy the vigorous banter and remain good colleagues after a heated discussion, many people are uncomfortable with the competing style.

Accommodating Style

When people subordinate their opinion to that of someone else to promote harmony in a relationship, they are using an accommodating style. This style develops when people are afraid of conflict, afraid to voice an opinion, or are so easygoing that they do not have a strong opinion about an issue one way or the other. However, if you have an opinion, you should not use this style. People who repress their opinions may become hostile or depressed. If their nonverbal behavior portrays them as suffering for their accommodation, others may be annoyed with the self-induced martyrdom.

You should always articulate your opinions appropriately. For example, if Maureen asks Andrei what PowerPoint background he'd like used for their presentation, and he says he doesn't care, he should not say, "Oh I hate that" when she picks one and designs the presentation. If he has only one dislike, he can say, "Anything is fine with me as long as it isn't pastel." If he has a list of things he dislikes, then he should not use the accommodating style. You should only use this style if you truly don't have an opinion and are willing to do whatever the other person wants to do without question or comment.

Remember that some people have a hard time sharing an opinion and just want to go along with a decision made by others. Try to create an atmosphere that encourages everyone to contribute.

Avoiding Style

When people walk away from conflict, they are using an avoiding style. When a heated argument begins, people using the avoidance style say, "I'm outta here." They physically remove themselves from the situation. This style is important to use whenever there is any threat of physical or verbal abuse either to you or from you. When abuse is not an issue, the avoidance style is one of the least useful styles because nothing is resolved. One person leaves, but the problem remains.

There are two subsets of the avoidance style. Someone might **withdraw** from a conflict because (1) The person has no opinion on the topic or no needs that must be met. He or she simply doesn't care to engage in the conflict. (2) The person is truly afraid of conflict. The individual may have grown up in an abusive family and can't handle the emotional response brought on when people start raising their voices and arguing, even in good fun.

Another subset of the avoidance style is **delaying**. Delaying happens when someone is too upset to continue participating in the conflict at that moment. Whenever you feel you might say or do something that you'll later regret, it is wise to delay the conflict until you calm down and can express yourself appropriately. If you become emotional during conflict, delaying is a useful strategy to avoid a breakdown at the office. Saying something like "I need to talk about this tomorrow" or "I'll come back in an hour to discuss it" lets the other person know that you aren't simply walking out. A break is acceptable as long as you return to continue the discussion and resolve the issue.

If you find yourself welling up with tears in the office, dig your fingernails into the palm of your hand. The pain in your hand diverts the emotions and helps stop the tears. We don't know why it works, but it often does!

Compromising Style

When both people give in slightly to reach a solution, they are using a compromising style. In the PowerPoint background example, Maureen might want a blue background, while Andrei wants a red tone. They could decide to compromise on a combination of red and blue for the background and choose a shade of purple. In this case, neither of them is getting what they really want, but they are both getting a little of what they want. A compromise can work well in various situations where there is no other resolution. In this example, both individuals could feel slightly cheated artistically.

Collaborating Style

When people work through the problem-solving process to reach the best solution for each of them, they are engaging in a collaborating style. The collaborating style mirrors the The Standard Agenda approach to problem solving discussed in chapter 8. By slightly changing the terminology of that model and applying it to conflict resolution, we get a six-step collaboration process:

1. **Define the problem.** Each party needs to identify that there is indeed a problem requiring attention.
2. **Explore the facts.** Both parties must state their needs. Even more importantly, they must listen carefully to truly understand the needs of the other person. If you cannot get through this step, collaboration cannot take place. Both parties must self-disclose honestly and completely.
3. **Brainstorm for possible solutions.** Generate as many solutions as possible and write them down.
4. **Set criteria to determine the best solution.** Generate a list of criteria that satisfies each person to determine the best solution. The first criterion should always be, "Any solution must be acceptable to both of us."

5. **Evaluate and select a solution.** Each solution is evaluated against the list of established criteria to determine which solution might work best.
6. **Finally, test the solution.** Put the solution into action and see if it is effective.

Collaboration is very effective when each person needs to feel involved in resolving an issue. It does, however, take more time and communication than the other conflict-resolution styles.

Think about the number of people who must try to resolve conflicts with one another in the workplace. You pick your romantic partner, but you usually don't get to pick your business colleagues. How will you get along? There is no simple answer. Sometimes, two competitors will resent each other because no one can "win" the argument. We know two competitors, however, who get along well because they love to argue.

Putting a competitor in a relationship with an avoider may sound promising as a way to solve problems. In reality it isn't. Think about people you know who use the competitive conflict-resolution style. How do they react when someone walks away from them? Most of them probably scream "DON'T YOU WALK AWAY FROM ME!" Two accommodators would get nowhere—"How do you want to format the report?" "I don't care. How do you want to format it?" "I don't care." What other combinations of conflict-resolution styles do you think would be particularly effective or ineffective?

REALITY ☑

How I Survived a Conflict Situation

Small group communication texts outline conflict resolution strategies, but things don't always go as planned. You might not always get an A+ group or even a C+ group. Sometimes the only thing you can do is push through it, no matter how bad the conflict situation or situations get. And by pushing through it, I mean grin and bear it. Conflicts are not always resolvable, and mine was definitely one of those situations.

As I looked at whom my team would be composed of for class I felt that I was given some great group members. And, I definitely was. A lifelong friendship was made through that course. However, I was also shown what it's really like working with different people and personalities in the real world. I learned what it was like to deal with an irrational person.

(continued)

As part of our final grade for the capstone project, our peers were given the chance to evaluate each other on a number of different categories—service, commitment, communication, and conflict just to name a few. In a sense, this was where "the gloves came off" for some. We were able to voice a semester's worth of poor decisions through this system.

When it was time for the points to be revealed one of our group members, Katie, was shocked by her low score. She did not hold back in voicing that shock to the group when the rest of the class went home. I knew I needed to listen to Katie's feedback, so I asked to hear her justification as to why the group should reconsider her total. I waited calmly while she described she was being treated unfairly and even targeted. When asked to explain what she had contributed to the group, which was a subpar amount but not zero, she had little knowledge of what she had contributed and what other members had picked up in her absence. For a total of about 45 minutes, my team members, along with the instructor, sat patiently to try to work through this conflict. In this case, patience was really key. We waited and waited and waited for a reasonable response with details that justified a point increase. She deserved the respect of us listening to why she felt she deserved more points. However, we did not receive that same respect back. The best she could do was reiterate how she was targeted and treated unfairly. Her irrationality towards the situation started to take a toll on the group. Finally, I said to her: "what would you like out of this situation?" She demanded we bump up her grade to a C instead of a D-. Her request was not out of the question, but I requested details on why she felt this was reasonable. The long and never-ending cycle we just sat through began to start all over again. At this point, I think I can speak for all of the group members that we would've all sacrificed points from our own grades, which entailed hours of hard work, to break that cycle and get out of that room.

In this situation, I realized the real-life value of patience. This conflict situation was one of the worst I've ever experienced, and I'm not sure what will top this. Some conflict situations aren't about "winning." They're about getting what you might want out of the situation but also realizing what the other person wants. Not everyone is going to be happy with the outcome, and you have to be ok with them not "liking" you or being happy if evidence is not provided. Stay calm and be cool. Likely, the person on the other end is fueling off of your emotions. Although that situation was not pleasant, I believe everyone's calm attitudes kept Katie in line.

After a major dispute like this, don't forget to debrief with your group. Even if it's a simple group chat via GroupMe or iMessage. A simple text saying "great job today" helps a lot. The days that followed that event, I was reassured by my team that we made the right decision, and I would've gladly accepted their feedback if they thought we could've handled it better or have done something differently. I also wanted to reassure them of how proud I was of their attitudes during that time and in the days that followed.

—Emily K. Schamel
Residency Program Coordinator; Mansfield University alum

Reflections on Conflict-Resolution Styles

It is important for you to think about your own style. Are you happy with it? Do you feel confident in your conflict-resolution skills, or would you like to change? Anyone can learn these styles and use them, if they want to improve. But you also need to think a little about why you use your current style. Most traditional-age college students spent the last 20 years developing their style through interactions with their families and friends. Nontraditional students have spent even more time developing their style because they have life experiences in business and with families and friends.

If your personal style is to accommodate others, ask yourself whether you are doing this because you honestly don't have an opinion, you are very easygoing, or you were conditioned to use that style because of an abusive family situation. Children who grow up with alcoholic, drug-addicted, or verbally abusive parents learn very quickly to be accommodators so they can stay out of harm's way. However, you can change your personal style once you understand the reasons for your behavior. Start asserting your opinion. Each time you do, it gets easier.

If you are a competitor, you probably grew up in a family where arguments and discussions were openly encouraged. You not only were allowed to speak your mind but you also were encouraged to do so. Think back to the discussion about the communication process. It is essential for you to understand the other person's circumstances in interpersonal communication—whether in a social or a business situation. But in the workplace, you may need to back off. Stop talking and ask yourself if this particular battle is important or if you could just go along with what others would like to do.

Let's examine the styles of coworkers, Nicole and Tiffany. Nicole grew up in an abusive family. Tiffany did not. When Tiffany wants to talk through a disagreement, Nicole simply acquiesces to Tiffany's viewpoint. Tiffany perceives Nicole as spineless with no opinion. With Tiffany's background, these characteristics are not desirable in a coworker. Nicole, on the other hand, is reminded of her abusive parent whenever Tiffany raises her voice and gets excited during a discussion. Once these colleagues talk about their personal circumstances (for example, their backgrounds), they can begin to alter their communication styles. Altering their styles keeps the work relationship collegial. If they do not make adjustments, the relationship may gradually fall apart. Even if Nicole and Tiffany are unwilling to change their styles, exploring their backgrounds should allow them a greater understanding of each other's style.

You may not always get to know your coworkers well enough to gain an understanding of why they do what they do, but the effective use of the five styles of conflict resolution will help you smooth over conflict in work relationships. Since no style is appropriate in every situation, build your problem-solving skills so that you have options. You should practice using various styles in different situations. Having the knowledge and adaptability to use the appropriate style for a particular interpersonal situation contributes to being an effective communicator.

It is important to remember some conflicts can never be resolved completely. Occasionally, we are simply stuck working with people we dislike; unpleasant people are part of the workforce. It may be necessary to keep your employment options open throughout your career, so you never feel trapped in a negative environment. For example, working in a situation where a manager yells and screams at subordinates daily is stressful, and you may dread going to work. Difficult work situations are simply that—difficult. Confidence in your own ability to communicate well helps you remain strong throughout moments of conflict in your career. Maintaining a positive attitude allows you to move smoothly into a new career and alter personal perspectives.

Sexual Harassment

The workplace pays much more attention to sexual harassment claims today than it did in the past. In fact, the term didn't exist 50 years ago. Journalist Lin Farley taught a course on women and work at Cornell University in the mid-1970s (Swenson, 2017). She quizzed her students about their workplace experiences and learned that every woman in the class had either been forced to quit a job or had been fired because they had rejected the sexual overtures of a boss. She worked with her colleagues to create a name for the physical and emotional abuse and pressure women faced on the job. She settled on *sexual harassment*. The term became public in 1975 when Farley testified about her work at Cornell before the Commission on Human Rights of New York City. She testified that "sexual harassment of women in their place of employment is extremely widespread. It is literally epidemic."

In the late 1980s, the Supreme Court decided that sexual harassment was a form of sex discrimination, which is prohibited by Title VII of the Civil Rights Act of 1964 (Murad, 2020). The law recognizing sexual harassment as a form of sex discrimination applies to private employers with 15 or more employees, as well as government and labor organizations. In 2017, the #MeToo movement created a new focus on sexual harassment in workplaces. More than 7,500 sexual harassment claims were filed with the U.S. Equal Employment Opportunity Commission (EEOC) in 2018—a 14 percent increase over the prior year. The EEOC (n.d.) defines sexual harassment as unwelcome sexual advances and other verbal or physical conduct of a sexual nature that affects an individual's employment, unreasonably interferes with an individual's work performance, or creates an intimidating, hostile, or offensive work environment. Harassment is not confined to remarks of a sexual nature; it includes offensive remarks about a person's gender. For example, it is illegal to harass a woman by making offensive comments about women in general. Many states go beyond federal regulations to prevent workplace harassment. Eight states require employers to provide sexual harassment training in their workplaces.

Sexual harassment is most often defined as "any unwanted sexual attention." If you think back to our previous discussions of communication, you're aware that attention can come in the form of verbal or nonverbal communication. And it comes in the form of intentional or unintentional communication. Your workplace should have a policy for sexual harassment, but we will mention a couple of specifics just to get you thinking about the future.

Verbal harassment includes suggestive remarks. There is nothing wrong with telling a colleague that he or she looks nice today, or that you like their outfit. However, certain paralanguage could make those same comments lecherous and illegal.

REALITY ☑

Try it in class. Have someone read the following statement in two different ways—once as a compliment and again with inflection that would qualify as sexual harassment: "Wow, you look really great today."

More blatant than suggestive remarks are outright sexual references: commenting about body parts, telling sexual jokes, and making inappropriate invitations. Any requests that are quid pro quo (something for something) fall under this category also: "You will get promoted if you do X for me."

Nonverbal harassment can include any kind of inappropriate eye contact, gesture, touching, and so on. It is best to keep in mind a mantra you learned in kindergarten: Keep your hands to yourself. Brushing up against someone, if truly an isolated accident, is not a problem. If it happens repeatedly and it is unwanted, it is sexual harassment.

In addition to nonverbal gestures or facial movements, your artifacts may create a **hostile environment**. If office decorations make the workplace an uncomfortable place, that is a form of hostile environment sexual harassment. A colleague may display a sexy calendar or poster that makes you uncomfortable. Or they may give you a sexual gift (such as an adult magazine or product). Not everyone has the same sense of humor, and it is important not to cross these social lines. These behaviors are actionable under corporate policy and law.

REALITY ☑

One of our alums shared the following: Experienced a super bad case of sexism today. We went to visit a foundry and the two women that I was with were the Human Resources directors of the company where I intern. The person who came out to meet us for the tour assumed that because I was the male of the group, I was the Human Resources director and must just have the name "Kelly." Even after I told him my name was not Kelly, he kept only addressing and making eye contact with me until I got him sort of alone and said, "You need to stop. I am literally just an intern!" It was disgusting.

There is also an issue called **third-party sexual harassment**. Let's say that two of you are perfectly comfortable with flirting and sexual innuendo at work. You banter back and forth in front of other employees. If what you are doing is uncomfortable for anyone else who may be hearing or seeing it, then third-party sexual harassment has occurred. This is also actionable.

Remember that sexual harassment is a receiver-oriented phenomenon based on perception. One person may be offended while another is not. Not knowing that you are offending someone is not an excuse, as we have seen with the #MeToo movement. Quite often the people in power decades ago who are being accused now gave little thought to what it was like to be compromised. And most employees decades ago simply put up with the harassment as part of the job because there was nothing else to do but quit. Now that people have a voice, they can take action.

Ethical Encounter

Some people proclaim themselves to be huggers. They will invade your space without warning or asking your permission while stating "I'm a hugger" as if that excuses the behavior. Is this ethical?

While you certainly need to address sexual harassment with the proper authorities, be certain that you have analyzed behaviors accurately. Communication can be intentional or unintentional, and we can sometimes resolve a misunderstanding by asking a question or alerting someone to the situation. Sometimes people are truly clueless that they are offending you. Below are some possible comments to consider:

> "I'm not sure if you realize you are looking at my chest when you talk to me. Please look at my eyes when we are speaking."
>
> "Would you be offended if I asked you to take down that poster?—it really makes me uncomfortable."
>
> "I feel uncomfortable with that kind of language. Please don't use it around me."

Naturally you run the risk of the other party thinking you are overly sensitive. But no one should have to put up with sexual requests/language/jokes/pictures in the workplace if it makes them feel uncomfortable.

Be sure to follow your company's sexual harassment policy. Most policies begin by stating that **you should clearly tell the offending**

person to stop the behavior. If that doesn't work, inform them in writing that you want the behavior stopped or you will report them. If harassment continues, follow the company policy and report it. One incident generally does not constitute sexual harassment. There has to be a documented pattern of behavior. You should read the company's procedure regarding sexual harassment when you are hired initially. Then, you will know what to do if it happens.

Performance Reviews

Your company may provide a written document as **a performance review** that states your strengths and weaknesses based on a manager's observation and analysis of your work. When you receive it, read it carefully and evaluate the information. If any of the statements in your review are incorrect or written in ambiguous language, ask your manager for a meeting and discuss its details. How can you improve your performance for the company if you do not know what a manager is criticizing? Address all inaccuracies by checking your documentation of messages, meetings, dates, etc. Since performance reviews are necessary in the workplace, you need to remember to keep meticulous records of everything you do from the moment you begin working for a company until the day you leave. Good record keeping makes the performance review process easier and less stressful because you can easily resolve inaccurate statements. Once you check your records to confirm what you thought was true, address the inaccuracies by meeting with your supervisor or putting them in writing.

Meet briefly with your manager to go over a performance review, whether the material is positive or negative. The meeting to discuss a performance review allows you to demonstrate that you appreciate the time your manager took to write the document. At the same time, it gives you the opportunity to build a relationship with your manager as a thoughtful, concerned employee hopeful about your future with the organization. Always pay attention to the nonverbal behavior of the manager throughout the discussion. If you notice a reaction that does not match the verbal discussion, you can ask for immediate clarification. Your ability to analyze the verbal and nonverbal aspects of interpersonal communication is truly critical for your survival in business. As a professional person, don't assume anything and make sure you understand everything clearly. It's difficult to improve if you aren't sure what a manager is asking you to do.

Never get defensive. Some people like to make excuses for why they did something the way they did. Just listen. If something is inaccurate simply ask for clarification in a calm manner. Thank them for the advice.

After your meeting with the manager, write a summary of the various points you discussed in the meeting and send it to him or her. Your written summary serves as an affirmation that you heard everything correctly and know how to proceed in your position until the next performance review.

Performance review approaches differ from organization to organization, but there are some universal principles that apply to assessments of job performance. The principles apply to daily conversations and to periodic formal meetings. Effective managers discuss areas for improvement, as well as complimenting positive performance regularly. The review process is helpful because it lets you know how your communication and work is perceived by others. In many cases, it allows you to see if your interpersonal style is as effective as you think it is. Your daily social language and behavior as well as your ongoing business communication determine your value. It is important to remain professional and credible the entire time you are working among peers. Ask your manager how you can improve if there are any negative statements in your review.

If you are an employee receiving the evaluations, remember that self-evaluation is a component for employees in the review process. Document the feedback you receive and review it before the next scheduled assessment. Employees should review projects completed (including whether the outcome met expectations), areas of exceptional performance, areas of growth, and extra responsibilities assumed. They should also assess whether deadlines were missed, areas that need improvement, and challenges in meeting goals. Management may solicit performance feedback from colleagues. Be prepared to provide organized, useful responses to such inquiries.

The first step in the performance review process should be a discussion of goals so that the employee knows exactly what is expected and how work will be evaluated (Heathfield, 2019). Both managers and employees need to prepare for formal performance reviews. Managers should plan the main points of the discussion. The more patterns identified and examples given, the more the employee will understand the feedback and the actions to take. Emphasize positive aspects of the performance and how the employee can continue to grow. Don't neglect areas that need improvement; state them precisely—especially for underperforming employees. If you are not direct, the employee may not grasp the seriousness of the deficit.

While we stated above that effective managers discuss areas for improvement and give compliments, unfortunately ineffective managers handle performance reviews quite differently. You may find yourself in a meeting receiving a lot of negative feedback or reading a review that only lists negatives. In this situation, the key is to remain as calm as possible. You should make sure to (1) listen carefully without argument or defensive statements (taking notes is a good way to divert eye contact and keep busy with recording what the supervisor is saying while you bite your tongue; (2) thank the supervisor for the feedback and state that you will review it; (3) sleep on it. Make sure that you are not responding until you are past the initial angry/disgruntled/shocked stage.

If you are the one giving the review, remember the following. To provide current feedback, performance reviews should not be limited to an annual event. In the past, annual performance reviews were often a requirement. Many organizations abandoned that process because it too often resulted in revisiting the past rather than focusing on present and future efforts and because it lacked collaboration and innovation (Capelli and Tavis, 2018). About one-third of U.S. companies have replaced annual reviews with frequent, informal check-ins between managers and employees. In a comparison of weekly versus annual feedback, Gallup found that team members were 5.2 times more likely to strongly agree that they received meaningful feedback, 3.2 times more likely to strongly agree that they were motivated to do outstanding work, and 2.7 times more likely to be engaged at work (Sutton and Wigert, 2019). Effective performance reviews work best within a culture of honest feedback. Thoughtful, frank conversations facilitate discussion of uncomfortable topics. Managers with strong communication skills create opportunities for genuine dialogue and collaboration. Employees feel that their opinions matter and that they are evaluated fairly.

Conversation is a key element in a performance review. The discussion should not be a lecture. Approach the review as an exchange to help employees improve and to reinforce positive relationships. The review should highlight positive aspects of employees' ability so they are motivated to continue to grow and contribute (Heathfield, 2019). Encourage the conversation by asking questions such as: What support can the department provide to help you reach the goals we have set? How often would you like to receive feedback? How can I be a better manager for you? After the performance review, both parties should retain notes about topics discussed and should evaluate the effectiveness of the interaction. The evaluation will help determine what, if anything, should be done differently for future meetings.

Final Thoughts

Employment would be much easier if you could hire yourself, make all of the decisions, take credit for everything that happens in the company, and give yourself lavish bonuses. Sadly, a career doesn't work that way. A productive working life depends on excellent communication skills to assist you in maneuvering effortlessly with diverse colleagues as you follow a career path. Those same communication skills are also used to face and conquer each challenging moment experienced in personal conflict, sexual harassment, and performance reviews. Your image management during cycles of tense communication reflects your credibility and maturity as a professional.

The concepts expressed in this chapter are easy to interpret as moments that happen due to the actions of others. While aspects of the assumption are true, it is also true that communication occurs between two or more people. This fact means that your language and behavior may have been at least a partial cause of the challenging situations you find yourself in occasionally. Therefore, analyzing your own communication first is an excellent way to approach problem solving. Once you understand potential communication errors you may have made, you can more accurately resolve a conflict with a colleague or manager, a sexually uncomfortable confrontation, and clarify factual/perceptual language in a performance review. You are a key partner in every communication exchange and must accept responsibility for your actions. Professionalism requires constant use of appropriate language and behavior with others. Be prepared to handle situational conflict; plan in advance how to react to sexual harassment; reflect on how to handle a performance review in a professional manner.

Key Terms

Accommodating	Interest conflicts
Avoiding	Moral conflicts
Bullying	Performance review
Collaborating	Relationship conflicts
Competing	Sexual harassment
Compromising	Structural conflicts
Conflict	Value conflicts
Data conflicts	Withdrawing

Exercises

1. Describe a conflict situation you experienced and the personal style you used at the time. How would you change your communication now?
2. Describe a situation in which you experienced or observed sexual harassment. What did you do? How would you handle it now?
3. Write a personal performance review of your work (attendance, written work, class participation) up to this point in the term. How can you improve your professional image before the end of the term?

CHAPTER
ELEVEN

Take Nothing for Granted
Everything Matters

Goals

- Differentiate between networks and networking
- Describe how you can use storytelling in the workplace
- Explain key differences in masculine and feminine communication
- Explain the implications of working with people from different cultures
- Identify effective strategies for dining out

Knowledge is power, but it's acquired with time. Hard work alone does not solidify a career. Peers and managers constantly evaluate you for your ability to communicate in a responsible manner. Therefore, it is useful to know something about the additional topics mentioned in this chapter. There is no better time than now to begin thinking about a professional way of life and how to effectively use communication opportunities to remain viable for continuous employment.

Networks and Networking

Networks are comprised of individuals with similar philosophical thoughts, personal goals, or belief systems. They consist of professional organizations, nonprofit organizations, corporations, religious groups, unions, fraternal societies, support groups, neighborhood organizations, and so on. Connecting to people and keeping in touch with them is a great way to share thoughts, ideas, job opportunities, and promotions.

Networking is the act of connecting with people and developing a relationship with them. Whereas people once networked via a contraption called a Rolodex (where you physically recorded the name and contact information of people you had met), networking is a much easier concept with the advent of the internet and electronic social networking venues such as Facebook, LinkedIn and other digital platforms.

Networking is a cumulative action. It requires a portion of your mental and personal time. At the beginning of a career, you will spend a lot of your time networking with individuals and organizations as you demonstrate to others that you have the passion and interest for a long-term career. The following are a few suggestions to help you make the most of initial networking opportunities.

- Be curious about the organization. Meet new people in every division of the company to deepen your understanding of how the business works. People will recognize your interest in learning about the company as a whole. These visits also broaden your understanding of other career opportunities within the company, so you can make informed decisions about growth, advancement, or moving on.
- Be polite to everyone you meet. The professional world is smaller than you realize, and you never know who belongs to what network or knows the same people. Connections drive careers, so make sure everyone who meets you has a positive experience and remembers your name.
- Attend some of the after-work social functions with colleagues. This is a strategic way to unwind and talk to colleagues in a social setting. Social sessions can build strong personal bonds. By the way, you do not have to drink alcohol; bars serve ginger

REALITY ☑

One of our alums went to work at an enormous complex in Manhattan. Each day when he checked in, he chatted with the man checking security badges. He asked him about his day, joked with him, and brought him coffee about once a week. Sometime later he met one of the VPs in the building. When he introduced himself, the VP said, "Oh! You are the one who has been so nice to my brother-in-law." You never know who is connected.

ale and club soda, so go and have some fun. If you do indulge, do so carefully. In larger cities, many employees and managers frequent specific bars or restaurants. If you do the same, you may have an opportunity to meet people you would never meet otherwise. Over time, you can decide which of these individuals should make your "good-colleagues-to-know" list. Employees and managers change companies and advance in rank; networking with them may be helpful in the future.

- If you get an opportunity to meet with someone important, avoid a hard sell on what you can do. Instead tell a compelling and memorable story (Feloni, 2015).
- Find a way to remain in touch with people whose company you enjoy throughout your life. Everyone uses a different way to keep in touch, so find the method that works best for both parties.
- Join professional and community organizations as a volunteer. This activity builds work experience away from the company and gives you new contacts and ideas for self-development. Listen as others are talking about their volunteer groups and join those organizations that have the potential to advance your career. Sometimes the contacts you make are useful if you choose to change careers. Every contact you make can be valuable in the future.
- Remain up-to-date on all of the literature about your professional area, both nationally and internationally. This information allows meaningful participation in conversations at work and demonstrates your curiosity and expertise.
- Remain active in activities you enjoy; those experiences will help you contribute to informal conversations at work. A large

majority of business personnel talk about various sports teams, so if sports trivia is a passion of yours—terrific. Business colleagues also meet socially for golf, tennis, racquetball, etc. If you play any of these sports, you might be invited to join those groups. Professional people have many, and varied interests. Some like to discuss literature; others coach young people in the community; some train seniors to use a computer to stay connected to the outside world, and so on. The key to any interest you possess is your commitment to reach out to others. Numerous interests make you more valuable to the business sector.

- If someone goes out on a professional limb to give you the contact information of a trusted colleague, keep the name, address, and phone number of that person in a private place no one else can access. Above all, do not "reshare" those contacts with others. These individuals are your contacts only, so protect their privacy. Maintain contact with them for advice, mentoring, and information throughout your life.
- Make sure to follow up with people you meet. Recently, a marine biology student watched a presentation by someone working in a regional program that she was interested in. She took a deep breath and made herself go talk to him after the program. When he asked her where she was from, they discovered they had some unusual connections. They chatted, and he said to contact him anytime. She sat down and wrote a follow-up email the next day saying who she was and reminding him what they talked about; she thanked him for his advice. He instantly sent her a number of links to employment opportunities that she would not have otherwise had! We recommend always thanking people, following up, checking in, etc. This is the best way to remain fresh on someone's mind.

Networking requires time and financial resources for food, beverages, and commuting. The expansion of your knowledge base and career contacts makes the investment a wise one. The more professionals who know you personally, the more likely you are to have someone alert you to a career advancement possibility. Networks can make a tremendous difference in your enjoyment of professional life.

Storytelling in Interpersonal Settings

We talked about the importance of storytelling to make yourself stand out in an interview, but these skills can be used elsewhere in a corporate setting as well. Storytelling skills are an excellent tool to use in business to boost morale, deliver information, and assist others in understanding new concepts. This intellectual skill allows you to be more creative during presentations because adjectives and adverbs are added more frequently to present colorful images to the audience. **Storytelling** usually involves an emotional description of time, events, action, and places that translate factual information into life experiences audience members have in common and will remember. The oral traditions of many cultures include stories, which present messages of hope, stewardship, ethical behavior, leadership, and problem solving. The key to good storytelling is a thorough understanding of the audience and the common experiences and beliefs they share. You simply mold the story for a business model.

Consultant Steve Denning (2011), a former World Bank executive, describes the power of narrative. "Storytelling is often the best way for leaders to communicate with people they are leading. Why? It is inherently well adapted to handling the most intractable leadership challenges of today—sparking change, communicating who you are, enhancing the brand, transmitting values, creating high-performance teams, sharing knowledge, taming the grapevine, leading people into the future." Denning also believes storytelling liberates innovation by generating the energy needed to change. "Storytelling is a key leadership technique because it's quick, powerful, free, natural, refreshing, energizing, collaborative, persuasive, holistic, entertaining, moving, memorable and authentic. Stories help us make sense of organizations.

Enhance an informative presentation by weaving in storytelling elements to support your information.

Strong work experience and life experience becomes the background for the stories you develop. You, family members, friends and/or an organization itself become the characters used in the message you create. When an audience believes you are tied to the tale, they are more likely to listen to what you are saying. This creative speaking style is completely different from the factual presentational style normally used in business. It can't be used in all corporate scenarios. When appropriate, storytelling becomes a refreshing, effective way to exchange information with others and to motivate them—and to be remembered.

Gender Communication

Extensive research in the field of **gender communication** has revealed that men and women typically have different and distinct communication styles. This is no surprise if you have fought with someone of the opposite sex or have been frustrated by the way people spoke to you. There are numerous books on this topic, and we recommend Deborah Tannen's *You Just Don't Understand* and *Talking from 9 to 5* if you want an in-depth look at some differences in gender communication. We'll briefly review some helpful tips for familiarizing yourself with gendered communication in the workplace.

There are masculine and feminine speech styles. The styles usually correspond with the speech patterns of men and the speech patterns of women, but not always. Language styles are changing rapidly. Why? Some gender theories trace patterns of communication to the games that people play when they are young. Boys, in general, play sports. When they go out to play, there is not much talking necessary because the rules of the game specify the expected behavior. Everyone knows what to do, and they do it. The goal is to win. Girls, in general, enact social situations (playing school, playing house). In this game, they do a lot of talking to negotiate how to play the enactment. "Winning" is not an outcome. The goal is to discuss, to create scenarios, and to enjoy one another's company.

Growing up with distinct models of communication influences adult speech patterns. Men, in general, talk when it is absolutely necessary; they talk to win, and they are very direct. Women, in general, talk more often; they talk to enjoy one another's company, to build relationships, and to be inclusive in their communication.

Gender communication theories are evolving as girls' behavior changes. Girls now play more sports and develop mechanical skills as quickly as boys. The women in our classes who played sports with the boys typically possess more masculine speech qualities than women who played exclusively with dolls and weren't physically active when they were children. Boys brought up with more creative play often exhibit the supportive/inclusive style of speaking. Gaming is also shifting communication styles. Everyone fights hard and wins when playing digital games. Men and women playing popular first shooter games are having similar experiences.

Brenda Allen (2011) makes the point that organizations themselves are gendered.

> The gendered nature of organizations is evident in many communication practices, policies, and preferences. Women and men learn to conform to formal expectations or unspoken norms about aspects of appearance, such as types of clothing, grooming, and acceptable body weight. Many, if not most, of these policies and norms persist without challenge and are based on masculinist, white, middle-class and middle-age ideals and aesthetics. (p. 56)

Feminine styles of communication—inclusive, collaborating, and cooperating—are often linked with subordinate roles in an organization. Organizational structure often includes hierarchies and chains of command, similar to the military. Organizations tend to value masculine ways of communicating. "A masculine ethic of reason and rationality underpins images of professionalism in organizations. . . . Ideas of professionalism usually encompass masculine ways of being, including assertion, independence, competitiveness, confidence, competition, domination, and winning" (Allen, 2011, p. 57).

Allen notes that we produce, reproduce—and sometimes challenge and change—expectations and stereotypes about gender in organizational contexts. As more women become leaders, CEOs and business owners, the organizational context may move away from traditional masculine communication styles. The word *compromise* has a negative connotation if winning is seen as the goal—giving up anything is viewed as a loss (Goman, 2019). In collaborative feminine communication, compromise means listening to understand the other person's needs and then finding a solution that works for everyone.

No communication style is best for all business interactions. In collaborative environments where listening skills, inclusive body language and empathy are more highly valued, the feminine style is viewed as more effective (Goman, 2016). In environments where decisiveness is critical, a male "take charge" attitude is valued.

REALITY ☑

Carol Kinsey Goman (2016) researched how communication differences were displayed in the workplace. She found that men and women both identified the same sets of strengths and weaknesses for themselves and for each other. Have you experienced similarities or differences with the following findings about gender and communication?

Strengths for women	**Strengths for men**
(1) reading nonverbal cues; (2) good listening; (3) effective display of empathy.	(1) commanding physical presence; (2) direct; (3) effective display of power.
Weaknesses for women (1) overly emotional; (2) meandering—not direct; (3) not authoritative.	**Weaknesses for men** (1) overly blunt; (2) insensitive to audience reactions; (3) too confident in own opinion

Remember, in the workplace, people assess communication styles for warmth (empathy, likability, caring) and authority (power, credibility, status).

Women's nonverbal behaviors are warmer. They lean forward when someone is speaking, smile, synchronize their movements with others, and nod. Men are more likely to send status signals. They stand tall and spread their materials on conference tables. Men's relative discomfort dealing with emotion prompts them to seek a solution; women understand that people sometimes just want to be heard.

Any style can be interpreted as a weakness if overdone. Women are viewed as weak if they smile too much or downplay their ideas and achievements. Women often believe that their good work will be noticed (a "good student" mentality); men are more aware that they need to promote themselves (Goman, 2016). When men's expansive postures infringe on other people's personal space, they may be seen as aggressive. Women use approximately five tones when speaking and their voices rise under stress, which makes them sound more emotional. Men use approximately three tones. Their deeper voices sound more confident but the lack of vocal range can also make them sound monotonous.

There are specific and harmful stereotypes for both women and men in corporate culture (Fixmer-Oraiz and Wood, 2019).

- *Sex object*—defined by looks rather than by accomplishments
- *Mother*—assumed responsibility to take care of everyone
- *Child*—stereotyped as needing to be taken care of
- *Iron maiden*—negative characterization as ambitious, directive, and competitive

Obviously these stereotypes are not flattering, and they encourage workers to treat women as less than equals.

The male stereotypes are equally troubling.

- *Sturdy oak*—expectations that men will always be strong and self-reliant
- *Fighter*—stereotype of taking charge and fighting all battles
- *Breadwinner*—judging men on their abilities as the wage earner

While these stereotypes are not as demeaning as some of the female stereotypes, they limit men's abilities to show an emotional or sensitive side, to take advantage of paternity leaves, or to stay home to care for sick children. They also impose a negative stigma for a man whose wife is employed in a position where she earns more money than he does.

Keep the previously mentioned cautions in mind while considering the following scenario. He comes in and gets right to the task that needs to be done. She wants to talk a little about the day, ask how things are going, etc. She nods and says "uh huh" while he talks (showing inclusiveness and encouragement for him to keep talking). He is annoyed by the interruption. When he communicates with her on the phone, he simply listens while she talks. He does not interject a reinforcing "uh-huh" or "ok." She gets angry at the silence assuming that he is not listening to her. Their perceptions of each other could be corrected by understanding different communication styles.

The gender roles learned in childhood need to be tempered so that communication is more effective and all employees can feel at ease while contributing to common goals. Excellent communication skills and intelligence are not restricted to one gender. Talent, credibility, and leadership are genderless traits. Examine your personal communication style. Compare your strengths and weaknesses to the gender differences discussed here (remembering that these are general tendencies not exact descriptions). Learn to assess situations so that you use the most effective style in those particular circumstances.

Watch out for sexist language. Even minor errors can make you look bad. For example, never introduce a woman as a chairman. Chair works just fine.

Intercultural Communication

Today's workplaces are comprised of individuals from different ethnic, religious, social, and educational backgrounds, necessitating an awareness of different communication patterns across cultures, which is the focus of **intercultural communication**. It is important to remember that people from other cultures interact in communication situations according to the patterns they learned—which may well differ from social patterns you learned. This statement may sound obvious. However, it is easy to forget cultural differences. For example, if an individual speaks English flawlessly with no accent, we may automatically assume that all other aspects of the individual's interactions match our own. Yet, nonverbal behaviors such as managing time have nothing to do with proficiency in English as a second language. If someone falls short of your expectations of a colleague, cultural differences may be the cause rather than a deficiency.

Working with people from diverse backgrounds occasionally requires some language and behavioral problem-solving skills. Try to analyze cultural nuances before reaching any conclusions about the other person. For instance, Americans tend to get straight to business while Mexicans tend to want to talk a little bit about their families before they get started. People from India may say they can do a task, even if they can't. They view this verbal reaction to a speaker as being polite—similar to Americans who nod their head while someone is speaking to them as a polite way to signal nonverbally that they are listening. So for someone from India, it is polite to say that they can finish a 50-page report by tomorrow, even if it is impossible for them to complete the task.

Touch is one of the areas of nonverbal communication that varies tremendously from one culture to the next. You need to be perceived as professional when you travel, so it is useful to know how to greet business colleagues during an international business meeting. A little research before you travel can assist you in knowing what to do.

The handshake dates back to ancient Greece; it was a symbol of peace and a gesture to show neither person was carrying a weapon (PSOW, 2019). The western handshake has become an internationally accepted greeting, but there are some notable variances. Learning the local custom demonstrates that you value the culture and people with whom you are interacting. If you are conducting business outside the United States, make sure to shake hands with and greet everyone in the room. Failure to do so is considered a rejection of anyone you omitted—and attendees will notice your behavior. It is customary to shake hands on arrival and departure. Here are some of the international nuances for handshakes.

- **China.** The western handshake involves a lighter grip and less of a pumping motion. Chinese people lower their eyes slightly as a sign of respect when meeting someone. Refrain from staring into someone's eyes during the handshake; the behavior can be perceived as a sign of disrespect.
- **Japan.** Both handshaking and bowing are accepted forms of greeting. Take your lead from the person you are meeting. If shaking hands, do so lightly.
- **Korea.** Men greet each other with a slight bow and a handshake. Support your right forearm with your left hand to show respect. Women rarely shake hands; they typically nod.
- **Russia.** Russians use a firm handshake and customarily kiss their guests' cheeks. Women only shake hands.
- **Latin America.** The handshake is light and lasts about twice as long as a U.S. handshake. Pulling away too soon is interpreted as rejection. A man may offer his hand to a woman and may kiss the top of a woman's hand.

REALITY ☑

In March 2020 as the COVID-19 pandemic news became a global story, the WHO and the CDC strongly discouraged handshakes. American government officials began using elbow bumps rather than handshakes. Alterations in business and cultural touching behaviors are changing rapidly. Interpersonal greetings that have existed for centuries are evaporating. By the time you read this book, the "next generation" of professional and social touching behaviors (handshakes, hugs, and kisses) will be evident. Adapt quickly to this change to stand out.

Corporate employment involves global culture. Even if you don't travel for an international division of a company, you will probably participate in a virtual meeting with global colleagues. You need to inform yourself about the cultural traditions of colleagues as well as employers to avoid communication mistakes that can be costly to your career and costly to your employer. Natalie Kienzle and Shane Husar (2007) state, "Cultural intelligence is defined as being skilled and flexible about understanding a culture, learning increasingly more about it, and gradually shaping one's thinking to be more sympathetic to the culture and one's behavior to be more fine-tuned and appropriate when interacting with others from the culture" (p. 84). They list five stages involved in developing cultural intelligence.

1. Reactivity to external stimuli.
2. Recognition of other cultural norms and motivation to learn more about them.
3. Accommodation of other cultural norms and rules.
4. Assimilation of diverse cultural norms into alternative behaviors.
5. Proactivity in cultural behavior based on recognition of changing cues that others do not perceive.

Cultural competence refers to your ability to interact effectively with people from other cultures—understanding and accepting the beliefs, values, and ethics of others plus developing the skills necessary to work with diverse individuals. Allen (2011) highlights the following four components of cultural competence.

- *Awareness*. Examine your own cultural background, including values and prejudices. Become aware of the impact of culture on your life and of how you perceive and respond to other cultures.
- *Attitude*. Respect others. Be sensitive to and open-minded about cultural differences.
- *Knowledge*. Recognize power structures and institutional barriers that prevent individuals from using organizational resources.
- *Skills*. Develop and improve verbal and nonverbal cross-cultural communication skills.

"By becoming culturally competent, you learn more about yourself as well as others, thereby expanding your horizons and gaining a better understanding of multiple views and experiences that form the foundation from which others see the world" (p. 75).

Today's technology allows you to communicate instantly around the world. To stand out in your profession, you must be knowledgeable in how to use language effectively with individuals from other cultures and adapt to new behaviors. Cultural intelligence is important to develop as the finances of the corporate world mingle globally to a greater extent than at any other time in world history.

The Art of Business Dining

Whether you attend lunch or dinner during an interview or schedule a meeting with a client or a manager at a restaurant, be aware of expectations for your behavior. It may seem odd to talk about dining in a communication book. However, changing family interactions and increased informality today have lessened the likelihood that parents require perfect table manners at home or taught children the fine art of dining.

Many job offers and business deals are conducted at a dining table. Hosts watch prospective job candidates to see how they conduct themselves and how they will represent the company as an employee. Potential clients gain insight into the professionalism of the company with whom they are contemplating a business deal. Table manners set hosts and guests apart in a positive or negative way (Gottsman, 2017). Therefore, a little etiquette information becomes useful knowledge. Some of you may know the following information, but many students are clueless on how to conduct themselves when it comes to eating at restaurants other than fast-food or casual, family-style establishments.

Some basics that everyone should know: Turn off your cell phone. Never talk with food in your mouth. Chew with your lips together. Keep the conversation light and free from objectionable topics. Sit up straight and keep your elbows off the table.

The person who invites another person(s) to dine out is the host for the event. Host duties include personally extending the invitation, making the reservation, arriving early, creating atmosphere, and deciding when to bring up serious discussion. Guest duties include confirming the meeting, arriving on time, coming prepared, being prepared to pay if necessary, and sending a thank-you note. If you are the host, put your guests at ease.

> Your conduct over the meal will determine your professional success. If you pay attention to the details and make every effort to see that your clients have a pleasant experience, they will assume that you handle their business the same way. (Ramsey, 2013)

Behavior During the Meal

While it is absolutely proper manners to have your guests order first, it is uncomfortable as a guest to order and then watch everyone else choosing something much less expensive. Aim for the middle to lower price end of the menu if you are the guest. For instance, if entrées run from $12–35, shoot for something around $15–18. If you find that you've made a huge faux pas when your boss orders something far smaller, there is nothing wrong with saying, "Oh I didn't see that—I think I'd like that instead." If you are on an interview, we recommend asking "What is good here? or What do you recommend?" If there are salads, sandwiches and full dinners, the answer can help guide you to an appropriate choice.

Familiarize yourself with fancy table settings; the following lists a few basics to remember.

- Salt and pepper should always be passed together
- Your bread is on the left, and your drink on the right. You can remember this with BMW—Bread-Meal-Water or by placing your index fingers on your thumbs and extending the rest of your fingers. You'll see you have a "b" on the left hand and a "d" on the right hand.
- If there are multiple forks and knives work from the outside toward the plate. Your salad fork will be the farthest on the left. Your meal fork will be next to the plate. Your dessert silverware will be across the top of a place setting or arrive with the dessert.

Put your napkin in your lap. Use your napkin to blot your lips (don't swipe across your face). If you must leave the table, place the napkin in your chair. When you leave, place the napkin beside your plate. You should never place it on a dirty dinner plate.

Be prepared that in fine restaurants plates are served from the left and removed from the right. When you arrive, enter your chair from the right; when you leave, exit the chair to the left. And always remember to push your chair in when you exit.

Don't begin eating until everyone is served. This is an important sign of respect. However, if there are multiple people being served and your host says "Oh please—eat before it gets cold" then you should follow the request rather than the rule of etiquette.

If you must use the restroom or make a call, keep it brief. You should not leave your dinner companion alone, particularly if the person is your superior. But let's be honest about human physiology; there are those rare and unfortunate events that occur when nature interferes. If you know you will be in the bathroom for a while, it may be best to excuse yourself with "Would you excuse me? I'm terribly sorry, but I may be a little while." This gives the other person a polite head's up not to worry if you aren't back in the normal time frame. They can use their phone to do some business or chat with others.

Managing Food

Some of the following advice may seem silly, but people who know proper etiquette notice when others violate basic tenants. You might as well err on the side of being too formal rather than put someone off.

- It is wise to avoid ordering messy or hard to eat foods. No club sandwiches or huge burgers that you can't bite easily. Sloppy sauces look great on the plate but not on your clothing.
- When you eat bread, you should tear a bite-size piece, butter it, consume, repeat. Never chop open a roll and slather butter over the whole thing.
- Make sure you know how to cut salad with a fork and knife. If lettuce and other vegetables come in large chunks, you need to get them to bite size pieces before consumption. Choosing a large salad during a business lunch/dinner may mean that you are still eating when everyone else is finished.
- When you eat soup, you should carefully skim away from yourself over the very top layer. This eliminates blowing and making a mess. If you've never been taught this, you'll need to practice. Many college students shovel the liquid toward themselves.

Alcohol

While some articles say to avoid alcohol, we would argue that moderation, if acceptable in your company, is certainly appropriate. There are some bosses who do not like to drink alone and feel a little miffed if you don't join them for a cocktail. You have to judge this decision one meal at a time and know your limit! However, if you don't drink, don't compromise. There is nothing wrong with ordering a club soda or simply drinking water.

> If you are tired of people questioning your choice to abstain from alcohol, put a lime in a club soda, and it looks like an alcoholic beverage.

If you are going to drink alcohol (and it is fine to never touch the stuff), make sure that you understand your own limits, the pronunciation of what you are ordering and the perception of your drink. Typically, students have some drinking experience in college before their first job. Others don't. Take the time to drink socially with friends before trying this in a workplace setting. Keep in mind that alcohol hits harder on an empty stomach or when mixed with a carbonated beverage. Account for these things as you order. One drink per hour is plenty for a business outing.

Learn correct pronunciations. We've heard cognac (kohn-yak) pronounced cog-nick and merlot (mer-lo) pronounced as mer-lo**t**. If you can't say it properly, then just don't. There are many pronunciation guides on the web for you to consult.

And finally, think about the nonverbal perception of the drink you are ordering. Look at your instructor and imagine them with a neat scotch in one hand and a cosmopolitan in the other. Does that change your image of them? Typically, we recommend no red cocktails (for many people, the color signals femininity). A vodka and tonic is visually more sophisticated than a cosmo. A dry wine is more sophisticated than the cheap sugary types. A darker beer can be perceived as more sophisticated than a cheap lite can. As bizarre

> Never switch to something that might be perceived as more sophisticated without having tried it before. If you are used to drinking a white zinfandel, a merlot will pack a lot more punch. Red Bull and vodka? Nothing says you are a rambunctious person more clearly. And "I'll buy a round of shots" screams "I am still a college student."

as this nonverbal dialogue may seem, someone's attitude about you is usually based on perceived qualities rather than fact.

As you can see from the protocol outlined above, there are definite business rules of etiquette to follow for anyone issuing or receiving an invitation to dine out. Guests are expected to behave in a professional fashion. Therefore, the casual offer to have lunch with someone may not be quite what it seems. Even in this seemingly relaxed eating environment, there are interpersonal rules of conduct for professional people. Remember that you are working; the business meal is an extension of your workday (Gottsman, 2017). Be sufficiently relaxed to put others at ease but remember the purpose for the meal and the desired outcome. Be aware of your body language; show you're engaged by sitting up straight. Be ready for conversation. Demonstrate a genuine interest in learning about your dining companion(s). Be ready with generic questions to find areas of common interest: How long have you been with the company? How did you get into the industry? Where did you go to college? Dining etiquette involves more than knowing which fork to use. Effective interactions at a meal means creating a favorable impression that sets the stage for the next steps in the relationship.

Ethical Encounter

If people are not drinking, leave them alone. They may turn down a drink because they are alcoholic, are using prescription drugs, have a religious restriction, need to drive, or maybe just don't like alcohol. Never ask questions that would force someone to reveal personal information or make them defensive. A "no thank you" is just that—a polite refusal with no invitation to explore the reasons why.

Final Thoughts

The concepts mentioned in this chapter are a reminder to perfect interpersonal skills for the challenges faced throughout a successful working career. You may feel you have the skills and knowledge to do a job well, but you need to measure your personal opinion versus the impressions of other people, who continually assesses your credibility and your value to the organization. Your career path is inescapably linked to the perceptions others make about your abilities. The manner in which you perform work tasks is as important as the tasks themselves, and requires vigilance on your part: networks need constant monitoring; storytelling makes you an interesting, valued colleague; knowledge about gendered communication will aid your interactions with others; respectful, informed dining etiquette reveals your social skills; and cultural intelligence makes a great impression on everyone. Employees with sound judgment and excellent communication skills add value to an organization.

Throughout this book, we have highlighted certain behaviors and asked whether they were appropriate. You make ethical decisions daily; as a member of an organization, your communication impacts colleagues. Patricia Andrews and John Baird (2005) address the question of why it is important to behave ethically if unethical behavior might provide a competitive advantage professionally. They point out that honesty in business dealings creates an environment of trust, which is an essential component for organizations to function effectively. Trust is a fundamental requirement for communities, organizations, and societies. “Knowing that you are honest, that you behave humanely in your dealings with your fellow employees, that you are fair in your evaluations of others, and that you are concerned for the welfare of the whole organization and the society it serves are important self-perceptions that truly are priceless” (p. 6). If you behave ethically, the people with whom you work are more likely to engage in ethical behavior. Conversely, unethical behavior can have serious ramifications. Unethical practices affect everyone; companies fail, and employees lose their livelihood when reputations are ruined because of unethical behavior.

Personal development continues throughout your lifetime. Work experience becomes your greatest ally because practical experience captures the attention of employers. Once you develop your intrapersonal strengths and skills, your ability to communicate well and adapt to new business opportunities guide your future path. A variety of new employment opportunities will be driven by new technology and global finance. In addition, your working life will probably involve interactions with people from other countries and new cultures in the virtual world. It is easy to adapt to change even though it may seem awkward at first. You must understand yourself thoroughly and what motivates you to establish a satisfying lifelong career. Who are you? What do you want? Establish a personal brand that displays confidence; be the type of person with whom other people enjoy working. Consistent communication throughout your working life will provide answers to the philosophical questions you currently ask yourself regarding your ability and worth to the corporate world. Employment is challenging, but with constant monitoring of your communication and behavioral skills, it is also extremely rewarding.

> Do not go where the path may lead. Go instead where there is no path and leave a trail.
>
> —Ralph Waldo Emerson

Key Terms

Cultural competence
Gender communication
Intercultural communication
Networking
Networks
Storytelling

Exercises

1. Describe your networking strategy to gain employment or attend graduate school.
2. Conduct an informative interview with a student from another country. Ask the interviewee to describe the language and behavioral differences between his or her culture and U.S. culture. What did you learn that you can apply to your professional life?
3. How does your behavior and attitude change when working for a male versus female manager or teacher? Why?
4. Eat lunch or dinner with peers and pay attention throughout the experience. Discuss the possible changes you need to make when eating out.
5. Attend a social function produced by an organization. Analyze the conversations and behaviors you observe. What perception do you have of the organization and its members as you leave?

APPENDIX

Additional Resources

New employees may have a number of questions that are not covered in the employee manual. Here are some questions you might have and some suggestions for handling common situations, as well as sources to explore for more information.

How do I accomplish the huge task that my boss just handed to me?

To keep from being overwhelmed by challenging projects, break the large task into manageable pieces that can be accomplished relatively quickly. Working on one small task at a time makes the project seem less formidable. Set a timer for half an hour and prime yourself to stay totally focused until it goes off (Patel, 2018). You'll be surprised by how much you can accomplish in a short time if you eliminate distractions and interruptions. When finished, take a short break and then move on to the next small task.

How do I keep moving forward in my career?

One of the keys is to have a list of goals of what you want to accomplish in your career. List your short- and long-term goals for both your career and personal life and a timeline for achieving them. You can also summarize actions to take to achieve your goals. As you complete actions and achieve short-term goals, add new ones—and reflect on your long-term goals to determine if you would change anything after gaining experience. The lists and timeline will help you remain focused.

I am so angry about something that happened at work. Can I let my friends know about it on social media?

Steve Daily, Associate Producer with Fox Sports South and one of our alums, offers the following advice. "Don't broadcast it: Don't go on your Facebook page and post anything about the company that you work for, especially something negative. Companies monitor these websites now and check up on what their employees are saying. If you put on your Twitter feed that the VP really annoyed you today with his long speech, he could be reading that in the next few days. Keep those profiles on a private setting. Eliminate those tags on photos of you doing shots from back in college. You might think, hey it was a long time ago. Your boss doesn't know that. Finally, don't use media sites while you are on the clock unless it is part of your job! If you post that you are bored at work, you just told your boss 'I'm not working.'"

I'm not really up on the latest technology of tweets, social networking, apps, etc. Do I really need to know this stuff?

Yes. Most people expect a business to have a social media presence (Casselbury, 2018). Social media enhances a company's brand by bringing attention to products and services and connecting the company with its consumers. Numerous businesses are using apps, LinkedIn, Twitter, Instagram, Snapchat, and other social networking sites to drive business their way. If people working on social media for the company don't know how to use it appropriately, the company's image suffers. An uninformed Tweet or Facebook post that can be misinterpreted can make the local or national news. Going viral may be the goal for positive news, but it can also be devastatingly negative. If you don't know how to use social media wisely, you are going to be left behind for someone who does.

Employee advocacy is the promotion of a company by its team members (Fisher, 2019). Employee advocacy programs play a critical role in an organization's social media activities in an increasingly connected economy. There are potentially positive results for marketing, sales, recruiting, employee relationships, and the company's brand. The more people share content about a company, the stronger the position of the company with search engines and the greater the reach to target audiences (Scates, 2018). Individuals looking for employment use social media to learn about a company and culture.

Encouraging employees to promote their companies on social media extends the reach of a brand and increases online engagement. When shared by employees, messages are five times as effective as the same message on the company's social channels—and employee messages are re-shared 24 times more frequently (Fisher, 2019). Both companies and employees can benefit from employees being active on social media; companies enjoy increased brand awareness while employees build their personal brands and can establish themselves as thought leaders. Advocates also serve as an excellent example for other employees and feel rewarded when they can serve as role models. Empowering employees to promote a company via social media demonstrates trust and loyalty.

How do I get my dream job?

—Joanie Cole Berney, Mansfield University alum

After staying at home with my two daughters for many years, I decided to return to the workforce full time. I heard that the local sports and entertainment arena was in the need for a receptionist. I got an interview for that receptionist position and was offered the job. I actually turned the job down. In my mind it was almost like that receptionist job was a bit beneath me. At my age I thought I should be able to do better; did I really want to be tied down to a desk and answer phones all day? The minute I turned the job down, I regretted it.

I felt I had made one of the worst mistakes of my life. Well, I have never been one to burn bridges or give up, so I contacted the arena and told them I had made a terrible mistake in turning down the position and if the person they hired instead of me didn't work out to keep me in mind. Months passed and I forgot about the position. Sure, I would see an ad for a concert and think to myself, I could be working there—but life went on. One day out of the blue, the arena called and said that the person they hired for the reception position left and if I wanted the position this time, it was mine.

I did not hesitate at all and accepted the position. This time I looked at the receptionist position as a foot in the door, and once I got in that door there was no telling where it could lead me. I offered to help people in other departments when they were busy. I took on the tasks that weren't getting done or that no one else wanted to do. I made that reception position a professional position; I took pride in answering those calls. I always had a smile on my face. It paid off. At my first yearly review I was told I was the best receptionist they ever had. I was given more and more responsibility and moved from the receptionist to the website coordinator to the marketing assistant to the current position I have now—marketing coordinator. I hope someday the opportunity arises for me to be the director of marketing at the building I am currently at or maybe even another building.

I have always told my daughters and the interns who work for me that there is nothing wrong with having a dream or a goal. It is good to set goals for yourself, and if you don't reach those goals right away, don't give up. Take each job you have and make the most of it. Never lose contact with people; you never know when you might need them. Always be friendly and helpful and willing to give 100%. No one remembers that person who frowned all the time; they remember the person with the smile on their face who made sure to say good morning to them every day.

I can honestly say I look forward to going to work each day. I don't know if there are a lot of people in the world who can really say that. Do I have the perfect job? No. Would I like to make more money? Yes. Would I take a job that I hated if it paid more than the one I have now? No. For me to be truly happy, I have to do what I love. I love promoting concerts. I love working with media outlets. I love the inner workings of the entertainment world. I love, love, love a show day! I love when the artist takes the stage and the crowd goes wild. In my eyes I have found my dream job. Will I be at this job forever? Who really can see into the future like that? For right now, I just enjoy doing the best that I can at a job that I truly love.

I've only seen old-looking formats for résumés. Is there anything that would set me apart?

Yes. Try www.blueskyresumes.com, which offers a number of different formats for different professions. We think it is a terrific way to explore visual formats that may be different from what you've seen in the past.

A colleague did a favor for me. Is it really necessary to make a big deal out of thanking them?

Yes, yes, and yes. A thank you note, a surprise coffee, or a small box of nice chocolate is a lovely way to say thank you.

I just started working at a company, and I really enjoy my coworkers. The problem is that every time I turn around I'm being asked for a gift donation. There is a cake fund for birthdays, holiday gifts for cleaning people, shower gifts for new babies, etc. I don't want to be a spoilsport, but my budget is extremely tight. What are the expectations?

This is a tough problem. It is no fun eating beans for dinner while shelling out large amounts of money for "unnecessary" items. You could be using the donations to pay the electric bill. On the other hand, when an employee refuses to donate, the gesture does not go unnoticed. You might see if you can contribute a lesser amount. In the long run, you have to figure out which consequence is worse—being perceived as a noncontributor or cutting back more on your own spending. If you plead poverty, make sure you don't parade around your new iPhone or talk about the latest item you purchased. Sometimes it is best to just chalk up the donations as the price of being employed—not unlike needing proper attire and transportation.

My boss is touching me on the shoulders, and I don't like it. What should I do?

If the behavior happens again, immediately respond by saying, "Please don't touch me. Thanks." If the behavior continues, consult with your HR department if there is one and/or put your concern in writing. If the pattern continues, then it is time to get legal advice.

What really happens in the interview process?

—Becca Bogle, Mansfield University alum

This morning I accepted an offer. The process wasn't easy at all. When I started my senior year, the question I asked the most people was, "When do I start applying for jobs?" I got a lot of mixed answers. I am also relocating to a different state which was a topic about which I had questions but found few answers. Also, I started applying for jobs in late September.

Let's call these companies A, B, C, and D based on the order in which I was contacted. Company A said "no" after my first phone interview.

Company B had three phone interviews, then flew me down for an on-site interview (in December the week after graduation) with my presenting a 10-minute presentation about myself (educational and professional) past and present. I would like to note that there were five people in the panel interview, and four of them came in late and in the middle of my presentation. None of them other than my original contact asked ANY questions. I did not feel welcomed at all, which made me not want to work there. This company did not hire me because they went with someone with more experience. However, someone that I interviewed with at this company emailed me on 2/1/2018 because her friend who is also in our field is looking to fill a position on her team and thought I would make a great addition. This lead was not in the area I am looking to live in, so I sent her a nice email thanking her and explaining such.

I applied to Company C on 9/11/2017 and had three phone interviews between mid-November and mid-December. Just before Christmas, they invited me down for an on-site interview during the first week in January due to plant shut down between Christmas and New Year's. This company was much better, very welcoming, they paid for everything, took me out to eat, etc. This was a two-day interview with two more phone interviews while I was there with people who couldn't make it, a nine-person panel interview, a meal with all nine people together, and another meal with fewer people. After I came home and waited, I was told that due to fiscal forecasting, this position was being put on hold. **add dramatic sobbing** They called me back a week later saying they have been trying to fill this position for a while and after further review, the forecast will not be as bad as anticipated so they are proceeding with this position and my next interview will be with none other than the CHIEF OPERATIONS OFFICER of the company. Oh boy . . . anyway, I guess I did well because they offered me employment as the Environmental, Health, and Safety Specialist; $60,000 plus bonuses, benefits, and relocation assistance (which is all that I asked for in my second interview), no negotiation needed. I did a lot of research ahead of time of what I can live on and what the position is valued at. My first day will be 2/26/2018.

I have had 3 phone interviews with Company D. Their right hand doesn't talk to their left hand. They said they wanted to have another interview with me a month ago, but the women who is supposed to schedule it rarely answers and when she does, she is wicked rude. In my second phone interview with this company, I was asked what my salary requirements were where I said the same as above. The man scoffed and said they were looking for about $20,000 less. I explained the difference in salary expectations between what their job description said was needed and my qualifications in comparison. After this conversation with them, they reposted a job ad with higher qualifications needed.

How do I stand out in the interview process?

—Erica Frank, Mansfield University alum

Hi Dr. Young!

I just wanted to share my recent interview experience with you in case it would be helpful for future students.

I went in for an initial interview for a new bartending job last week. It went really well and was a typical interview. I had to fill out a bartending questionnaire at the start, but I didn't know the answers to two questions. At the end of that interview they invited me for a second interview the next day. Amanda, who interviewed me, said, "You'll be meeting Josh tomorrow. I won't be here but I'm sure I'll be seeing you again." So obviously I was excited because this brand-new bar opening up seems like the perfect place for me compared to where I am now and with better money, hours, and atmosphere.

I go in the next day and meet Josh. He said, "Amanda said positive things, let see if they are true." and he pulled out the questionnaire. And I said, "Oh! I looked up those answers I didn't know yesterday!" He said, "please tell me." I gave a ten-minute explanation about the differences between scotch, whiskey, Bourbon, and single and blended malts.

Get this, he said, "I love someone willing to learn—you're hired; I need ten more just like you."

And that's it! I start training next Thursday and we open the 16th! Can't wait!

Business and Professional Communication did me well.

How do I professionally and effectively ask for a promotion?

—Chelsea L. Thomas, Christie Buyer, Breanna G. Murphy, Mansfield University alums

Almost everyone reaches a time in their careers when they believe they should be promoted to the next level. Although we may differ in our reasoning for feeling this way, *Harvard Business Review* suggests that we should all be taking the same seven steps towards asking for a promotion (Knight, 2018). The seven steps include: reflect, research, build your case, consider timing, plant the seed, nurture the seed and be patient.

Step 1: Reflect—what do you want?

This may seem a bit backwards from what we are used to but reflecting comes first because you must decide what you want from the promotion. This may include a variety of answers including more money, more power, more managerial responsibility, a new position, etc. One must decide exactly what is desirable before moving forward in the process.

Step 2: Research—get outside intelligence.

Before asking for a promotion, it is important to do some outside research on the matter. Three key research steps should include: (1) How people in your position got promoted in the past; (2) Do other seniors aside from your direct manager think you are ready; and (3) Do your peers think you are ready enough that they will support and follow you? If you do this research and still feel as though asking for a promotion is appropriate, move on to step 3!

Step 3: Build your case—why should you get promoted?

At this point in the process, it is time for you to start physically putting together proof that you are ready to be promoted. Preparing a personal portfolio is an excellent way to do so. First, you want to make sure your portfolio looks professional by using a leather padfolio or a visually appealing cardstock folder if making multiple copies. Second, add documents to the portfolio that reflect your skills including your résumé, letters of recommendation, certifications, and completed project results. Next, make sure the portfolio is easy to navigate by including labeled sections, bolded words and chronological order of importance. Last, you should make sure to include only information that stands alone without explanation in case you are not able to be there when the portfolio is reviewed.

Step 4: Consider timing—is the timing appropriate?

Now that you know you are ready and deserving of a promotion, you must also consider if the timing is right for the company. Two situations that can imply the timing would be good for the company are when the position you desire is open and when the company is on stable ground. Find out if a job is open is by searching the company's career page or by asking a manger. It is not always clear when a company is stable, but key signs that point toward instability are mass layoffs, bad press, and not paying bills/paychecks on time. Showing you considered the company before just pushing for your own interests demonstrates value as an employee, which may help with your eventual promotion.

Step 5: Plant the seed—start the conversation.

Once you have completed steps 1 through 4, you can start the conversation with your boss about why you deserve this promotion. You can discuss why you are a good fit for the promotion and the experience you have that will make you the best option for the position. It is always best to remember that actions speak louder than words, and you want to be able to continue to show your boss you are ready and want this promotion.

Step 6: Nurture the seed—continue the conversation through feedback.

It is important to remind management that you are looking to get the promotion. A good way to do that is by asking for advice on what you are doing well and what you can do to improve. This is effective because there is always room to improve yourself, but it also shows the boss you are willing to change if it benefits the company. This in the end could help push management toward the decisions to promote you.

Step 7: Be patient—Do not be pushy, but also do not get pushed aside.

If you do not get an immediate answer from your boss, ask when would be a good time to revisit the promotion. Do not bring up the topic too often or you may become irritating and despite your qualifications be rejected for the promotion. Additionally, remember that it is important to continue working hard each day to prove that one day you deserve to be at the next level.

What not to do

Do not expect a promotion to be handed to you based only on your experience and work ethic. Always ask for the promotion or put the thought in your superiors' ear. Secondly, don't compare yourself to others. Do not drag other employees into your interview or compare yourself to their successes or shortcomings. You are your own person; believe in yourself and your capabilities.

Never ever think you are entitled to the promotion. The company does not owe you anything; if they don't appreciate you, take your work somewhere else. In addition, do not do other coworkers' or your boss's work. Stepping on other people's toes or doing more work than you should be doing can be seen as threatening or disrespectful instead of being helpful or beneficial. Lastly, your relationship with your boss does not guarantee a promotion. A good relationship with your boss does not mean that you don't advocate for yourself; explain the reasoning and value in promoting you.

How to handle rejection

If you are not offered the promotion there are several ways to handle rejection. One of the most important is not to get emotional. Getting angry, upset, or disappointed is a normal reaction, but do not show it in front of other employees. It looks unprofessional and may make you seem incompetent. The best thing to do is handle these emotions outside of the office, on your own personal time, instead of at work. Next, make sure to seek feedback. After learning that you did not receive the job, ask your boss or superior what you could have done instead. Learning what you can improve on or what you are missing for the promotion will be beneficial for future opportunities. Implement the feedback. Receiving feedback is great, but if you do not implement the changes it will go to waste. Reassess and figure out what you could do better or differently in the future. Consider why the other candidate may have gotten the promotion. The most important aspect of this stage is having honest self-communication. Make yourself a better employee. This entails learning new skills and making yourself as much of an asset to your company as you can.

There are a couple of people whom I supervise that don't do what they are supposed to do. What's wrong with just making a blanket statement to everyone instead of singling them out?

—Dean A. Marker, Mansfield University alum

It's easy to understand why you may want to issue a blanket statement to your employees. It keeps both you and the specific employees out of a potentially awkward situation if things were to go awry. The problem is blanket statements are the least effective way to communicate need for improvement to individuals. More often than not, these generalizations will fall on deaf ears. In my experience, without expressly communicated expectations, individuals are either ignorant of the fact that they aren't performing, or they are simply content with the effort they put forth.

With generalizations, not only do you run the risk of your points not being understood but also the risk of unintended parties believing the shortcomings apply to them. Employees who care a lot about their jobs may take these statements to heart and start second-guessing their work. Now, instead of communicating directly to resolve a potentially minor issue, the initial problem hasn't been solved and there is a secondary issue that's cropped up because of it.

The most effective way to ensure that the expectations are understood is clear and direct communication. As an employee, most of us would be a lot more driven to complete work or make improvements with our supervisors breathing down our necks. While that may be a bit extreme, the concept still applies. The increase in personal accountability ensures that there is a clear reduction in opportunity for misunderstanding.

The notion that it's uncomfortable to address specific people is perfectly understandable, and there's definitely a chance that more tension could arise if you speak to individuals directly. Employees may feel that they can't trust you, which will further the divide between you and your employees. However, in many cases this is not very likely to happen. In professional work environments, most employees should be mature enough to realize the benefits of constructive criticism and that there are always opportunities for growth. While broad generalizations may seem like the safest way to communicate your expectations, they can cause more problems than they fix. The firm recommendation is to stay away from them as much as possible.

What kind of interview questions should I expect?

Here are some of the top questions we have found.

1. Where would you like to be in your career five years from now?
2. Tell me about your proudest achievement.
3. Give me an example of a time when you had to think outside the box.
4. What negative thing would your last boss say about you?
5. What can you do for us that other candidates can't?
6. What are the responsibilities of your current or previous position?
7. What do you know about this industry?
8. What do you know about our company?
9. How long will it take for you to make a significant contribution?
10. What is your most significant accomplishment?
11. Why did you leave your last job?
12. Why do you think you would like to work for our company?
13. If it were your first day, what would you say to the associates you will be working with?
14. What have you done to overcome major obstacles in your life?
15. Are you willing to relocate?
16. How would you describe your work style?
17. Tell me about yourself.
18. Why do you think we should hire you for this job?
19. How do you define success?
20. What was the last book you read?
21. What area of this job would you find most difficult?
22. What leadership/supervisory roles have you held?
23. What is your weakness?
24. What accomplishments are you most proud of?

25. What has been your greatest crisis, how did you solve it?
26. What person has had the greatest influence on you, why?
27. What do you like best about your job/school . . . what do you like least?
28. How has college prepared you for this career?
29. Describe your ideal job.
30. Why did you choose this particular field of work?
31. What have you done that shows initiative?
32. In what areas of the job would you expect to be most successful . . . least successful?
33. What are your salary requirements?
34. What frustrates you?
35. Describe a situation with an irate customer and how you handled it.
36. What aspect of this job do you consider most crucial?
37. What are your long-range career objectives and how do you plan to achieve them?
38. How do you think a friend would describe you?
39. What motivates you?
40. How many hours a week do you need to work to get the job done?
41. How do you work under pressure?
42. What two or three things are most important to you in your job?
43. Tell me about other jobs you've had. In hindsight, how could you have improved your performance?
44. What makes a good supervisor?
45. What skills do you want to improve?
46. What qualities do you look for in a boss?
47. What have you learned from mistakes on the job? What experience do you have in this field?
48. What motivates you to do your best on the job? Do you consider yourself successful?
49. What do coworkers say about you?

50. What has disappointed you about a job?
51. Tell me about a problem you had with a supervisor.
52. Are you a team player?
53. Have you ever had to fire anyone? How did you feel about that?
54. What is your philosophy toward work?
55. Explain how you would be an asset to this organization.
56. What would your previous supervisor say your strongest point is?
57. Tell me about a suggestion you have made.
58. What irritates you about coworkers?
59. Describe your management style.
60. What is your greatest strength?
61. Tell me about your dream job.
62. What kind of person would you refuse to work with?
63. Why do you think you would do well at this job?
64. How do you propose to compensate for your lack of experience?
65. Tell me about a time when you helped resolve a dispute between others.
66. Describe your work ethic.
67. Tell me about the most fun you have had on the job.
68. How do you react to negativity or gossip from coworkers?
69. If you were unable to meet a commitment or deadline, what would you do?
70. Do you prefer to work alone or in a group?
71. What have I forgotten to ask?

Behavioral Interview Questions

Top Echelon is a website offering recruiting software and services. Kaylee DeWitt (2017), a content writer for Top Echelon, published an article discussing the benefits of behavioral interviewing, with multiple suggestions for questions on a number of topics. There are no "correct" answers to behavioral interview questions; responses differ depending on past experiences. The goal is to learn how the candidate reacted in real-life situations, which helps recruiters identify whether a person's personality matches the requirements for a particular job. Read DeWitt's suggestions to prepare for questions about your communication skills, attention to detail, analytical ability, time management, interpersonal skills, teamwork, decision making, handling stress, adaptability, integrity, resilience, initiative, leadership, innovation, goal setting, sales ability, and customer service aptitude.

Attention to detail interview questions

1. What do you do to verify that your work is accurate?
2. Describe a time you made an error. Why did you miss the mistake? How did you handle the situation?
3. Describe a time when you discovered a coworker made a mistake. What did you do?

Analytical skills interview questions

4. Describe a project that demonstrated your analytical skills.
5. Tell me about a time when you had to analyze information. What was your process?
6. Have you used your analytical skills to find a problem? What did you do after you discovered it?
7. Tell me about a time when you used your problem-solving skills to find a solution to a problem.

Interview questions about decision making

8. What steps do you take before making a decision?
9. Talk about a time you had to make a decision with limited information. How did you determine what would be the best decision?
10. Tell me about a time when you had to make an immediate decision.
11. Have you felt pressure while making a decision? How did the pressure affect you?
12. What's the most difficult decision you've made at work? What factors made the decision difficult?
13. Have you made a decision that impacted your coworkers? How did you arrive at your choice?

14. Describe an unpopular decision you made. What did you do when you learned about the negative reaction?
15. Describe a decision that you regretted. What contributed to your regret?

Leadership interview questions

16. Describe a time when you were in charge of a project. Would you do anything differently?
17. Describe a project that didn't have a leader when you took charge. Describe the process of taking charge and what you accomplished.
18. Have you had a difficult group to lead? What did you do to manage them?
19. What was the toughest project you had to lead? Why was it difficult?
20. What is the most difficult part of being a leader for you? What do you do about that?
21. Describe something that challenged you as a leader. Were you changed by the challenge?
22. What was your greatest achievement as a leader? What aspects were you most proud of?
23. Talk about motivating your team. How did you do it? Were your efforts effective?

Interview questions about taking initiative

24. Describe a time when you saw a problem at work and created a solution for it.
25. Tell me about a change you made at work?
26. Talk about a project you started. What process did you follow? What were the results?
27. Tell me about a project that was implemented because of your work.
28. Were you bored at work and asked for more or different work? What steps did you take?

Interview questions about goal setting

29. Describe the process you use to set personal goals.
30. Describe a career goal and how you reached it. What obstacles did you encounter?
31. Describe a career goal you failed to reach. What caused the failure? How did you feel?
32. What goals did you set for your team? How did you keep people on track to meet the goals?

Interview questions about sales

33. What have you done to increase your number of customers?
34. What is your greatest accomplishment in sales? How did you achieve that?
35. Tell me about a time you convinced a reluctant customer to make a purchase. How did you do it?
36. Talk about a time when you had to negotiate with a customer. What did you do? What was the outcome?

Customer service interview questions

37. Describe the steps you take to develop a relationship with a customer.
38. In a situation when you were unsure about a customer's request, what did you do?
39. Talk about a miscommunication between you and a customer. What did you do to repair communication?
40. Describe an incident involving an upset or angry customer. What did you do? Is there anything you would have done differently?
41. Tell me about a time you convinced a customer not to switch to another company. What steps did you take?
42. Describe a time when you went out of your way to please a customer.
43. Have you ever defended a customer? Why? How did your coworkers or boss react?
44. Did you inherit a coworker's customer? How did you inform the customer about the change? How did you build trust with them?

Communication interview questions

45. Tell me about how you communicated with your previous bosses.
46. Describe your communication with a person you didn't like. Was the interaction effective? Why or why not?
47. Talk about a time when your communication failed. What caused the problem? How did you handle the situation?
48. Describe interactions with a remote coworker. What communication channels did you choose? What difficulties did you experience?
49. Have you ever given a speech or presentation for your job? How did you prepare? How was the presentation received?
50. Describe a time when you had to give an impromptu presentation. What did you do?
51. Give examples of using your written communication skills. Were the reports or memos well received? What aspects were the most effective.
52. Describe a time when you used a communication method that was outside the norm for a particular activity. Why did you choose that channel? Was it effective?

Interview questions about interpersonal skills

53. Describe a conflict with someone at work. What did you do?
54. Describe dealing with a coworker you didn't like. What skills helped you maintain an effective working relationship?
55. How do you communicate with someone who doesn't like you?
56. Tell me about a disagreement with a manager. What did you do?
57. How have you maintained relationships with former coworkers? What skills do you use?
58. Describe a situation in which you didn't get along with a customer. What did you do?

Interview questions about teamwork

59. What role do you normally take on a team? Why?
60. Tell me about your most recent experience working with a team. What was your role? How did you interact with the other team members?
61. Talk about a time when team members disagreed with you. What did you do?
62. Describe a situation in which you tried to resolve a dispute within the team. What was the result?
63. Have you been part of a team where members didn't get along? What happened? What did you do?
64. Talk about a time when your team members had to compromise. What was the result?
65. Describe a time when a team member wasn't doing his work. What did you do?
66. Describe a situation in which you had to delegate work among team members. How did you decide who would do each task? Is there anything you would do differently?
67. Have you ever let your team down? What did you do? How did you react?

Time management interview questions

68. When scheduling your work, how do you decide what to do first?
69. When in charge of a project, how did you organize the tasks and make sure everything got done?
70. Describe being part of multiple projects simultaneously. How did you handle the workload?
71. When you have multiple requests from customers or coworkers, how do you prioritize them?
72. Tell me about a time when you missed a deadline on a project. What did you do?

Interview questions about handling stress

73. Describe a stressful work situation? How did you handle the challenges?
74. What was your most stressful project and why? What did you do to manage the stress? How did the project turn out?
75. Tell me about a time when you were concerned that a situation could become stressful. What did you do to prevent it?
76. Describe a time when you tried to reduce stress for a coworker.

Interview questions about adaptability

77. How did you handle your transition between different jobs or positions in the past?
78. Describe a time when changes happened that you couldn't control. How did you react?
79. Tell me about a time when you experienced rapid change. How did you handle the situation?
80. Describe a situation when you changed the course of a project. How did you relay the changes to your team? Were there unanticipated repercussions?
81. Talk about a time when you had to adapt to a coworker's work style to finish a task. Why was it necessary? What did you do?
82. Think of a time when you weren't comfortable with a change. What did you do?

Interview questions about innovation

83. Describe a time when a manager asked you to come up with a creative way to complete a project. What steps did you take?
84. Tell me about a problem you solved in a unique way. What happened?
85. Describe a project where none of the usual paths to completion worked. What alternatives did you choose?
86. Talk about a time when you presented a creative idea to your coworkers.
87. Tell me about a time when your coworkers resisted a creative idea. How did you react? How did you feel?

88. Tell me about a time when your creative idea failed. How did you feel? What would you do differently?

Interview questions about integrity

89. Describe a time when a coworker or customer questioned your honesty. What did you do?
90. Tell me about a time when you followed a rule with which you didn't agree. Why did you comply? How did you feel?
91. Talk about a time when it was difficult to be honest.
92. Was there ever a time when you weren't honest at work? What happened?
93. Has there ever been a situation where you thought it was better to be dishonest? Why? What did you end up doing?
94. Tell me about a time when you found out that a coworker was doing something wrong. What did you do?

Resilience interview questions

95. Talk about a setback you had at work. What did you do?
96. Describe a time you faced a problem at work. What did you do? What would you do differently?
97. Tell me about a time you had to work under a lot of pressure. How did you handle the situation?
98. Describe a time that you faced a challenge at work. How did you feel? What steps did you take?
99. Did you ever have to compete against coworkers? What were the results?

References

Allen, B. (2011). *Difference Matters: Communicating Social Identity*, 2nd ed. Long Grove, IL: Waveland Press, Inc.

Andersen, P. A. (2008). *Nonverbal Communication: Forms and Functions*, 2nd ed. Long Grove, IL: Waveland Press, Inc.

Andrews, P. H., and J. E. Baird (2005). *Communication for Business and the Professions*, 8th ed. Long Grove, IL: Waveland Press, Inc.

Baird, J. (2010, January 28). "An Unquiet Nation." Retrieved from http://juliabaird.me/an-unquiet-nation/

Bell, T. (2018, April 17). The Secrets to Beating an Applicant Tracking System (ATS). CIO.com

Bennett, J. (2010, November 1). "Privacy Is Dead." *Newsweek*, pp. 40–41.

Bishop, J. (2019, January 21). "5 Positive Affirmations to Help You Smash That Job Interview." Retrieved from https://www.glassdoor.co.uk/blog/5-positive-affirmations-help-smash-job-interview/

Brokaw, L. (2017, August 8). "Four Habits of Highly Effective Virtual Teams." *MIT Sloan Management Review*. Retrieved from https://sloanreview.mit.edu/article/four-habits-of-highly-effective-virtual-teams/

Burns, J. M. (1978). *Leadership*. New York: Harper & Row.

Business Dictionary (2020). Retrieved from http://www.businessdictionary.com/definition/behavioral-interview.html

Campbell, S. (2018, March 15). "7 Inspiring Traits of Compassionate Leadership." *Entrepreneur*. Retrieved from https://www.entrepreneur.com/article/310391

Capelli, P., and A. Tavis (2018, October). "The Performance Management Revolution." *Harvard Business Review*. Retrieved from https://hbr.org/2016/10/the-performance-management-revolution

Casselbury, (2018, June 28). "The Impact of Social Media in the Workplace: Pros and Cons." Chron. Retrieved from https://work.chron.com/impact-social-media-workplace-pros-cons-22611.html

Chen, C. (2020). "Skype Hype: The Key to Acing Your Virtual Interview." Daily Muse Inc. Retrieved from https://www.themuse.com/advice/skype-hype-the-key-to-acing-your-virtual-interview

Dehne, S. (2010, October 1). "Lacking Confidence? That May Be the Reason You're Still Job Searching." Retrieved from https://www.aol.com/2010/10/01/lacking-confidence-that-may-be-the-reason-youre-still-job-sear/

Denning, S. (2011, June 8). "Why Leadership Storytelling Is Important." *Forbes*. Retrieved from https://www.forbes.com/sites/stevedenning/2011/06/08/why-leadership-storytelling-is-important/#6bba428878Of

Dewey, J. (1910). *How We Think.* New York: D. C. Heath.

DeWitt, K. (2017, June 21). "100 Behavioral Interview Questions to Help You Find the Best Candidates." Top Echelon. Retrieved from https://www.topechelon.com/blog/placement-process/top-behavioral-interview-questions-list-examples/

Doyle, A. (2018). "Why You Should Keep Your Resume Honest." The Balance Careers. Retrieved from https://www.thebalancecareers.com/why-you-should-keep-your-resume-honest-2063304

Doyle, A. (2019a). "Cover Letter Samples & Writing Tips." The Balance Careers. Retrieved from https://www.thebalancecareers.com/cover-letters-4161919

Doyle, A. (2019b). "How to Prepare for a Behavioral Job Interview." The Balance Careers. Retrieved from https://www.thebalancecareers.com/behavioral-job-interviews-2058575

Doyle, A. (2019c). "What Is the Star Interview Response Technique?" The Balance Careers. Retrieved from https://www.thebalancecareers.com/what-is-the-star-interview-response-technique-2061629

Doyle, A. (2019d). "How to Write Job Descriptions for Your Resume." The Balance Careers. Retrieved from https://www.thebalancecareers.com/how-to-write-job-descriptions-for-your-resume-2063182

Doyle, A. (2020a). "What Are Talent Assessments and How Do Companies Use Them?" The Balance Careers. Retrieved from https://www.thebalancecareers.com/what-are-talent-assessments-and-how-do-companies-use-them-2059814

Doyle, A. (2020b). "What Exactly Are Soft Skills?" The Balance Careers. Retrieved from https://www.thebalancecareers.com/what-are-soft-skills-2060852

Driver, S. (2018, October 7). "Keep It Clean: Social Media Screenings Gain in Popularity." *Business News Daily*. Retrieved from https://www.businessnewsdaily.com/2377-social-media-hiring.html

Enelow, W., and L. Kursmark (2010). *Cover Letter Magic: Trade Secrets of Professional Resume Writers*, 4th ed. St. Paul, MN: Jist Publishing.

Feloni, R. (2015, October 27). "A Master Networker Shares His Top 20 Networking Tips." *Business Insider*. Retrieved from https://www.businessinsider.com/master-networker-top-networking-tips-2015-10

Fisher, A. (2019, August 23). "How to Encourage Employee Advocacy on Social Media." *Forbes.* Retrieved from https://www.forbes.com/sites/theyec/2019/08/23/how-to-encourage-employee-advocacy-on-social-media/#266e1e5550b7

Fixmer-Oraiz, N., and J. Wood (2019). *Gendered Lives: Communication, Gender, and Culture*, 13th ed. Boston: Cengage.

Gallo, A. (2014, February 4). "How to Write a Cover Letter." *Harvard Business Review.*

German, K. M. (2017). *Principles of Public Speaking*, 19th ed. New York: Routledge.

Goffman, E. (1959). *The Presentation of Self in Everyday Life.* New York: Anchor Books.

Goman, C. K. (2016, March 31). "Is Your Communication Style Dictated by Your Gender?" *Forbes.* Retrieved from https://www.forbes.com/sites/carolkinseygoman/2016/03/31/is-your-communication-style-dictated-by-your-gender/#5dbdcb9feb9d

Goman, C. K. (2019, September 18). "Should You Bring Your Femininity to Work?" *Forbes.*

Gottsman, D. (2016, September 26). "10 Professional Texting Etiquette Rules." Retrieved from https://www.huffpost.com/entry/10-professional-texting-e_b_12154416

Gottsman, D. (2017, January 18). "How to Master the Art of the Business Meal." *Inc.* retrieved from https://www.inc.com/diane-gottsman/mastering-the-art-of-a-business-meal.html

Grant, A. (2011, January 3). "Want More Clout? Stand Up Straight." *Chicago Tribune*, sec. 6, p. 3.

Haefner, R. (2009, October 6). "More Employers Screening Candidates via Social Networking Sites." Careerbuilder.com. Retrieved from http://sites.dreamingcode.com/dccontentnet/Content/Newdata/pdf/75_55Ab.pdf

Hasan, S. (2019, December 5). "Top 15 Leadership Qualities That Make Good Leaders," TaskQue. Retrieved from https://blog.taskque.com/characteristics-good-leaders/

Hatfield, M. (2017, November 14). "How to Tell When a Robot Will Be Reading Your Resume before a Human Ever Sees It." *Business Insider.*

Hayes L. (2018, August 9). "More Than Half of Employers Have Found Content on Social Media That Caused Them NOT to Hire a Candidate, According to Recent CareerBuilder Survey." Retrieved from http://press.careerbuilder.com/2018-08-09-More-Than-Half-of-Employers-Have-Found-Content-on-Social-Media-That-Caused-Them-NOT-to-Hire-a-Candidate-According-to-Recent-CareerBuilder-Survey

Heathfield, S. (2019, June 25). "10 Key Tips for Effective Employee Performance Reviews." The Balance Careers. Retrieved from https://www.thebalancecareers.com/effective-performance-review-tips-1918842

Indeed (2017, May 10). "139 Action Verbs to Make Your Resume Stand Out." Retrieved from https://www.indeed.com/career-advice/resumes-cover-letters/action-verbs-to-make-your-resume-stand-out

Indeed (2019). Winding River Production Animator Job Posting. Retrieved from https://www.indeed.com/cmp/Winding-River-Productions/jobs/Production-Animator-a9bcb239d3ba8553?sjdu=QwrRXKrqZ3CNX5W-O9jEvTHK_qwVIn-tz6nDN_ABFtt3emEmGA4WKdNPb3qzhhYsKH-ikorn8mr_2b5aCfJLiQ&tk=1dccp5prp51h7802&adid=281309831&vjs=3

Ivy, D. K., and P. Backlund (2012). *GenderSpeak: Personal Effectiveness in Gender Communication*, 5th ed. New York: Pearson.

Jansen, J. (2016). *I Don't Know What I Want, but I Know It's Not This*. New York: Penguin Books.

Johannesen, R. L., K. S. Valde, and K. E. Whedbee (2008). *Ethics in Human Communication*. Long Grove, IL: Waveland Press, Inc.

Johnson, C., and M. Hackman (2018). *Leadership: A Communication Perspective*, 7th ed. Long Grove, IL: Waveland Press, Inc.

Johnson, S. (2008, January 17). "Reacting to Facebook, Sites Prove We Love to Hate." *Chicago Tribune*, sec. 5, p. 1.

Jolly, D. (2010, August 26). "German Law Would Limit the Use of Facebook in Hiring." *The New York Times*, sec. B, p. 8.

Kellerman, B. (2008). *Followership: How Followers are Creating Change and Changing Leaders*. Cambridge: Harvard Business School Press.

Kienzle, N., and S. Husar (2007). "How Can Cultural Awareness Improve Communication in the Global Workplace?" *Journal of Communication, Speech & Theatre Association of North Dakota*, 20, pp. 81–85.

Kilmann, R. H. (2015). "A Brief History of the Thomas-Kilmann Conflict Mode Instrument." Retrieved from https://kilmanndiagnostics.com/a-brief-history-of-the-thomas-kilmann-conflict-mode-instrument/

Kilmann, R. H., and K. W. Thomas (1977). "Developing a Forced-Choice Measure of Conflict-Handling Behavior: The MODE Instrument." *Educational and Psychological Measurements*, 37, pp. 309–325.

Kleiman, J. (2020). "Showing Up Late—Plus 4 More Interview Mistakes Smart People Make Every Day." Retrieved from https://www.themuse.com/advice/showing-up-lateplus-4-more-interview-mistakes-smart-people-make-every-day

Knight, R. (2018, January 29). "How to Ask for a Promotion." *Harvard Business Review*. Retrieved from https://hbr.org/2018/01/how-to-ask-for-a-promotion

Krames, J. A. (2008). *Inside Drucker's Brain*. Penguin Books: London.

Lamson, M. (2018, July 25). "How to Manage Gender and Culture in Virtual Teams." *Inc*. Retrieved from https://www.inc.com/melissa-lamson/5-tips-for-managing-gender-culture-in-virtual-teams.html

Littlejohn, S. W., and K. Domenici (2007). *Communication, Conflict, and the Management of Difference*. Long Grove, IL: Waveland Press, Inc.

Lorenz, K. (2010, June 29). "10 Attitudes of Successful Workers." Retrieved from https://footnote4.com/2010/06/29/10-attitudes-of-successful-workers-by-kate-lorenz-careerbuilder-com-editor/

Lucas, S. (2019, May 1). "Why Soft Skills Are a Manager's Most Significant Skills." The Balance Careers. Retrieved from https://www.thebalancecareers.com/why-soft-skills-are-important-for-managers-4158692

Martin, M. (2018, July 6). "Illegal Job Interview Questions to Avoid." *Business News Daily*. Retrieved from https://www.businessnewsdaily.com/4037-illegal-interview-questions.html

McCallum, J. S. (2013, October). "Followership: The Other Side of Leadership." *Ivey Business Journal*. Retrieved from https://iveybusinessjournal.com/publication/followership-the-other-side-of-leadership/

McKay, D. R. (2019, November 20). "Rules for Using Cell Phones at Work." The Balance Careers. Retrieved from https://www.thebalancecareers.com/rules-for-using-cell-phones-at-work-526258

Moody, J., B. Stewart, and C. Bolt-Lee (2002, March). "Showcasing the Skilled Business Graduate: Expanding the Tool Kit." *Business Communication Quarterly*, 65(1), p. 21.

Murad, K. (2020, February 17). "Sexual Harassment in the Workplace." National Conference of State Legislatures. Retrieved from https://www.ncsl.org/research/labor-and-employment/sexual-harassment-in-the-workplace.aspx

Muse Editor (2020). "The 31 Best LinkedIn Profile Tips for Job Seekers." Retrieved from https://www.themuse.com/advice/the-31-best-linkedin-profile-tips-for-job-seekers

OWL (n.d.). "Writing the Basic Business Letter." Retrieved from https://owl.purdue.edu/owl/subject_specific_writing/professional_technical_writing/basic_business_letters/index.html

Patel, D. (2018, July 16). "How to Accomplish More in 4 Days Than Most People Do in 4 Weeks." *Entrepreneur*. Retrieved from https://www.entrepreneur.com/article/316393

Poundstone, W. (2003). *How Would You Move Mt. Fuji? Microsoft's Cult of the Puzzle—How the World's Smartest Company Selects the Most Creative Thinkers*. New York: Little, Brown.

PSOW (2019, November 12). "The International Nuances of Handshaking." The Protocol School of Washington. Retrieved from https://www.psow.edu/blog/the-international-nuances-of-handshaking/

Ramsey, L. (2013, August 19). "Sealing the Deal over the Business Meal." Business Know-How. Retrieved from https://www.businessknowhow.com/growth/bizmeal.htm

Reh, J. (2019, June 3). "Management Skills Pyramid." The Balance Careers. Retrieved from https://www.thebalancecareers.com/management-skills-pyramid-2275888

Roberts, C. (n.d.). "Checklist for Personal Values." Retrieved from https://eu.themyersbriggs.com/~/media/Files/PDFs/Miscellaneous/Checklist-for-Personal-Values-May-27.pdf?la=en

Salm, L. (2017, June 15). "70% of Employers Are Snooping Candidates' Social Media Profiles." Career Builder. Retrieved from https://www.careerbuilder.com/advice/social-media-survey-2017

Scates, K. (2018, April 17). "5 Must Have Social Media Guidelines for Employees." Randstad RiseSmart. Retrieved from https://www.randstadrisesmart.com/blog/5-must-have-social-media-guidelines-employees

SimpleTexting (2019, May 29). "Rules of Office Texting Etiquette." Retrieved from https://simpletexting.com/rules-of-office-texting-etiquette/

Slack, M. (2019, December 22). "How to Write a Cover Letter for a Job Application." Retrieved from https://resumegenius.com/blog/cover-letter-help/how-to-write-a-cover-letter

Sutton, R., and B. Wigert (2019, May 6). "More Harm than Good: The Truth about Performance Reviews." Gallup. Retrieved from https://www.gallup.com/workplace/249332/harm-good-truth-performance-reviews.aspx

Swenson, K. (2017, November 22). "Who Came Up with the Term 'Sexual Harassment'?" *The Washington Post*. Retrieved from https://www.washingtonpost.com/news/morning-mix/wp/2017/11/22/who-came-up-with-the-term-sexual-harassment/

Tahmincioglu, E. (2009, October 26). "Employers Digging Deep on Prospective Workers." Retrieved from http://www.nbcnews.com/id/33414017/ns/business-careers/t/employers-digging-deep-prospective-workers/

Tannen, D. (1990). *You Just Don't Understand: Women and Men in Conversation.* New York: Harper-Collins.

Tannen, D. (1994). *Talking from 9 to 5: Women and Men at Work*. New York: HarperCollins.

Thibodeaux, W. (2018, July 23). "Let's Talk about Communication: Tips for Building a Great Business Relationship at the First Meeting." *Chicago Tribune*, sec. 2, p. 1.

U.S. Equal Employment Opportunity Commission (n.d.). "Sexual Harassment." Retrieved from https://www.eeoc.gov/laws/types/sexual_harassment.cfm

Vozza, S. (2020, February 24). "Show Off Those Soft Skills." *Chicago Tribune,* sec. 2, p. 3.

Woloshin, M. (2009, February). "Writing Cover Letters—The Perfect Personal Pitch." *Tactics*, p. 7.

Young, K. S., J. T. Wood, G. M. Phillips, and D. J. Pedersen (2021). *Group Discussion: A Practical Guide to Participation and Leadership*, 5th ed. Long Grove, IL: Waveland Press, Inc.

Zojceska, A. (2019, March 25). "Everything You Need to Know about Skill Assessment Tests." TalentLyft. Retrieved from https://www.talentlyft.com/en/blog/article/278/everything-you-need-to-know-about-skill-assessment-tests

Zupek, R. (2010, February 24). "Nine Things that Seal the Deal for Hiring Managers." Retrieved from http://www.cnn.com/2010/LIVING/worklife/02/24/cb.seal.job.interview/index.html

Index